OPEN SECRETS

THE NEWS TV WON'T TELL YOU

Marjorie and Don Gray

Pacific Press Publishing Association
Boise, Idaho
Montemorelos, Nuevo Leon, Mexico
Oshawa, Ontario, Canada

Edited by Ken McFarland and Marvin Moore
Designed by Tim Larson
Cover illustration by Nery Cruz
Type set in 10/12 Korinna Medium

ISBN 0-8163-0667-2

In Appreciation

The authors wish to express their appreciation to many who have knowingly or unknowingly contributed to the production of this book by their lives, words, works, or inspiration:

George E. Vandeman, Roy Naden, C. Mervyn Maxwell, Samuele Bacchiocchi, William Shea, H.M.S. Richards, Sr., Siegfried H. Horn, George Cornell, Andrea Steele, Lynn Mallery, William Fagal, Beryl Johnson, Roy Allan Anderson, Phillip Knox—and especially to our editor, Ken McFarland, and to Bob Kyte of Pacific Press.

Finally, our appreciation to all who helped with typing, proofreading, and otherwise encouraging this publication.

Preface

TV will never tell you all the news. Not that it wouldn't if it could. But it *can't*.

TV newscasts can tell you what has already happened, but they can't tell you what *is going to* happen.

TV can echo your most-asked questions, but only rarely can it come up with satisfactory answers.

TV can report on war and crime and disaster—the bad news. But it doesn't seem able to find much good news.

Recently Bell and Associates—a national research and polling firm—conducted a series of surveys to determine today's most-asked questions. Questions such as—

> *"How can I cope with loneliness?"*
> *"How can I manage stress?"*
> *"Why is there so much suffering?"*
> *"How can I have financial security?"*
> *"Is the world coming unglued?"*

The book you are about to read offers answers to these and many more of today's most-asked questions. It presents more good news in one place than you have probably read in a long time.

This good news—these answers—are drawn from history's all-time best seller. To most people today, these things have been like well-hidden secrets. But for you who read these pages, they will become OPEN SECRETS!

Contents

How Nick Found Answers to His Questions

As the deafening blast of gunfire rang out, Nick's body lifted straight into the air—then he slumped in a heap to the floor. His legs would not move, and blood ran freely from his back. His friends watched in stunned horror, convinced he was dying!

It was Thursday, February 13—a day Nick will never forget as long as he lives. A day that would bring staggering and lasting changes into his life.

"I had a strange premonition that morning that something drastic was going to happen," Nick recalled, a slight frown creasing his forehead. "I can't explain it. And I couldn't stop it—it was just there."

Nick couldn't seem to shake the foreboding sense of uneasiness. It hung on like an Arctic chill. For some inexplicable reason, he had a strange compulsion to clean his bedroom.

"I started looking through all my things," Nick explained, "thinking that if something did happen to me, my parents would be going through all my stuff—and they would think everything had some meaning for me. But as I looked at most of my things, I realized they didn't have any meaning for me at all. I just threw them out. No need having them around, you know."

The strange premonition stayed with him. Looking

back, Nick finds it rather odd that he didn't tell his parents what was going on in his mind.

"I just thought, Well, tomorrow will be all right. This feeling will pass."

Nick, twenty-six years old, was a native of a large city in the Pacific Northwest—the son of loving, caring, middle-class parents. He had three older sisters, the youngest seven years his senior.

"I was a spoiled brat," confessed Nick with an engaging smile. "My dad used to call me the Crown Prince. I got whatever I wanted whenever I wanted it, so I had life really easy. I did have a nasty, bad temper, but mostly I was just a sweet little blond kid."

Nick attended military school in grades six through eight. "My father thought it would straighten me out. I never thought I needed to be straightened out, really, looking back on it. But my parents thought it would do me some good."

After high school, Nick got a job at the phone company. He had a lot of friends at work, and he enjoyed running with the fellows and having a good time. "I took a drink once in a while when the guys were sitting around having a beer. I didn't particularly like the taste of it, but later I got drunk with the guys occasionally."

On February 13, after cleaning his room, Nick met some of his friends and went to shoot pool at a local tavern. "I was pretty good at pool," Nick chuckled, "but that day I blew it. I couldn't even beat a woman I shot against! Everything seemed out of balance. I felt as if I were walking into something, with no power to stop. Somehow I didn't seem able to change my plans—I just felt compelled to go on."

Later that evening Nick and his friends decided to go to the house of a man who had a drug deal coming down, to buy some drugs. Soon another young fellow came in. No one paid any attention to him. "We had seen him around before. We figured he was OK—that he was there to buy drugs," Nick said, shifting a little in his chair.

But the young man had other plans! Whipping out a gun, he ordered, "All right, you guys—line up against that wall! Now, take off your clothes—and make it fast!"

"He had no intention of permitting us to follow him," Nick explained.

Stunned by the turn of events, Nick and his friends lost no time complying with his request. "You don't ask many questions when you're looking down the barrel of a gun," Nick added knowingly.

As Nick began stripping, he ran into problems. He had on high-top laced boots, and he couldn't seem to slip his tight Levis over them. Hurriedly he sat down to unlace his boots. And that's when it happened!

The intruder pulled the trigger, and a bullet crashed through Nick's shoulder, lodging against his spinal cord. The impact sent Nick straight up into the air—then he toppled to the floor.

He lay in the blood gushing from his back. And though shivering in shock, Nick never lost consciousness. Instantly he knew he was paralyzed. No one had to tell him.

Nick was rushed to the hospital, where everyone thought he was dying—the doctors, the nurses, his friends. But Nick knew differently. "I felt I would live—I just had that feeling." He did live, but it was a long, painful recovery. The Crown Prince would not have life really easy again for what would seem an eternity.

Young Nick's fun-loving, athletic lifestyle was gone forever. The emotional and mental impact of his paralysis was staggering! As he began taking inventory of the far-reaching consequences of his condition and contemplated his unsettling future, he began to seethe inwardly. Everything inside him began to rebel. He was angry—so angry he seemed incapable of controlling his turbulent feelings. He threw his food on the hospital walls.

"It's hard to believe, but I actually did that," Nick admitted, hanging his head in disbelief. "A kind nurse tried to help me cope. She thought it might help if I read the Bible. Do you know what I did with it? I threw it in the trash can! I was hurting—really hurting. My frustration had reached a breaking point."

Tormented by the thought of spending life in a wheelchair, Nick began to think of a way out. "Well, I thought, people say there's life after death—a good life—and if that's right, then why sit around in a wheelchair? I began thinking of suicide."

Nick shared his hospital room with two other young men, both quadriplegics. One of them, perhaps unwittingly, helped turn Nick's thinking around.

"I'll never forget it," Nick reflected. "I was having a bad time trying to dress myself. Everything seemed so difficult without the use of my legs. I became more and more frustrated and angry. I griped and grumbled, cursed and shouted—loud and long. Finally, one of the quadriplegics said, 'I'd be happy to trade places with you. I'd gladly take where you're at!' "

That seemingly backhanded reproach cut him to the quick. "It really shook me up. I knew right then that I couldn't continue to wallow in self-pity. So many other people were much worse off. I felt I just couldn't complain ever again."

Of course, Nick wanted more than what seemed apparent at that time. He could never be content just rocking and reminiscing about the past. He was young and wanted to live life to the fullest. He started searching for another way out of his seemingly impossible situation.

He thought of trying the Bible. Maybe it would help. But when he began reading, it didn't seem to make any sense at all.

Then one day he watched a movie about faith healers in the Philippines. Apparently people with all sorts of physical problems were being healed. Hope surged through him. If others were being healed, why not himself? He learned of a woman who was organizing a group of people to take to Manila for healing. The possibility appealed to him. True, it was a long shot, but it was tantalizing.

In mid-November Nick and his mother, with keen anticipation, boarded a plane for Manila. The trip proved an agonizing one for Nick. His skin began to break down as a result of sitting so long on the plane. By the time he and his mother arrived at their hotel in Manila, Nick was physically and emotionally spent. The pain he experienced was agonizing.

Because of his condition, Nick was taken to his room where he could lie down. The others in the group were taken to a large room in the hotel where many faith healers came to interview them. "All in all, there were probably sixty to seventy people in the group—maybe more," Nick guessed.

Later, some of the faith healers came to Nick's room. As he recalled it, some of their rituals bordered on the bizarre. And though they returned several times attempting to heal him, they were unable to do so.

During the time the faith healers were coming and going, someone gave Nick some books to read on spiritualism. "Part of the reading made good sense," Nick said, "but I had the unsettling feeling that something was wrong after I studied it—it just didn't all fit."

When the regular faith healers were unable to heal Nick, they announced that they had asked the chief healer to visit him. Surely *he* could help Nick. A few days later, the most important of the healers arrived with several of his protégés. After trying several times, the man frankly admitted, "I can't do anything for you. The only thing for you to do is pray and read the Bible."

"He didn't even heal me so I could sit without pain!" Nick added. "I began to pray—'Please heal me. I want to be healed.' Over and over I prayed, but nothing happened."

The Christmas holidays were now approaching, so a discouraged Nick and his disappointed mother returned to the United States. The trip back proved even more torturous for Nick than the trip to Manila had been. He felt as if he were sitting on a searing hot iron all the way. By the time the plane landed, Nick's nerves were nearly shattered—he was too weak to go home. From the plane, he was taken back to the hospital. But the reception his doctors gave him there was less than enthusiastic.

"Well, here's the kid that went to the faith healers in the Philippines to get healed," they seemed to be thinking. "Now he's back, worse off than ever, for *us* to heal."

But through all his ordeal, something had happened to Nick. No, he wasn't healed. But at least something had changed. He no longer lashed out in his frustration. His inward seething had simmered to a more controllable level. "My desire to commit suicide was gone," Nick said. "And I had also made a decision to live with my problem. I started reading and studying in earnest—searching for meaning to my life.

"I read Eastern philosophies, one by one, and decided that some parts were nice, some parts were true—but that ultimately they didn't hold water. All the while I felt as if something were missing. My heart ached with emptiness. I couldn't shake it, and I didn't understand it."

Nick wanted to return to work. He tried to get on again with the phone company where he had worked, but they wouldn't take him back. Through one of his counselors, he found a job with the local art museum on their admissions desk. The job was pleasant. Nick felt good about working again, but the ache in his heart was still there.

In his new position, Nick had plenty of time, between admissions, to read. He read about various religions. And again he discovered some things that sounded good and seemed right, but something seemed to be missing from each of them.

Nick became friends with some of the guards at the museum. They were always interested in what he was reading and offered suggestions that they felt might help him. One day a guard brought him a book called *The Desire of Ages*—a book on the life of Christ.

"It took me six months to read that big book," Nick remembered. "But it had a certain ring. I knew it was all true. As I studied the life of Christ, it did something to me. I decided that I wanted to become a Christian—to do what God wanted me to do. I wanted to accept Him and become His follower, but I wasn't sure how to do it."

Again Nick picked up the Bible and started to study and read in earnest. Now it was thrilling. It made sense—good sense. He couldn't seem to study enough. The Bible had come alive!

Soon Nick attended some religious lectures and listened to some tapes about becoming a victorious Christian. What he learned melted his heart. "I didn't like everything I heard," Nick admitted, "because I knew I'd have to change my lifestyle—eliminate some things from my life, you understand. But I knew that at last I had found what I was searching for—TRUTH. I now had discovered meaning to my life. I had hope for the future—and a peace I can't explain. I truly have been blessed."

Today Nick is still in a wheelchair. The bullet is still lodged against his spinal cord. But he has a peace, a radiance, and joy beyond all description.

"It's strange, but the dull ache is gone," he says. "It left me. I'm not saying that I like where I'm at—but I am saying that I wouldn't trade what I know now for the ability to be back walking again."

Nick would like nothing more than to share what he has found with everyone everywhere—for millions are longing and searching for peace in this troubled world. Millions are seeking answers to troubling questions that seem to have no real answers.

Nick found what he was searching for in the study of the Bible—and in a book given to him by a friend. The truth and hope he found is clearly presented in the upcoming chapters of this book.

So friend—if you search for solutions to your problems—if you seek answers to your questions—if you need help where you're hurting—if you look for something to fill your inner emptiness—the end of your search could be as simple a matter as turning to the next chapter.

As with Nick, what you desire too deeply for words may seem to be an ever-retreating mirage—an elusive secret. But be assured that if indeed it is a secret, it is an *open* secret.

How Can I Cope With Loneliness?

Lonely voices crying in the city,
Lonely voices sounding like a child.
Lonely voices come from busy people,
Too disturbed to stop a little while.

"Oh, God, I'm so lonely!" How often this agonizing cry goes out from people plagued by a loneliness that eats away at their very souls. Loneliness is a disease of our age. The world is full of lonely people.

So many lonely people! Solomon once observed, "Woe to him that is alone when he falleth; for he hath not another to help him up." Ecclesiastes 4:10. Psychologists tell us that at all times in our lives we must have at least one person who cares about us and whom we ourselves care for. Much unhappiness, depression, and many suicides are the result of people feeling lonely and unloved. If the past holds no meaning, the present no joy, the future no hope, and no one seems to care—what is there to live for?

Evidently David felt this utter loneliness in his life at one time, for he wrote, "I am like a vulture in a far-off wilderness, or like an owl alone in the desert. I lie awake, lonely as a solitary sparrow on the roof." Psalm 102:6, 7, LB.

Many people embark on dangerous trips, desperately searching for a means of escaping loneliness. Some pop pills, some inject heroin, others join street gangs. Some turn to alcohol, some to fun and games. Some turn to prostitution, while others busy themselves acquiring things. All of them are chasing fragile bubbles, only to have them burst, leaving a greater void, a deeper loneliness than before.

Is there more to life? Is there meaning to it at all? Is there anyone who really cares? Yes, life is more than a meaningless pause between two eternities. There is Someone who cares!

Jacob, driven from his home, threatened with death by his angry brother, separated from his loved ones for the first time in his life, lay down on the ground with a stone for his pillow. In his utter loneliness he felt that even God might have forsaken him. With deep agony and weeping he confessed his sins and begged God to give him some evidence that He still cared for him. In that lonely moment in Jacob's experience, God spoke these words of comfort and assurance: "I am with you and will watch over you wherever you go, . . . I will not leave you." Genesis 28:15, NIV.

Don't you like that? What God said to Jacob so long ago He says to every man and woman today. You are never alone! God is right there with you when you need Him. You don't have to make an appointment with Him. You don't have to stand in line because He is busy somewhere out there running the universe. He is always there!

"But," some say, "He is so far away. How can I trust a God I cannot see? A God I do not know?" Can anyone really know what God is like? We need to know!

Job said, "Acquaint now thyself with him, and be at peace." Job 22:21. We are invited to become acquainted with God. Furthermore, the Bible says that when we get to know Him, we find peace. You can call off your search for peace of mind and find a solution for loneliness when you get to know Him.

How do we know that there is a God? What evidence do

we have that He exists? The prophet Isaiah felt that there was evidence: "Lift up your eyes on high, and behold who hath created these things, that bringeth out their host by number: he called them all by names by the greatness of his might." Isaiah 40:26.

Through the centuries man has marveled at the mysteries of the heavens, wondering what secrets lie hidden in outer space. During the Dark Ages the church tried to keep men from looking at the universe through the telescope. The church leaders were afraid that if man studied the heavens too closely he might discover things that would shake his faith in God.

However, as man has invented bigger and better means of probing the heavens, his faith in God has increased, for "the heavens declare the glory of God; the skies proclaim the work of his hands. Day after day they pour forth speech; night after night they display knowledge. There is no speech or language where their voice is not heard." Psalm 19:1-3, NIV.

There is no language barrier to the message splashed across the Heavens telling about God. "Without a sound or word, silent in the skies, their message reaches out to all the world." Psalm 19:3, LB.

Before the invention of the telescope, men counted the stars they could see and concluded that there were exactly 5,119 stars. No more! But for centuries the Bible had stated, "The host of heaven cannot be numbered." Jeremiah 33:22. Today, as we swing our giant telescopes toward the heavens, we discover that many of the those tiny dots of light twinkling in the sky are not just stars, but whole galaxies made up of millions of blazing suns like our own. And surrounding these innumerable suns are numberless planets, traveling through space together.

As you gaze up at the Milky Way, you are looking at the edge of our own galaxy, a star system shaped like a saucer.

Astronomer Fritz Conn says, "Our home in the universe is a spiral of 200 billion stars, a unit of suns whirling through space like a fiery pinwheel." Every 24 hours our galaxy travels a million and a half miles through space at more than 66,000 miles per hour. Feel a little tired? Anyone who has traveled that far in a day has a right to be tired! Beyond our Milky Way system, stretching above, below, and around us, are millions of other galaxies. If we divide the sky into windows the size of the moon, our telescopes can find 1,000 galaxies in each windowpane. Photographs have been made with more than 10,000 such galaxies on one plate! "The huge 200-inch Hale reflector on Palomar Mountain . . . can see as many as a million galaxies inside the bowl of the Big Dipper alone!"—*National Geographic,* May 1974, page 592. If the island universes are distributed equally, we arrive at a figure of 100 billion galaxies—each composed of 200 to 500 billion stars, each star one million times as large as our Earth.

Inconceivable? So it seems! Yet God used two illustrations that help us to comprehend a little better the immensity of it all. God took Abraham outdoors and challenged him to count the stars. "Look up at the heavens and count the stars—if indeed you can count them," God said. Then He added, "So shall your offspring be." Genesis 15:5, NIV.

Evidently God took Abraham down by the shore of the Dead Sea at another time and said to him, "I will multiply thy seed as the stars of the heaven, and as the sand which is upon the sea shore." Genesis 22:17.

Recently an astronomer said that if you could count all the grains of sand by all the seashores in the world, you would have approximately the same number of grains of sand as there are stars in the heavens. The next time you are at the beach you might try counting the number of grains in a bucketful of sand. Better allow plenty of time! Is it any wonder that David said, "When I consider thy heavens, the work of thy fingers, the moon and the stars, which thou hast ordained; what is man, that thou art mindful of him?" Psalm 8:3, 4.

Have you ever wondered if a powerful God who rules and sustains such a vast universe is actually concerned with man and his problems here on Earth? Jesus said that not even a sparrow falls to the ground that God does not notice. "So don't be afraid," He said, "you are worth more than many sparrows." Matthew 10:31, NIV. As if to emphasize God's love and care, Jesus said, "Even the very hairs of your head are all numbered." Matthew 10:30, NIV.

What a God!

Impressive as the innumerable suns and galaxies may be, the size of the universe in which we live is even more awesome. Man has already traveled almost 250,000 miles into space in *Apollo II*. Neil Armstrong and Edwin Aldrin walked on the moon, but that was not really much of a trip. The moon is our nearest neighbor. The nearest star to Earth, the sun, is more than a million times the size of our Earth and is 93 million miles away. Yet we are still in our own neighborhood!

Aside from the sun, the star nearest Earth is Proxima Centauri—more than four light years away, or approximately 24 trillion miles from Earth. If we traveled in a rocketship at a speed of 25,000 miles per hour, it would take us 120,000 years to reach this star! Are you beginning to sense the immeasurable expanse of space?

The Mount Palomar telescope can pick up light that started on its way through space more than 2 billion years ago! Radio telescopes are able to pick up waves that started on their way to Earth over 20 billion years ago! That is not to say that our Earth was here 20 billion years ago, but that the light started on its way 20 billion years ago and is just now reaching us! No wonder the prophet of old said, "Behold the height of the stars, how high they are!" Job 22:12.

It is difficult for the human mind to comprehend innumerable worlds, immeasurable space, and the intricate design evident everywhere in the universe. Yet this incredibly complex universe is as smooth running as a delicate, finely tuned watch. Just think! Billions of galaxies, each traveling at phenomenal speed in its appointed course through the skies, sometimes passing right through one another, like water-skiers in a ballet. Yet timing is so precise that astronomers can predict the location of these heavenly bodies thousands of years into the future. What a master Intelligence that demands!

Isaiah reveals the power behind the Hand that winds the mighty mainspring, keeping the heavenly clock in motion: "To whom can the holy God be compared? Is there anyone else like him? Look up at the sky! Who created the stars you see? The one who leads them out like an army, he knows how many there are and calls each one by name! His power is so great—not one of them is ever missing!" Isaiah 40:25, TEV.

Dr. Edwin B. Frost, who for many years was the director of Yerkes Observatory, wrote: "There is no evidence that the universe is automatic, or that it has within itself the power to make the laws which govern it. Mere matter cannot be endowed with such capacity. The universe is not a haphazard aggregation of accidental bodies moving without system or order. It is the work of Omnipotence."—Phillip L. Knox, Wonder Worlds, page 13.

Paul recognized this when he said, "In and through Him the universe is one harmonious whole." Colossians 1:17, Weymouth.

Whether we study tiny atoms or giant galaxies, we find the incredible design and order of a Master Intelligence—a Master Designer. All creation witnesses to a Creator! The very first sentence in the Bible clearly pinpoints this Creator: "In the beginning God created the heaven and the earth." Genesis 1:1.

Nobel prize-winning physicist, Dr. Arthur Compton, wrote, "For myself, faith begins with a realization that a supreme intelligence brought the universe into being and created man. It is not difficult for me to have this faith for it is incontrovertible that where there is a plan, there is an intelligence. An orderly unfolding universe testifies to the truth of the most majestic statement, 'In the beginning God.'"—*Chicago Daily News,* quoted in *New Life Guide,* number 2.

"By the word of the Lord were the heavens made." "For he spake, and it was done; he commanded, and it stood fast." Psalm 33:6, 9. God took His unlimited energy and congealed it into matter. Jeremiah tells us how He did it: "He hath made the earth by his power, he hath established the world by his wisdom, and hath stretched out the heavens by his discretion." Jeremiah 10:12.

God has given us many evidences of His existence. "His eternal power and deity, has been clearly perceived in the things that have been made." Romans 1:20, RSV.

When Robinson Crusoe discovered fresh footprints in the wet sand, he knew there was another person on the island, even though he had not seen the person. "If one print of a bare foot in the sand is absolute proof of the existence and presence of a human being, what are we to think when we see the prints of the Master's shoes, as John Bunyan calls them, covering the whole world?"—*Does God Exist?* page 5.

Although deteriorated by the curse of sin and by man's careless pollution, the world still reveals a breathtaking display of God's footprints. We catch a glimpse of the fingers of our Creator's majesty at the most unexpected moments and places:

In brilliant sunsets, each uniquely beautiful, crowning the last steps of day.
In tiny snowflakes—each with its intricate, geometric design.

In the profusion of fragrant flowers—delicately tinted, dotting the landscape.

In lofty redwoods and picturesque Joshua trees.

In scented pines and autumn maples.

In winter's frost and snow-capped peaks—on every opening bud and tiny seed—we see the prints of the Master's shoes covering the whole world.

We can but echo David's praise, "Great are the works of the Lord." "Glorious and majestic are his deeds." Psalm 111:2, 3, NIV.

God not only made man and gave him a beautiful universe to live in, but He is also mindful of man's needs: "The eyes of all look to you, and you give them their food at the proper time. You open your hand and satisfy the desires of every living thing." Psalm 145:15, 16, NIV. "He maketh his sun to rise on the evil and on the good, and sendeth rain on the just and on the unjust." Matthew 5:45.

Let us take a look at just a few of the ways God cares for the needs of His creatures. The water you drink is older than the pyramids, as old as the hills. Water may be polluted by chemicals or wastes, but let the sun evaporate or lift it into the atmosphere, and it becomes clean and usable again and again, distributed by rain, dew, or snow. What a tremendous water system God designed!

Then, there is God's great power plant in the sky. If the sun were a little bigger or a little closer to Earth, our oceans would boil away. If the sun were a just a little smaller or a little farther away, our atmosphere would freeze. Either way, life could not exist on Earth. But God not only created all things, He sustains all things.

"In his hand is the life of every creature and the breath of all mankind." Job 12:10, NIV.

The air we breathe is a gift of God, an evidence of His care and love. God designed the universe, and He knew just the right formula for the air we breathe to sustain life and health on Earth. He knew just the right amount of nitrogen, oxygen, argon, and carbon dioxide to mix into the atmosphere.

And as God supplies our needs from the atmosphere, He does it with such consummate beauty! He colors the sky blue with oxygen molecules in the air that scatter the shortest wavelengths of visible light. He makes rainbows, beautiful cloud formations, varied sunrises and sunsets—all through atmospheric conditions. Our whole world is amazingly adapted for human habitation, with scenes to delight our senses.

God did not create this beautiful world and magnificent universe in vain. He created it for beings who could appreciate and enjoy it. That is what the Bible means when it says, "He created it not in vain, he formed it to be inhabited." Isaiah 45:18.

There is no end to the wonders in our natural world, no end to God's care for His creatures. Think of the migration of the birds, one of the greatest puzzles of nature. How can birds weighing less than an ounce navigate thousands of miles nonstop to a destination they have never seen? How can fish find streams where their lives began, 1,200 miles across featureless oceans? How did they learn when and where to go? Who taught the honeybee to make the honeycomb which is such an engineering marvel—and with a brain no larger than a pinhead! Who is the mastermind behind it all?

Job tells us: "But ask the animals, and they will teach you, or the birds of the air, and they will tell you; or speak to the earth, and it will teach you, or let the fish of the sea inform you. Which of all these does not know that the hand of the Lord has done this?" Job 12:7-9, NIV.

Yes, God did it all! In fact, our duty and privilege to worship God is based on the fact that He is our Creator, and to

Him all things owe their existence. "Know that the Lord is God. It is he who made us, and we are his; we are his people, the sheep of his pasture." Psalm 100:3, NIV.

As we view all the marvels in nature, we once again have evidence that the God of the universe does care about us and is anxious to help us. He knows all of our needs, and He has the power to supply those needs. "Ah, Sovereign Lord, you have made the heavens and the earth by your great power and outstretched arm. Nothing is too hard for you." Jeremiah 32:17, NIV.

Doesn't it give you peace of mind to know that God can handle everything in the universe and in your personal life? No problem is too small to bring to the God of the atom, nor too large to bring to the God of the galaxies. God knows everything, and He even knows it all ahead of time. He says, "I am God, and there is none like me, declaring the end from the beginning, and from ancient times the things that are not yet done." Isaiah 46:9, 10.

What peace and confidence we can have—knowing that nothing can happen to us that is too hard for God to take care of. Because He is all-wise and always dependable, He will do what is best for us.

But best of all, "God is love." 1 John 4:8. Jesus Himself said, "The Father himself loves you." John 16:27, NIV.

Does it surprise you that the mighty God who created and sustains such a colossal, complete universe could be concerned about you? It is staggering to contemplate God's unlimited power. It is equally difficult to understand His inscrutable wisdom and His ability to be everywhere. But love is something we can understand. And there is nothing in all the world than can separate us from God's love. "I am convinced that neither death nor life, neither angels nor demons, neither the present nor the future, nor any powers, neither height nor depth, nor anything else in all creation, will be able to separate us from the love of

God that is in Christ Jesus our Lord." Romans 8:38, NIV.

God loves us when we are lovable—and when we are unlovable. He loves us whether we are black or white, male or female, beautiful or ugly. There is nobody else like that! But most important, He loves us forever! "Yea, I have loved thee with an everlasting love." Jeremiah 31:3. David wrote, "The Lord is good and his love endures forever." Psalm 100:5, NIV.

As if there still might be some doubt in our minds about His love, God explains it in such simple terms that we can easily understand: "Can a woman forget her nursing child, and have no compassion on the son of her womb?" Isaiah 49:15, NASB. Strange as it may seem, that has happened. But God says, "Even these may forget, but I will not forget you. Behold, I have inscribed you on the palms of My hands." Isaiah 49:15, 16, NASB.

God tried to demonstrate His love to man, but words and messages sent by prophets and angels were not enough. We did not get the message. So God sent His Son. Jesus was a perfect revelation of the personality and character of God. He said, "He that hath seen me hath seen the Father." John 14:9.

If we really want to know what God is like, we should study the life of Jesus. He took our nature that He might reach our needs. He preached the good news of salvation to the poor. He healed the brokenhearted and gave sight to the blind. He fed the hungry and ate with people in their homes. He forgave their sins and gave them hope for the future. His face was the first face many saw—His voice the first many ever heard. He spread life and joy through the villages and towns where He walked.

His life was one of self-denial and thoughtful care for others. As we see Him washing the feet of the one who betrayed Him; as we see the shame, the insults, and humiliation He endured, the death at Calvary and His broken heart, we begin to understand a little bit of the love of God for His children.

"For God so loved the world, that he gave his only begotten Son." John 3:16.

God gave His son to a fallen race—to a planet in rebellion. What more could He do to show His tender love? Christ died in your place and mine. He suffered the cruel lashing, the thorns driven into His forehead, the nails driven through His hands and feet, without protest. He could have called ten thousand angels to set Him free, but He could not save Himself and save others too. This was the ultimate gift of a loving, caring God for guilty man—for you and for me. As His bruised and bleeding body hung on the cross, He prayed, "Father, forgive them; for they know not what they do." Luke 23:34.

That is what God is like!

And listen, friend, the suffering of God did not begin or end at Calvary. Ever since man chose to go his own way, God has suffered. He feels the separation, the pain of loneliness, more deeply than we, because He loves more deeply. God longs to restore Earth's inhabitants, His children, back to His family. He is pleading right now,"Look unto me, and be ye saved, all the ends of the earth: for I am God, and there is none else." Isaiah 45:22.

He is the only One! The One who garnishes the valleys with wildflowers and sees the sparrow fall. The One who claims ownership of the cattle upon a thousand hills and numbers the hairs upon our heads. The One who sees each tear that falls.

> And while He guides the Universe
> By miracle divine
> And calls a million stars by name,
> He's not forgotten mine.
> —Anonymous

What a God! "He's big enough to rule the mighty universe, yet small enough to live within my heart."

With such an all-wise, all-powerful, all-loving God who sustains and controls the whole universe, yet numbers the very hairs on our heads, we need never feel that we are alone or fear for our future survival. He certainly is capable of protecting us.

"But," you say, "if a loving God is in control of things, why is the world in such a mess?"

That is a good question. The next chapter answers that very important question from God's Holy Word. You may be surprised by the answer!

Why Is There So Much Suffering?

From the university classrooms and bookstores of San Francisco to the plush cinemas and shabby tenements of New York, we are being bombarded by the mystic deeds of the supernatural, the bizarre world of the occult, the zany rituals of Satan worship.

Spectacular headlines, theater marquees, and supermarket tabloids blaze with supernatural intrigue. The bewildering predictions of supermarket psychics and syndicated astrologers tantalize man's curiosity. No longer is it the superstitious who check their daily zodiac sign. Astrology is a $200 million-a-year business! Forty million Americans seem to have "stars" in their eyes.

More than forty universities in America offer courses in witchcraft, ESP, or psychic phenomena—and all classes are full. The human mind seems to be absolutely captivated by the lure of the unknown. Indeed, we are living in an age when the supernatural almost seems natural!

One of the most surprising things about the psychic explosion is that many people assume that if it's supernatural, it's from God. But is that true? Or is there another sinister, misleading power also operating in the unseen world? To be uninformed is risky business!

"But," you say, "what about the predictions of the psychics? Some seem to show amazing accuracy—enough to suggest a supernatural power." True, yet the psychics' batting average is less than impressive.

Ralph Blodgett, while assistant editor of *These Times* magazine, wrote: "Counterfeit prophets annually fire buckshot into tomorrow's clouds, hoping to bag an occasional stray duck as it passes overhead. . . . What we found for 1978 completely shatters the oft-publicized myth of psychic accuracy. Out of 250 specific published predictions, we found less than 3 percent (i.e., six) that we could list as reasonably fulfilled and 97 percent (244) that missed the mark completely."—*These Times*, March 1979.

One newscaster said he could guess future events with 65 percent accuracy without any psychic or supernatural help—just by using good common sense and keeping informed.

Why is it that psychics have the ability to predict some events with accuracy, while at other times they miss completely? What pipeline do the seers use? Who is communicating with the psychics—if anyone? Are all supernatural manifestations mere trickery, or are some real? If they are real, is God the source of wisdom behind them?

You may be surprised to learn that the first recorded psychic experience occurred some 6,000 years ago, and that it is documented in the Bible. Let's read about it:

"Now the serpent was more crafty than any of the wild animals the Lord God had made. He said to the woman, 'Did God really say, "You must not eat from any tree in the garden"?' The woman said to the serpent, 'We may eat fruit from the trees in the garden, but God did say, "You must not eat fruit from the tree that is in the middle of the garden, and you must not touch it, or you will die."' 'You will not surely die!' the serpent said to the woman. 'For God knows that when you eat of it your eyes will be opened, and you will be like God, knowing good and evil.'" Genesis 3:1-4, NIV.

What would you do if you were approached by a talking

snake? Would you listen in stunned amazement, or would you run for your life? Eve did not run. You see, she had never experienced pain or harm or anything unpleasant. She did not know fear. Curious, she lingered. Eve did not realize the sinister power behind the serpent's voice. She never dreamed that the serpent was only a medium for another being.

Who was this power operating through the serpent? God Himself unveils the mystic power behind the psychic world—the world of the occult, spirit mediums, and devil worship: "The great dragon was cast out, that old serpent, called the Devil, and Satan, which deceiveth the whole world: he was cast out into the earth, and his angels were cast out with him." Revelation 12:9.

From what place were they cast out? The Bible says, "I saw Satan fall like lightning from heaven." Luke 10:18, NIV.

A devil in heaven? Incredible, but true! The Bible unveils a most tragic story. Satan, or Lucifer, as his name used to be, was a beautiful, powerful angel in heaven. Contrary to most artists' paintings, the devil is not an ugly monster with horns, a tail, and a pitchfork in hand. Nothing could be further from the truth.

Using the symbolism of the King of Tyre, the Bible describes Satan in heaven before he was cast into the earth: "You were the model of perfection, full of wisdom and perfect in beauty. You were in Eden, the garden of God; every precious stone adorned you. . . . You were anointed as a guardian cherub, for so I ordained you." Ezekiel 28:12-14, NIV.

Lucifer held an exalted position in heaven. He was a guardian cherub, or angel, who stood beside God's throne. But this angel was not content being next to God. Something happened that spoiled this close relationship. God said of him, "Thou wast perfect in thy ways from the day that thou wast created, till iniquity was found in thee." "Thine heart was lifted up because of thy beauty, thou hast cor-rupted thy wisdom by reason of thy brightness." Ezekiel 28:15, 17.

This beautiful, exalted angel became lost on an ego trip. He coveted the glory and homage due God alone. He was power hungry. In fact, this created angel had the bold-ness to challenge his Creator for the rulership of the uni-verse! "How art thou fallen from heaven, O Lucifer, son of the morning! how art thou cast down to the ground. . . . For thou hast said in thine heart, I will ascend into heaven, I will exalt my throne above the stars of God. . . . I will be like the most High." Isaiah 14:12-14.

As these arrogant words spilled forth from Lucifer's lips, the perfect love and harmony of heaven was shattered into a million selfish pieces. It wasn't long before Lucifer began to spread the spirit of discontent among the other angels. Insid-iously he undermined God's love and justice. Like a rotten ap-ple in a box, his rebellion spread to other angels in heaven.

God could have eliminated Lucifer and the angels who chose to join his revolution, in one blinding flash. But had He done so, all His creatures would have served Him out of fear. We know that God is a God of love. He can only be happy in a love relationship with His creatures, where they worship Him because they love and trust Him.

Lucifer questioned God's wisdom and justice—the way He ran the universe. He challenged God's laws and His fair-ness. But God did not place His laws in operation to show who was boss. He made them to protect His creatures, to ensure their peace and happiness. His laws are like stoplights and speed-limit signs—all planned for our safety and well-being.

But this most honored of all the angels thought that he could run the universe better than God, so Lucifer, "son of the morning," by his spirit of deceit and rebellion, became Satan, "the adversary of God."

Out of fairness and love, God has allowed Satan to demonstrate to the universe the way he would run the world. By this plan He shows the universe the result of disregarding His all-wise plans for perfect love and harmony. Satan has been allowed to demonstrate the true character of sin.

The insidious virus of doubt and deception spread by Satan infected one third of the angels of heaven, leading to open rebellion. And strange as it may seem, there was war in heaven! The Bible describes it:

"There was war in heaven: Michael and his angels fought against the dragon; and the dragon fought and his angels, and prevailed not; neither was their place found anymore in heaven. And the great dragon . . . that old serpent, called the Devil, and Satan, which deceiveth the whole world: he was cast out into the earth, and his angels were cast out with him." Revelation 12:7-9.

Heaven became the battleground of the first war, and Satan and his angels were thrown out of heaven. The conflict between Christ and Satan was not over. It just changed theaters! The battle that began in heaven moved to Planet Earth. Earth became the stage upon which the great controversy between good and evil would be dramatized, where Satan would demonstrate his kind of government and how he would run the world.

But why Earth? Why did our planet have to become "a spectacle to the whole universe, to angels as well as to men"? 1 Corinthians 4:9, NIV.

The earth had just come from the fingertips of the Creator's hands, in all its splendor and perfection, beautiful beyond description—a home designed and decorated by the Creator Himself! No home has ever been so lovely.

Evidently Satan thought so, too, for he saw this world as a prize worth capturing. He would not attempt to invade and control an established planet with millions of loyal, God-loving inhabitants. Rather, he would attempt to seize a planet of fragile beauty, a new-born world.

Although Adam and Eve were created perfect, they were not placed beyond the possibility of wrongdoing. They were free to choose to love and follow God—or to ignore His instructions. But their loyalty would be tested, and that test would focus on a single tree. God warned, "You are free to eat from any tree in the garden; but you must not eat from the tree of the knowledge of good and evil, for when you eat of it you will surely die." Genesis 2:16, 17, NIV.

That seemed a reasonable request. Perhaps they smiled and thought, "Fair enough. That's easy." They must have felt quite secure. But man is most vulnerable when he is caught completely off guard because he feels secure. That is what happened to Eve. Satan used his supernatural, psychic power to deceive her. Satan rarely works openly. He uses governments, organizations, people, or even a serpent. That is why Paul said, "Put on the full armor of God so that you can take your stand against the devil's schemes. For our struggle is not against flesh and blood, but against the rulers, against the authorities, against the powers of this dark world and against the spiritual forces of evil in the heavenly realms." Ephesians 6:11, 12, NIV.

Eve was deceived—she never suspected that the words from the talking snake came from Satan. The devil, speaking through the serpent, said to her, "Did God really say, 'You must not eat from any tree in the Garden'?" Genesis 3:1, NIV.

Eve quickly replied, "We may eat fruit from the trees in the garden, but God did say, 'You must not eat fruit from the tree that is in the middle of the garden, and you must not touch it, or you will die.' " Genesis 3:2, 3, NIV.

But the serpent scoffed. "You will not surely die" (Genesis 3:4, NIV), he said, as if the idea were ridiculous.

As Eve listened to the serpent, it must have crossed her mind that it was contradicting God. Who was right? Perhaps sensing that she felt confused, the serpent hurriedly added, "For God knows that when you eat of it your eyes will be opened, and you will be like God, knowing good and evil." Genesis 3:5, NIV.

The devil suggested that God was unfair, that He was holding back something good. To be like God had been Satan's consuming desire and his downfall. Now it sounded good to Eve, too, and in an impetuous moment, she sold out. "When the woman saw that the fruit of the tree was good for food and pleasing to the eye, and also desirable for gaining wisdom, she took some and ate it." Genesis 3:6, NIV.

Adam and Eve failed God's test of love and loyalty, and it was not long before they knew that something had gone wrong. For the first time in their lives they felt afraid, ashamed, guilty. In time they realized that by disobedience, they had lost everything: happiness, perfect love, fellowship with God, their garden home, and the dominion of Planet Earth. No longer masters, they had made themselves slaves!

Paul said, "Don't you know that when you offer yourselves to someone to obey him as slaves, you are slaves to the one whom you obey?" Romans 6:16, NIV.

Satan had hijacked the new-born world. From that moment he laid claim to dominion and the title, "Prince of this World" (see John 12:31)—the ruler of a planet in rebellion.

As this most tragic day in history drew to a close, God came in the cool of the evening as usual, calling for Adam and Eve. Until now this had been the happy time of their day. But not so this day. They ran and hid. Finally, Adam slipped slowly from behind some shrubs in the garden and confessed, "I heard you in the garden, and I was afraid because I was naked; so I hid." Genesis 3:10, NIV.

Adam had never been afraid before. But that is what sin does. It makes a person afraid, even of God. God replied,

"Have you eaten from the tree that I commanded you not to eat from?" Genesis 3:11, NIV.

Notice Adam's reply: "The woman you put here with me—she gave me some fruit from the tree, and I ate it." Genesis 3:12, NIV. A few hours before, Adam had been willing to die for Eve. Now he blamed her for his problems—and he blamed God for creating her. How sin shatters perfect love!

Eve was no less accusing: "Then the Lord God said to the woman, 'What is this you have done?' The woman said, 'The serpent deceived me, and I ate.'" Genesis 3:13, NIV. Eve put the blame on God too. "It's the serpent You made that got me into trouble," she said. Like Adam, she tried to justify herself by placing the responsibility for her sin on God.

That very day Adam and Eve were doomed to die. Immortality had been promised on condition of obedience. By disobeying, they forfeited eternal life. In order to possess an endless life, man must continue to eat of the tree of life. Deprived of this, his vitality would gradually diminish until life would end.

To keep Adam and Eve from eating the fruit of the tree of life and living forever to perpetuate sin, God evicted them from their garden home. "After he drove the man out, he placed on the east side of the Garden of Eden cherubim and a flaming sword flashing back and forth to guard the way to the tree of life." Genesis 3:24, NIV.

The devil had said, "Ye shall not surely die." But deprived of the tree of life, Adam and Eve did die. The Bible says: "Altogether, Adam lived 930 years, and then he died." Genesis 5:5, NIV. Too late, Adam and Eve discovered that the devil "is a liar and the father of lies." John 8:44, NIV.

Our perfect world was blighted with the curse of sin. Earth became a pesthouse of disease, cruelty, and death, engulfed in trouble, tears, and terror. And bewildered millions want to know why. Who is to blame? When will it end? Doesn't God care? Are we only a forgotten little planet out on the edge of the universe—a world that doesn't matter?

It is easy to blame God for the world's heartbreak and devastation, but Satan is really responsible for the havoc. He is the one who brought trouble to this planet and who has been pushing sin and suffering ever since.

Jesus unmasked the devil and the way he afflicts people. As He was teaching in the synagogue one Sabbath, He noticed a woman bent over with a crippling deformity. Touched by her pathetic circumstances, Jesus healed her. The rulers instantly criticized Him because the healing took place on Sabbath. But notice how He defended His actions: "And ought not this woman, being a daughter of Abraham, whom *Satan hath bound,* lo, these eighteen years, be loosed from this bond on the Sabbath day?" Luke 13:16, emphasis supplied.

Jesus said that Satan had bound this woman. He was the guilty one. In fact, he is the sinister force behind all disease and suffering, heartache and death.

Perhaps nowhere in the Bible are Satan and his strategy more clearly exposed than in the first chapter of Job, in a conversation between God and the devil. It was some time after the fall of Satan that the sons of God presented themselves before Him. Satan came too. Think of that: a meeting of the "sons of God," and Satan crashed the party!

"The Lord said to Satan, 'Where have you come from?'" Job 1:7, NIV. In other words, "Who invited you? What right do you have to be here?"

"Satan answered the Lord, 'From roaming through the earth and going back and forth in it.'" Job 1:7, NIV. Satan claimed complete dominion over the earth and its inhabitants! He had taken over Adam's position.

Adam is called a "son of God" (see Luke 3:38), just like the others who came that day for a meeting with God. Could it be that they were appointed heads of other worlds, just as Adam was originally the head of our world? At any rate, Satan's claim to represent Earth did not go unchallenged. "Then the Lord said to Satan, 'Have you considered my servant Job? There is no one on earth like him; he is blameless and upright, a man who fears God and shuns evil.' " Job 1:8, NIV.

The Lord was saying, "Wait a minute, there's Job. He hasn't chosen to serve you. He serves me!"

"Well," sneered Satan, "why shouldn't he? You've given him riches and honor. He's the greatest man of the East! No wonder he worships you. But take away all the things You've given him, and he'll curse You to Your face."

What a challenge! Satan claimed that the only reason Job was loyal to God was because of what God did for him—not because he loved and trusted Him. The Lord said, "Very well, then, everything he has is in your hands, but on the man himself do not lay a finger." Job 1:12, NIV.

Satan left, eager to get his hands on Job's possessions. The blows soon began to fall. First, the Sabeans stole Job's cattle and murdered his cowhands. Next, lightning struck, killing his sheep and shepherds. Then the Chaldeans came and plundered Job's camels. But the most heartbreaking news of all was yet to come: a tornado demolished the home of Job's oldest son. A party had been on; all ten of Job's children were killed!

Although overcome with grief, Job's loyalty to God was unchanged. He said, "The Lord gave and the Lord has taken away; may the name of the Lord be praised." Job 1:21, NIV.

Job thought that the Lord had taken away his possessions and caused all the heartache. He did not yet understand that Satan, the destroyer, was responsible. Although he could not understand the tragedies that devastated his possessions and family, Job trusted God's goodness just the same.

Again Satan challenged God, saying, "A man will give all he has for his own life. But stretch out your hand and strike his flesh and bones, and he will surely curse you to your face." Job 2:4, 5, NIV.

The Lord said to Satan, "Very well, then, he is in your hands; but you must spare his life." Job 2:6, NIV.

Would Job remain loyal to God when the going got rougher, or would he turn his back on God? The test was on. "So Satan went out from the presence of the Lord and afflicted Job with painful sores from the soles of his feet to the top of his head." Job 2:7, NIV.

But even though Satan had deprived Job of his possessions, his family, and his health, Job remained loyal to God. "In all this Job sinned not, nor charged God foolishly." Job 1:22.

Who was it that plagued Job? Satan. Who stole his livestock and killed his servants? Satan. Who brought the tornado that destroyed his sons and daughters? Satan.

The Lord may *allow* difficulties to come to test our loyalty and love, but Satan is the guilty one responsible for all the evil on Planet Earth. You and I are caught in the center of a bewildering cosmic drama, a conflict between authority and lawlessness, between the Creator and Satan, the original rebel. We are not spectators. We are involved, whether we want to be or not.

The idea that Satan is only a myth or an influence leaves us totally unprepared to confront the intelligent being he actually is. John said, "Woe to the inhabiters of the earth and of the sea! for the devil is come down unto you, having great wrath, because he knoweth that he hath but a short time." Revelation 12:12. And Peter warned, "The devil, as a roaring lion, walketh about, seeking whom he may devour." 1 Peter 5:8.

It was Satan, working through the jealous mind of King Herod, who tried to destroy the Christ child at Bethlehem.

Herod decreed that all male children two years old and younger be killed.

It was Satan who came to Christ in the wilderness, masquerading as an angel from heaven. If he could just get Christ to fail in some way or give up His mission of saving lost man, then Satan would have dominion of Planet Earth forever. But over each temptation, Christ was triumphant. Finally, in desperation, Satan showed Christ all the kingdoms of the world and said, "All these things will I give thee, if thou wilt fall down and worship me." Matthew 4:9.

"All these things" were stolen property! Satan had secured them by fraud and deceit. Jesus answered, "Get thee hence, Satan: for it is written, Thou shalt worship the Lord thy God, and him only shalt thou serve." Matthew 4:10.

Satan departed a defeated foe—for the moment. But he would return, for there was still Calvary! Satan determined to make Calvary the final hour of defeat, the death knell for Jesus and for mankind. All his power was bent on preventing Christ from restoring man's lost dominion, intercepting man's last chance for survival and happiness.

From the wilderness to Calvary, the fury of Satan's anger dogged Christ's steps. Finally, Satan managed to have Christ betrayed into the hands of the murderous mob, and Christ died on Calvary. So it was that God, with a loneliness that could never be healed except by the restoration of man, gave His only Son; and the Son gave Himself, to reverse your fate and mine. It was an hour of victory, a day to spell freedom for all the prisoners of the devil. That day Satan became a defeated foe! Christ, by His death, earned the right to destroy all evil and suffering.

"Since the children have flesh and blood, he too shared in their humanity so that by his death he might destroy him who holds the power of death—that is, the devil." Hebrews 2:14, NIV.

Satan demonstrated before all the intelligences of the

universe what kind of being he is. And he is still demonstrating the way he would run the world. Tornadoes, earthquakes, floods, crime, disease, heartache, and pain—these we see. But standing unseen behind them all is the supernatural working of Satan. These tragedies are not "acts of God"; they are "acts of the devil." Do you see how cleverly Satan and his angels can use the supernatural to deceive and destroy? "And no marvel; for Satan himself is transformed into an angel of light." 2 Corinthians 11:14.

It may never have occurred to you that devils—demons—can work miracles. But they can. "They are the spirits of devils, working miracles." Revelation 16:14. Satan works miracles. His angels can work miracles. And he can give men the power to work miracles whenever he chooses. "There shall arise false Christs, and false prophets, and shall shew great signs and wonders; insomuch that, if it were possible, they shall deceive the very elect." Matthew 24:24.

Do you see the real issue? The time has come when we cannot trust our senses, a time when the counterfeit resembles the genuine so closely that it is difficult to distinguish between them except by God's Word.

The good news is that this celestial planet, hijacked by Satan, is soon to be rescued. This knowledge should quiet the fears of nervous, anxious passengers on a planet gone wrong. Jesus is coming, and when He comes the prophecy of Ezekiel will be fulfilled concerning Satan, the rebel angel: "I will destroy thee, O covering cherub." "Therefore will I bring forth a fire from the midst of thee, it shall devour thee, and I will bring thee to ashes upon the earth." Ezekiel 28:16, 18.

Gone forever will be sin and suffering. Yes, friend, Jesus is coming soon. Not as a lowly Galilean, not as One ridiculed, spat upon, denied. Not as One hanging on a cross, but as King of kings, with the right to reign. Christ will return to this rebellious planet. We must be ready, for if we miss that, we miss everything!

The issue facing each of us today is, Whom will we believe? Whom will we follow? A loving God, or a fallen angel? The lines are being drawn; the whole world is being divided into two sides. Where is your loyalty? To every restless, lonely heart, to every aching, guilty soul, to all His children on a planet in rebellion, Jesus gives the loving invitation, "Come unto me." And, "Him that cometh to me I will in no wise cast out." Matthew 11:28; John 6:37.

Jesus longs to restore you to the family of God, to give you eternal life on a planet made new. But the decision must be made: Who will be your Lord and Master? Friend, your decision is a life and death matter! Won't you choose right now to let Christ be your King?

"But," you say, "I really don't know that much about Jesus. Many people call Him the Messiah. Can we know for certain that He is who He claimed to be?" Many people have been searching for the real Messiah. Let's turn to the next chapter and let the Bible answer that question through some very intriging prophecies and historical accounts.

Does Anyone Really Care About Me?

In the spring of 1960 a team led by Yigael Yadin, Israel's renowned archaeologist, made the most exciting discovery in the history of Israel. All excavations in the Holy Land are exciting, but this one—a discovery by Yadin's team on the treacherous slopes of Nahal Hever Canyon—held special significance. With the help of modern technology, they found, in two short seasons of digging, the evidence of a legendary hero of Israel's ancient past.

They found scores of papyrus rolls wrapped neatly and tied in sacking and goatskin. They also found silver and bronze coins, baskets, sandals, mirrors, jugs, and cooking utensils—all carried to this remote cave near the Dead Sea in A.D. 135 by Jews fleeing for their lives when the revolt against Rome failed. These archaeologists carefully unrolled and deciphered letters, legal documents, and dispatches—secrets that had been kept hidden for 1,800 years! When Yadin reported this discovery to Israel's leaders, he projected onto a screen a slide showing a portion of a document found in the Cave of Letters and read aloud the first line: "Shimeon Bar Kosiba, President over Israel."

Then, turning to President Ben Zvi, Yadin said: "Your Excellency, I am honored to be able to tell you that we have discovered fifteen dispatches written or dictated by the last President of Ancient Israel 1800 years ago."—*Bar-Kokkba,* page 15. Spontaneous shouts of joy filled the room, and the excitement spread throughout Israel by newspaper and radio.

Why would Israel be electrified by a name on a fragment of papyrus? The answer lies in the name—the name of a man treasured in Jewish folklore as more of a myth than a man of flesh and blood. As legend had it, he had led the last Jewish attempt to overthrow Rome and had won independence for his nation, at least for a time.

After Jerusalem's fall in A.D. 70, the Roman Emperor Hadrian built another city on the site of Jerusalem, naming it after himself. Later, he erected a shrine to the Roman god Jupiter on the very spot of the former Jewish temple. Then, as if adding insult to injury, Hadrian issued an edict forbidding the Jews from practicing their ancient rite of circumcision! These humiliating outrages were only bearable to the Jews because of their belief that soon the promised Messiah would come and deliver them from Roman oppression.

At this crucial moment of national humiliation, Bar-Kokkba, a charismatic young Jew, rallied thousands of young zealots to the cause of liberating the nation. The historian Eusebius says: "The Jews were at that time led by a certain Bar-Chochebas, which means, 'Star,' a man who was murderous and a bandit, but relied on his name, as if dealing with slaves, and claimed to be a luminary who had come down to them from heaven."—*Bar-Kokkba,* page 258.

Bar-Kokkba claimed to be the Messiah, "the Deliverer." Archaeologists have unearthed thousands of coins inscribed with Bar-Kokkba's given name, Shimeon. Some have the additional title, "President" or "Prince of Israel." Letters and dispatches by Bar-Kokkba found in the Cave of Letters verify his titles and position. They also reveal that he was tough and brutal. Yadin wrote:

"There is a story of his practice to test the prowess of

his soldiers by cutting off their fingers. The sages used to tell him: 'How long will you continue to make the men of Israel blemished?' "—*Bar-Kokkba*, page 23.

Bar-Kokkba demanded allegiance from everyone, torturing and killing Christians who refused to deny Jesus as the Messiah and accept him as their deliverer. For a time, Roman leaders ignored Bar-Kokkba, but when rebellion turned into revolt, the Emperor dispatched an army to quash the uprising. But much to his surprise, Bar-Kokkba enjoyed initial successes, established a Jewish state, and proclaimed himself President of Israel.

Furious with the turn of events, Hadrian sent more troops and laid siege to Jerusalem for three and a half years before the insurrection was finally put down. The revolt devastated the Jews. One historian wrote, "The revenge was ruthless, and Judea was almost depopulated. . . . Fifty fortresses and 985 villages were destroyed, and 580,000 men were slain, aside from those who died from hunger and disease."—Albert A. Trever, *History of Ancient Civilization*, page 524.

Liberation and independence for the Jews was short-lived. Bar-Kokkba was beheaded by the Romans. In some writings he is referred to as Bar Koziba, meaning "deceiver." He declared himself to be the Messiah, the Deliverer, but he was an imposter.

This was a common fraud in those times. A century before, another Jew claimed to be the Messiah. In fact, He claimed to be the Son of God. His name was Jesus—a young carpenter from the northern village of Nazareth.

Who was this Jesus of Nazareth? Was He a teacher? A philosopher? A physician? A humanitarian? A preacher? Yes, indeed! He was all of these—and more. When He walked the dusty roads of Palestine, those who saw Him felt awed by His presence. Those who heard Him exclaimed, "Never man spake like this man." John 7:46.

He never wrote a book, yet if you should read a book a week on the life of Christ it would take you a century to read those that are cataloged in the Library of Congress! He was not an artist, yet He inspired the greatest paintings in the world. He was not a musician, yet His life motivated some of the greatest masterpieces ever composed. He was not an architect or sculptor, yet some of the most beautiful buildings and statues in the world have been dedicated to Him. He earned no degree, yet some of the most prestigious universities in the world have been founded in His honor. He lived less than thirty-five years, but all history is dated from His birth.

One writer graphically summed up Christ's life in these words: "Nineteen centuries have come and gone, and today he is still the central figure of the human race. . . . All the armies that ever marched, and all the navies that ever sailed, and all the parliaments that ever sat, and all the kings that every reigned have not affected the life of man on this earth as much as that one solitary life."—Taken from the essay "One Solitary Life."

Few would disagree with these historical facts. But unless Jesus was more than all of this, He was not the true Jesus, the true Messiah.

Like Bar-Kokkba, Jesus claimed to be from heaven: "I have come down from heaven." John 6:38, NIV. Also like Bar-Kokkba, Jesus said He came to deliver the captives: "If the Son therefore shall make you free, ye shall be free indeed." John 8:36. However, Jesus was not speaking about liberating the Jews from Roman oppression. He was speaking of delivering them from the slavery of sin!

The Jews did not understand Jesus' statement. They said, "We are Abraham's descendants and have never been slaves of anyone. How can you say that we shall be set free?" John 8:33, NIV. Jesus replied, "I tell you the truth, everyone who sins is a slave to sin." John 8:34, NIV.

The Jews expected their Messiah to lead a movement to break the yoke of Rome and restore sovereignty to the Jewish nation. Bar-Kokkba attempted to deliver his people by force and brutality and to secure for himself an exalted position. But Jesus said, "My kingdom is not of this world: if my kingdom were of this world, then would my servants fight. " John 18:36. Jesus came to set men free from guilt and sin through love, not force, and He sought no political office.

But that still does not answer the great question! Was Jesus the Messiah? Many men appeared during the first century claiming to be the Messiah. What evidence proves that Jesus was what He claimed to be? Jesus Himself gave the answer when He said, "These are the Scriptures that testify about me. " John 5:39, NIV.

Of course, in Jesus' day the New Testament had not been written, so He meant that the Old Testament proved who and what He was. The New Testament, written after the death of Christ, is the history of His life written by His contemporaries.

Let's turn to the Old Testament prophecies concerning the Messiah, the Deliverer, and see if Jesus' life and death precisely fulfills them.

At the gate to the Garden of Eden, the Lord gave Adam and Eve the first promise of a Deliverer in His rebuke of Satan, the serpent. He said, "I will put enmity between you and the woman, and between your offspring and hers; he will crush your head, and you will strike his heel." Genesis 3:15, NIV. In other words, one day a child would be born into this world who would break the power of Satan, but in so doing, the promised Deliverer would Himself receive a painful wound.

No doubt Eve hoped that one of her sons would be that promised child. Many mothers in Israel must have wondered if their newborn sons might be the Promised One! As time passed, God added more details concerning the coming Messiah, like adding pieces to a jigsaw puzzle. Let's put some of the pieces together and see what the evidence reveals.

Seven hundred years before the birth of Christ, God predicted through Isaiah how the Deliverer would be born: "Behold, a virgin shall conceive, and bear a son, and shall call his name Emmanuel." Isaiah 7:14.

Did Jesus have a miraculous birth? Luke wrote concerning Jesus' birth: "God sent the angel Gabriel to Nazareth, a town in Galilee, to a virgin pledged to be married to a man named Joseph. . . . The virgin's name was Mary. . . . The angel said to her, . . . 'You will be with child and give birth to a son, and you are to give him the name Jesus.' " Luke 1:26-31, NIV.

Let us see if some other pieces fit around this piece. Centuries before the birth of Christ, Micah revealed the place where the Messiah would be born: "Bethlehem, . . . out of thee shall he come forth unto me that is to be ruler in Israel." Micah 5:2.

Wait a minute, you say! This part of the puzzle will not fit. Micah said the Messiah would be born in Bethlehem, but the angel Gabriel went to Nazareth, ninety-two miles away, to find Mary. True, up until a week before His birth it seemed that Nazareth would be the birthplace of Jesus. However, the Bible says that "in those days Caesar Augustus issued a decree that a census should be taken of the entire Roman world. . . . And everyone went to his own town to register. So Joseph also went up from the town of Nazareth . . . to Bethlehem. . . . He went there to register with Mary." Luke 2:1-5, NIV.

Luke describes the events after Joseph and Mary arrived in Bethlehem: "While they were there, the time came for the baby to be born, and she gave birth to her firstborn, a son. She wrapped him in strips of cloth and placed him in a manger." Luke 2:6, 7, NIV.

For centuries, patriarchs and prophets, priests and scribes, mothers and fathers had longed for that moment. Yet when He came, no trumpets sounded. Only the mooing of cows and the braying of donkeys welcomed His birth. Even though the time and the place of His birth had been foretold by the prophets, angels had to announce it to shepherds in the fields caring for their flocks. They sang, "Unto you is born this day in the city of David a Saviour, which is Christ the Lord." Luke 2:11.

Jesus worked as a carpenter in Nazareth till He was thirty years old. Then, in A.D. 27, He closed the door to His carpenter shop and set out for the Jordan River, where thousands had gone to hear His cousin, John the Baptist. After being baptized by John in the Jordan River, He entered upon a ministry that eventually led to Calvary.

Centuries before, Isaiah foretold the work of the Messiah in these words: "The Lord hath anointed me to preach good tidings unto the meek; . . . to bind up the brokenhearted, to proclaim liberty to the captives, and the opening of the prison to them that are bound; to proclaim the acceptable year of the Lord; . . . to comfort all that mourn." Isaiah 61:1, 2. Seven centuries later in His hometown synagogue, Jesus read this same passage from Isaiah. Then He rolled up the scroll and said: "Today this scripture is fulfilled in your hearing." Luke 4:21, NIV.

Was that an idle claim? What was Jesus' ministry like? Did He really meet men's needs? Does this part of the puzzle fit? Let us take a quick look at His ministry.

No record exists of anyone coming to Jesus for healing who was not made well. In fact, Luke says the people "sought to touch him: for there went virtue out of him, and healed them all." Luke 6:19. Crippled bodies were made whole. Withered muscles were renewed. By just a touch of His hand or a word from His lips, the blind were made to see, the dumb to sing, the deaf to hear.

And one day He stood before a tomb that cradled a man who had been dead for four days. He called, "Lazarus, come forth!" and mourning and tears turned to rejoicing. John 11:43. This was typical of Jesus' ministry. His messages were filled with joy and hope. He kept saying to the depressed, "Be of good cheer." John 16:33. To those who were burdened, He said, "Don't worry, take heart," or "Let not your heart be troubled." John 14:1.

Jesus accepted people as they were, whatever their frailties. Because He accepted them in love and understanding, they were changed!

One day a group of self-righteous accusers brought an adulterous woman to Jesus, hoping that He would condemn her to death. But Jesus stooped and began writing some embarrassing biographies of her accusers in the sand. One by one they stole away. Turning to the terror-stricken woman trembling on the ground, Jesus said, "Neither do I condemn thee: go, and sin no more." John 8:11. Isaiah had prophesied years before that the "anointed One" would "bestow on them . . . the oil of gladness instead of mourning, and a garment of praise instead of a spirit of despair." Isaiah 61:3, NIV. Surely Christ fit this part of the puzzle.

However, the most detailed evidence proving His divinity is found in the part of the puzzle concerning His death and resurrection. The book of Psalms predicted the identity of the one who would betray the Messiah a thousand years before the event took place: "Even my close friend, whom I trusted, he who shared my bread, has lifted up his heel against me." Psalm 41:9, NIV.

Matthew tells how this prophecy was fulfilled. As the angry mob with their clubs and swords climbed the mountainside, the disciples were amazed to see Judas, one of Jesus' own disciples, in front of the mob—as one of the leaders! He had eaten the Last Supper with them only a few hours before. As Jesus boldly walked toward the mob, He asked,

"Whom do you seek?" Back came the shout, "Jesus!" Then Judas said, "Hail, master; and kissed him. . . . Then came they, and laid hands on Jesus, and took him." Matthew 26:49, 50.

Even the price of the betrayal was prophesied centuries before, including how the money would be spent! "So they weighed for my price thirty pieces of silver. . . . And I took the thirty pieces of silver, and cast them to the potter in the house of the Lord." Zechariah 11:12, 13.

Matthew gives the details of the betrayal of Jesus: "Judas Iscariot, went unto the chief priests, and said to them, What will ye give me, and I will deliver him unto you? And they convenanted with him for thirty pieces of silver." Matthew 26:14, 15. But after Jesus had been condemned, Judas ran back to the chief priests, "And he cast down the pieces of silver in the temple, and departed." "And they took counsel, and bought with them the potter's field, to bury strangers in." Matthew 27:5, 7. Once again we see how the New Testament fulfills the Old Testament predictions. Only divine foreknowledge could give such precise details.

Isaiah had prophesied of the Messiah: "I offered my back to those who beat me, my cheeks to those who pulled out my beard; I did not hide my face from mocking and spitting." Isaiah 50:6, NIV. Matthew gives the details of that night. Jesus, bound as a common criminal, was taken before Annas and Caiaphas and tried illegally in the middle of the night. "Then did they spit in his face, and buffeted him; and others smote him with palms of their hands." Matthew 26:67. Certainly this portion of the puzzle fits!

The next morning they took Him to the Roman governor, Pilate. But while false witnesses testified against Him, Jesus never spoke a word. Next, King Herod mocked Him, and as a cruel joke dressed Him in a royal robe. Then He was sent back to Pilate, who said he found no fault in Him, yet had Him beaten.

Finally Pilate gave the angry crowd a choice: Should he release Jesus—or the notorious criminal Barabbas?

The crowd shouted back, "Barabbas!"

"What then shall I do with Jesus?" Pilate asked.

"Crucify Him! Crucify Him!" they shouted. See Luke 23:13-21.

Hundreds of years before the Romans invented crucifixion as a means of capital punishment, the psalmist predicted the manner in which Christ would be put to death. The ordinary means used by Jewish people in executing the death penalty was stoning, but David wrote, "They pierced my hands and my feet." Psalm 22:16.

Matthew tells us that a crown of thorns was smashed down over His forehead, and they smote Him on the head. See Matthew 27:27-30. At Calvary, Jesus meekly allowed the soldiers to drive the spikes through His hands and feet. The disciple Thomas witnessed this and later said, "Unless I see the nail marks in his hands and put my finger where the nails were, . . . I will not believe it." John 20:25, NIV. Yes, Jesus was crucified, and His hands and feet were pierced by nails, fulfilling the Old Testament prophecy. There is yet another prophecy that fits the puzzle. Isaiah predicted that in death the Messiah would be "numbered with the transgressors." Isaiah 53:12. In the New Testament, Mark said, "And with him they crucified two thieves; the one on his right hand, and the other on his left. And the scripture was fulfilled, which saith, And he was numbered with the transgressors." Mark 15:27, 28. Once again the Old Testament prophecy was fulfilled. King David told what would happen to Jesus' clothing a thousand years before His death: "They divide my garments among them, and for my clothing do they cast lots." Psalm 22:18, Berkeley. John, an eyewitness, told what happened at the cross: "The soldiers therefore . . . took His outer garments and made four parts. . . . Now the tunic was seamless, woven in one piece. They said, . . . 'Let us not tear it, but cast lots for it, to decide whose it shall be.' " John 19:23, 24, NASB. That portion of the puzzle also fits exactly!

The Old Testament even foretold some of the words the Messiah would utter as He suffered on the cross: "My God, my God, why hast thou forsaken me?" Psalm 22:1. And, "Into thine hand I commit my spirit." Psalm 31:5.

Matthew records that as Jesus felt the separation that sin brings from God, He cried out with a loud voice, "My God, my God, why hast thou forsaken me?" Matthew 27:46. That was Jesus' greatest moment of suffering. The guilt of all mankind weighed upon Him, and He felt cut off from God's presence. Then, according to Luke, He cried out in a loud voice, "Father, into thy hands I commend my spirit." Luke 23:46. Another piece of the puzzle fits! David predicted that none of Jesus' bones would be broken: "He keepeth all his bones: not one of them is broken." Psalm 34:20. Zechariah said, "They will look on me, the one they have pierced." Zechariah 12:10, NIV.

John, an eyewitness, gave the story in detail: "Now it was the day of Preparation, and the next day was to be a special Sabbath. Because the Jews did not want the bodies left on the crosses during the Sabbath, they asked Pilate to have the legs broken and the bodies taken down. The soldiers therefore came and broke the legs of the first man who had been crucified with Jesus, and then those of the other. But when they came to Jesus and found that he was already dead, they did not break his legs. Instead, one of the soldiers pierced Jesus' side with a spear, bringing a sudden flow of blood and water." John 19:31-34, NIV. Another part of the Old Testament puzzle fits exactly!

Many of the prophecies concerning the Messiah were totally beyond the human control of Jesus. For example, He could not have arranged the place of His birth, the manner of His birth, His betrayal, or the events surrounding His death.

However, a prophecy about the exact time of His coming 2,000 years ago provides one of the most decisive evidences that Christ was sent of God, that He was the real Messiah. After the Jews had been taken into captivity by Babylon, the angel Gabriel told Daniel, "Know therefore and understand, that from the going forth of the commandment to restore and to build Jerusalem unto the Messiah the Prince shall be seven weeks, and threescore and two weeks." Daniel 9:25.

Sixty-nine weeks equals 483 days, and in Bible prophecy a day equals a year. "I have appointed thee each day for a year." Ezekiel 4:6. So there would be 483 years from the command to restore and rebuild Jerusalem until the appearance of the Messiah. The decree was made by King Artaxerxes in the year 457 B.C. Adding 483 years brings us to A.D. 27. Now follow closely. "Messiah" in Hebrew, and "Christ" in Greek, both mean "the anointed One." When was Jesus anointed? Luke pinpoints the very year!

"Now in the fifteenth year of the reign of Tiberius Caesar," "when all the people were baptized, it came to pass, that Jesus also being baptized, and praying, the heaven was opened, and the Holy Ghost descended in a bodily shape like a dove upon him, and a voice came from heaven, which said, Thou art my beloved Son; in thee I am well pleased." Luke 3:1, 21, 22.

Jesus was anointed by the Holy Spirit at His baptism in the Jordan River. Paul states: "God anointed Jesus of Nazareth with the Holy Ghost." Acts 10:38.

Now, let's do one more bit of arithmetic. Tiberius Caesar began to reign in A.D. 12. Luke said Jesus was baptized in the fifteenth year of Tiberius' rule, which would bring us to A.D. 27, fulfilling the 483-year prophecy to the letter and proving that Jesus was indeed who He claimed to be. This piece of the puzzle matches perfectly!

The last part of the prophecy stated that the Messiah

would die in the middle of the seventieth week of this prophecy: "He shall confirm the covenant with many for one week: and in the midst of the week he shall cause the sacrifice and oblation to cease." Daniel 9:27. That prophecy was also fulfilled exactly. Jesus died on the fourteenth day of the first Jewish month in the year A.D. 31.

Mark records what took place in the temple at the moment of His death: "And the veil in the temple was rent in twain from the top to the bottom." Mark 15:38. This indicated that the Israelites no longer needed sacrifices to show their faith in a coming Saviour, for the Messiah, the true sacrificial Lamb, had been slain that day on Calvary! The sacrificial offerings were to cease. That part of the puzzle also fits.

The apostle Paul studied these Old Testament prophecies, and as he gathered evidence from eyewitnesses of the events surrounding the life and death of Christ, he wrote to his young protégé, Timothy, that Christ was more than a mere man. He declared, "God was manifest in the flesh, justified in the Spirit, seen of angels, preached unto the Gentiles, believed on in the world, received up into glory." 1 Timothy 3:16.

Yes, Jesus was truly all that He claimed to be—the Messiah! And, friend, as our Lord hung upon that cross—His back lacerated from the cruel beatings, His hands and feet driven through with spikes, His head pierced by the thorns, enduring the mockery and jeers of the crowd, "He could have called ten thousand angels to destroy the world and set Him free." But you see, He could not save Himself and us too!

Do you sometimes wonder if anyone really cares about you? Jesus does. Long ago, He proved just how much He cares as He poured out His life for you on a lonely hill just outside Jerusalem.

How Can I Get Rid of Guilt?

On a hot and sultry July day in the year 1505, a young law student trudged along the rutted road leading to the German village of Stotterheim. Suddenly, without warning, the sky became overcast, a gusty wind whipped through the trees, and a torrential rain unleashed its fury on the lonely traveler. Peals of thunder rocked the countryside—and then it happened! A bolt of lightning shot through the black clouds and sent the student reeling to the ground.

Terrorized by the thought that he had been struck down by the Almighty, Martin Luther cried out to his patron saint, "St. Anne, help me! I will become a monk."

Neither Luther's enraged father nor the persuasive arguments of his friends could change his mind. Two weeks later, Luther entered the monastery of the Augustinian order of Hermits to become a monk. There he was taught to fear God and the demons that surrounded him. However, his sense of guilt only deepened, and he zealously set about to rid himself of sin and save his soul by his own good works. He shrank from no sacrifice, whether physical pain or mental stress, in his quest to attain God's approval.

Luther wrote later, "I was a good monk. . . . If ever a monk got to heaven by his monkery it was I. . . . If I had kept on any longer I should have killed myself with vigils, prayers, reading, and other work."—Roland Bainton, *Here I Stand: A Life of Martin Luther*, page 45.

However, despite his rigorous efforts to satisfy what he thought to be an angry God, Luther never felt the ledger was balanced. The harder he tried, the more sinful he felt. Inner peace and tranquility eluded him. He felt he could not do enough to merit God's forgiveness and favor.

But does man receive forgiveness and eternal life by doing more good deeds than bad? Almost every religion outside of true Christianity teaches just that. In India, long-bearded men clad in scanty loincloths sit on beds of spikes, believing that by torturing their bodies they can earn God's favor. Flagellants beat and bruise their bodies with whips and chains. Firewalkers and skewer-wearers seek favor by unusual acts of physical abuse.

Buddhists believe they gain merit for a future life by building pagodas or feeding the holy men, and for the Moslem there is no greater joy or better way of earning favor with God than a pilgrimage to Mecca or dying in defense of Islam.

Strange as it may seem, many Christians unwittingly do the same thing. They attend church, give offerings, and follow the golden rule, thinking they earn favor with God and thus deserve eternal life. But is that possible? Can man, through some means of physical punishment, mental anguish, or deeds of kindness bribe God to grant him forgiveness and eternal life? Do we earn salvation, or win it as one does an Olympic gold medal?

Luther tried, but he finally concluded that if forgiveness rested on his own works, he was a lost man. When the Augustinian monasteries selected him to lead a delegation to Rome in 1510, Luther felt overjoyed! No city on Earth had so many holy relics or spiritual indulgences. Here was his chance to earn merit and secure the peace he so much desired. This is how Luther described the visit:

"In Rome I was a frantic saint. I ran through all the churches and catacombs. . . . I celebrated several masses . . . and almost regretted that my father and mother were still living, for I would have liked to redeem them from purgatory with my masses and other good works and prayers."—*The Reformation: A Narrative History*, page 24.

Determined to earn all the merit with God that he could while in Rome, Luther climbed Pilate's Staircase on hands and knees, repeating the Lord's Prayer and for good measure kissing each of the twenty-eight steps. But even as he climbed the stairs, a disturbing thought kept pressing into his mind: Was this a valid means of forgiveness? At the top of the stairs, Luther stood erect and voiced his question: "Who knows whether it is so?"—Roland Bainton, *Here I Stand: A Life of Martin Luther*, page 51.

This nagging doubt accompanied Luther back to the monastery in Germany, where he searched the Scriptures as never before, determined to find the answer to this most important question: How is man saved? To his amazement, as he studied God's Word, Luther found no teaching of trying harder or winning merit to make oneself righteous. Rather, he found the good news that forgiveness is free!

As he studied the book of Romans, Luther found a text that would forever quiet his troubled heart: "The just shall live by faith." Romans 1:17. Instead of seeking forgiveness by works such as prayers, vigils, scourgings, and climbing stairs on hands and knees, Luther found and took the simple steps of faith given by God in His Holy Word.

The first step to eternal life, Luther had recognized years before: that he was a sinner and he needed help. The apostle Paul had written, "There is none righteous, no not one." Romans 3:10. That included Paul and Martin Luther. It includes you and me.

"Wait a minute," you say. "I'm a good person. I don't steal or kill or commit adultery! I'm a good neighbor. I even give to the Children's Hospital and solicit funds for the Cancer Society!"

That may be true, but remember Jesus said that if we hate someone, we are sinners. And if we lie, cheat, or gossip, if we are unkind or uncaring, we are sinners. Have you ever disliked someone enough to wish something bad would happen to him? Have you ever told a "white lie" or cheated on your income tax? Have you ever been cross with your children or impatient with your husband or wife? Have you ever wished you had your neighbor's house or car? That is sin! It makes you a lawbreaker, for "sin is the transgression of the law." 1 John 3:4.

And as with the laws of our land, there is a penalty for disobedience. The Bible says, "The wages of sin is death." Romans 6:23.

We have all sinned. There is no doubt about that! In fact, if we only commit three sinful acts each day, we are guilty of 1,095 sins each year. Multiply that number by your age, and you have some idea of how sinful you may be! Shocking, isn't it? Yet it is good to recognize that we have a sin problem, for then we can seek help.

If a person had cancer and he never recognized his condition or sought medical assistance, he would eventually die. That is the fate of the sinner who fails to recognize his spiritual condition and seek aid. Isaiah says, "Your iniquities [sins] have separated you from your God." Isaiah 59:2.

God is the source of all life, and when the relationship between God and man was severed by Adam's rebellion, man began to die. Paul describes the result of Adam's sin: "Wherefore, as by one man sin entered into the world, and death by sin; and so death passed upon all men, for that all have sinned." Romans 5:12. What a predicament we are in! We are all sinners, under sentence of death.

But a God of love did not tell us the result of sin without giving us hope for salvation. Here is the good news: "The wages of sin is death; but the gift of God is eternal life through Jesus Christ our Lord." Romans 6:23. In this text Luther discovered that eternal life is a gift! It is not something you can earn or deserve, for Paul wrote, "For by grace [free love and favor of God] are ye saved through faith; and that not of yourselves: it is the gift of God: Not of works, lest any man should boast." Ephesians 2:8, 9.

You cannot save yourself by your own works; you must depend on God's grace, His love and favor, which are free. If you could earn salvation it would not be a gift! Suppose your employer gave you an envelope and said he had a gift for you. If you discovered your paycheck for the past two weeks inside, would that be a gift? Not if you had earned it!

But why would the mighty God who rules the universe be concerned about people on a planet out on the edge of space? Why did He not just abandon rebellious man and leave him to suffer the consequences of sin? The answer is found in John's first letter: "God is love." 1 John 4:16.

God's love for man, who is terminally ill with the disease of sin, can perhaps be best understood by a human illustration. A young couple excitedly bring their baby home from the hospital. Within a few days the infant begins to cry day and night with a severe case of colic. The parents follow the physician's advice, but nothing seems to help. They walk the floor with the baby until they are exhausted, but not once do they consider giving the child away or leaving her to suffer alone. Why? They love her! They love that little helpless child all the more because of the pain and suffering she has to endure.

That is what God is like. His children on Planet Earth developed the colic of sin, and the pain and suffering that they endure because of it only intensifies God's love for them. Never has God considered abandoning us. Never has He considered leaving us to perish and suffer the consequences of our rebellion. The Bible says, "The Lord . . . is longsuffering to us-ward, not willing that any should perish, but that all should come to repentance." 2 Peter 3:9.

Regardless of how good or bad you may be, God loves you and wants to save you. He is not willing that you should perish. However, we have all sinned. We have all rebelled against God and broken His law. Earthly governments cannot tolerate lawlessness and survive for long. Violators are punished. But violating God's law is even more serious because sin separates us from God, the source of life! Even though God is a God of love, He is also a God of justice. On Mount Sinai He described Himself: "The Lord, the compassionate and gracious God, slow to anger, abounding in love and faithfulness, maintaining love to thousands, and forgiving wickedness, rebellion and sin. Yet he does not leave the guilty unpunished." Exodus 34:6, 7, NIV.

God is a loving, forgiving, compassionate God, but He says it is impossible for Him to overlook man's guilt. He cannot just ignore sin. He cannot change His law. He cannot make wrong right. So those who sin will die because they separate themselves from God, the source of life.

Is there no solution? No way out?

Yes, friend, there is! A loving God found a way to save us and still be just. He found a perfect substitute to die in our place, paying the penalty for our sins so that we could live. John, the beloved disciple, explains it this way: "God so loved the world, that he gave his only begotten Son, that whosoever believeth in him should not perish, but have everlasting life." John 3:16.

Jesus came to live on Earth as a man, facing the same problems and temptations that every human has faced. He proved by His perfect life of obedience that there is no excuse for sin. Then, as the one sinless representative of the human race, Christ voluntarily took upon Himself the guilt of every person who would ever live, and died in their behalf. Paul says, "As by one man's disobedience many were made sinners, so by the obedience of one shall many be made righteous." Romans 5:19.

Jesus' death was in no sense intended to appease an angry God, as Luther first thought. Jesus offered to die to save us from our sins, and God loved us so much that He was willing to sacrifice His only Son as a ransom. Jesus was the Lamb of God, the sacrificial Lamb!

Under the shadow of Mount Sinai the people of God daily witnessed, through symbols and ceremonies, an enactment of God's plan to redeem fallen man. The desert tabernacle, built to God's specific instructions with services instituted by God, continually called man's attention to a future Calvary, where the true Lamb would be sacrificed for the sins of all mankind, giving to all the hope and assurance of forgiveness and salvation. The sinner came, bringing a sacrificial animal. He placed his hand on the head of the animal and confessed his sin. Then he took a knife and killed it, symbolizing that his sins caused the death of Jesus, the sacrificial Lamb.

Gruesome, yes. But the cross at Calvary that brought the promise of eternal life to the human heart was more gruesome still. However, by this act God demonstrated that sin brings death, either to the sinner or to the innocent sacrifice.

God's people in Old Testament times offered sacrifices to show their faith in the coming death of the Son of God, the One who would die in man's place as his substitute. Jesus was the true sacrifice. As Jesus came to be baptized, John said of Him, "Behold the Lamb of God, which taketh away the sin of the world." John 1:29.

How ironic that some of the men He came to save plotted to take His life! Jesus was beaten, mocked, and sentenced to be crucified—the cruelest form of execution ever devised. And that rough-hewn cross should have held Barabbas, the hardened criminal. Barabbas, the lawbreaker.

Barabbas, the sinner. Barabbas, deserving of the death penalty. Yet, as the Bible says, the One "who did no sin, neither was guile found in his mouth" (1 Peter 2:22) died on that cross!

In death He was identified with sinners. He was crucified between two thieves! And as God placed upon Him the sins of the whole world, He cried out, "My God, my God, why have you forsaken me?" Matthew 27:46, LB. He felt the terrible separation that sin brings. Jesus could not bear the agony of separation from the Father. It broke His heart.

The crowd shouted, "He saved others; himself he cannot save." Mark 15:31. And that was true. He could not save Himself and still save others. He was incarnate God paying the price for a lost race, a broken law, the wages of sin. Thus it was that God, with a love that could not be satisfied until man was restored to His family, gave His own Son to die in man's place, as his substitute.

Jesus was treated as we deserve that we might be treated as He deserves. He was condemned for our sins and suffered our death that we might have eternal life. In this way God could give us eternal life and still be just. Not because of any good thing we have done, but because God can give us credit for what Christ did—for the perfect life He lived.

Paul, the apostle to the Gentiles, said, "It is by grace you have been saved, through faith." Ephesians 2:8, NIV. This faith is the very heart of salvation. When the Philippian jailer asked Paul what he must do to be saved, Paul answered, "Believe on the Lord Jesus Christ, and thou shalt be saved." Acts 16:31.

However, mental assent to the historical fact of Christ's life and death is not saving faith. There is more to it than that. The Bible says that "the devils also believe, and tremble." James 2:19. To believe in Jesus means more than just acknowledging that He died 1900 years ago.

Saving faith is trusting in the sacrifice of Christ as the

full and complete atonement for every sin we have ever committed. It means believing that it is not what we can do that saves us, but what Christ did on Calvary. No human can ever boast that he saved himself. The glory is all God's. It is grace on God's part and faith on man's part, trusting God completely, willingly letting Him control our lives.

Receiving salvation is so simple, yet many make it seem so complex. We do not deserve it. We cannot earn it. But a God of love wants to give it to us, if we will reach out and accept it.

If a friend gave you a birthday present, would you try to pay him for it? Of course not! You would reach out and gratefully accept it. Jesus offers you His righteousness and salvation as a gift of love. Even if you wanted to, you could not pay for it. But you can reach out in faith and gratefully accept it by kneeling at the foot of the cross and praying this prayer:

"God, I recognize that I am a sinner and I need help. I want to accept Jesus as my Saviour and Lord. Please forgive every sin I have ever committed and take complete control of my life. Thank You for hearing and answering my prayer, in Jesus' name. Amen."

At that moment God gives you eternal life, for the disciple John says, "He that hath the Son hath life; and he that hath not the Son of God hath not life. These things have I written unto you that believe on the name of the son of God; that ye may know that ye have eternal life." 1 John 5:12, 13.

Jesus gives the invitation to everyone everywhere, so that "whosoever believeth in him should not perish, but have everlasting life." John 3:16.

Maybe you feel you are a hopeless sinner, but that is not true! God can turn the most impossible situation into victory. No life is too bad, no sin too great for Christ to forgive. On the cross Jesus hung between two sinners, both common criminals. At first they made fun of Jesus. But as the day wore on, one thief—whom tradition says had seen Jesus teaching and healing—now caught a glimpse of Jesus' love. He could see Jesus' hands and feet being nailed to the cross without a word of complaint. He heard Jesus' halting prayer coming from lips of agony, "Father, forgive them; for they know not what they do." Luke 23:34.

A strange feeling sprang up in the thief's heart. He had never seen such love. As his companion jeered, "If thou be Christ, save thyself and us" (Luke 23:39), his own life flashed before him. He recognized his sinfulness, sensed his hopelessness, and rebuked the other thief for his mockery. Then he turned his eyes back to Jesus. Jesus did not look like One who could help him. Yet there was a majesty about Him, even in His agony. Truly, he reasoned, this must be the Lamb of God spoken of by the prophets. The repentant thief cried out from the depths of his soul, "Lord, remember me when thou comest into thy kingdom." Luke 23:42.

Instantly Jesus answered, "You will be with me in paradise." Luke 23:43, NIV.

What a promise! Looking into the future when all who love Him will be gathered into His kingdom, Jesus promised to remember the repentant thief who reached out in faith, and in reaching out, found salvation. Today Jesus longs to give you the same assurance. In fact, in the last book of the Bible Jesus pictures Himself knocking at your heart's door, waiting to be invited in. He is listening and waiting. Why not open your heart's door today and invite Him to come in and be the Saviour and Lord of your life? He is waiting.

Does God Have Anything to Say to Me?

Suffocating heat! Dry, burning sand stretching mile after mile across the barren Sinai Desert!

For the weary caravan of travelers, the monotony is punctuated only by the lurching motion of the cantankerous camels. Joseph—eleventh son of Jacob, sold as a slave to a caravan of Ishmaelite traders by his jealous half-brothers—is on his way to Egypt.

Heartbroken as Joseph is by the cruel treatment of his brothers, the prospect of being sold as a common slave—of never seeing his father or home again—is even more terrifying. What a sad journey this is for Joseph. Even seeing the giant pyramids and the incredible Sphinx holds no interest for him because of the dull ache in his heart, as he remembers the events of recent days. Nearing the palace, Joseph wonders at the wealth and beauty of the cities of Egypt. Not for a moment does he dream that someday he will be a ruler in this rich nation.

In a short time the Ishmaelite traders have sold Joseph as a house boy to Potiphar, captain of the guard in Pharaoh's court. And so it has come about that the pampered son of one of the richest men in Canaan has become a helpless slave—at the beck and call of a heathen master.

Fearful and lonely, Joseph turned for comfort to his father's God, determining to be faithful to Him at all cost.

Potiphar quickly recognized Joseph's honesty and organizational ability, steadily increasing his responsibilities until Joseph became overseer of his entire estate.

"His master saw that the Lord was with him, and that the Lord made all that he did to prosper in his hand." Genesis 39:3.

But just when everything seemed to be going well, Potiphar's wife falsely accused Joseph of improper advances, and Potiphar had Joseph thrown in prison. Yet even there, Joseph's integrity and talent for organization were recognized. The warden put him in charge of all the prisoners.

Several years later Pharaoh had some strange dreams that disturbed him. Sensing their importance, he called for the magicians and royal priests, asking that they tell him the meaning of his dreams. But try as they might, they could not interpret Pharaoh's dreams.

Then Pharaoh's butler remembered Joseph, the young Hebrew in prison who had once interpreted one of his dreams accurately. Joseph was summoned to the royal palace, and Pharaoh told him that he had dreamed he was standing by the Nile River and saw seven fat, healthy cows come up out of the water. Then he said he saw seven thin cows come up and eat the fat cows, but they remained thin. Later, he told Joseph, he dreamed that he saw seven full ears of corn on one stalk and seven withered ones. Joseph explained that both dreams had the same meaning: "God has revealed to Pharaoh what he is about to do." "Seven years of great abundance are coming throughout the land of Egypt, but seven years of famine will follow them." Genesis 41:25, 29, 30, NIV.

Joseph advised Pharaoh to select a wise man to supervise preparations for the coming years of famine. Impressed by Joseph's ability to interpret dreams, Pharaoh made Joseph the prime minister of Egypt. At the age of 30, he became the second most powerful person in the land. Just as

Joseph foretold, Egypt enjoyed seven years of rich harvests. Joseph had enormous granaries built and stored the excess grain for the famine which followed.

Is the story of Joseph just a myth? Jewish folklore? Biblical legend? For many years skeptics and historians said so. They scoffed at the Bible's account of a slave boy becoming a ruler, and they rejected the Genesis account of a seven-year famine in Egypt, calling it "mere fiction." But inscriptions chiseled on a rock near the first cataract of the Nile River read, in part, "I collected corn. . . . I was watchful in time of sowing. And when a famine arose, lasting many years, I distributed corn."—George A. Barron, *Archaeology and the Bible*, page 369. And again, "The Nile has not overflowed for a period of seven years. . . . Herbage fails. . . . The storehouses were built. . . . All that was in them has been consumed."—*Ibid.,* page 306.

Also reminiscent of Pharaoh's dreams is a fresco found in an Egyptian tomb featuring seven fat cows and seven lean ones.

Some have said it is unbelievable that a foreigner—especially a hated Semite shepherd—could rise to such a high position in Egypt. However, as we search ancient history, we find a period of time when this could well have happened—when the Semitic Hyksos overthrew the Egyptian dynasty and ruled approximately 235 years, from about 1780 B.C. to 1545 B.C. These invaders established their own line of Pharaohs and ruled the country. Hated foreigners themselves, the Hyksos would trust Joseph, also a Semite, sooner than a native of Egypt. The timing fits perfectly.

The archaeologist's spade has opened the windows to the remote past, confirming repeatedly the biblical account of history by clay tablets, hidden manuscripts, stone cylinders, and hieroglyphics decorating steles, tombs, and temple walls.

Through the ages, skeptics and critics have derided the Bible's scientific statements, ridiculed its historicity, scoffed at its prophecies, and smiled at its spiritual authority. The trek of the Bible through the centuries has been a fascinating one all the way. Never has there been a book like it! Some have denied it, rejected it, outlawed it, spurned it, burned it, and buried it. Others have died for it.

The skeptic Voltaire once boasted: "I am weary of hearing people repeat that twelve men established the Christian religion. I will prove that one man may suffice to overthrow it."— George E. Vandeman, *Hammers in the Fire,* page 15.

Voltaire predicted that in a century the Bible would be unknown. The century came and went. What about his boast? Is the Bible an unknown book? Today a Bible depository stands on the very place where Voltaire made his prediction. The depository contains Bibles stacked by the thousands.

Never in the history of mankind have so many books been written. The marketplace is flooded with a torrent of books on every imaginable subject—and some unimaginable ones! Some are true; most are fiction.

In a year, Americans purchase more than a billion and a half books, spending more than six billion dollars. Yet many of today's best sellers will be tomorrow's throwaways! And yet heading the list of best sellers worldwide, year in and year out, decade after decade, is the Bible!

United States presidents take the oath of office with their hand on the Bible. British kings and queens take their coronation vows upon the Sacred Word.

What kind of book is it that captures the admiration and loyalty of so many? What lies behind the Bible's mystic power? What does it claim to be? First, it claims to be inspired by God. "All scripture is given by inspiration of God." 2 Timothy 3:16.

Next, it claims to be written by chosen men who were

inspired by the Holy Ghost. "For the prophecy came not in old time by the will of man: but holy men of God spake as they were moved by the Holy Ghost." 2 Peter 1:21.

These claims are either true or untrue. If they are true, then there is no greater authority on Earth! If they are untrue—well, then the Bible is just another book. However, as archaeologists quietly uncover the past in ancient tombs and buried cities, they find evidence that even the smallest details of Scripture are fact—not fiction.

Until the nineteenth century, little was known about the ancient past except for the biblical record. Its history seemed locked forever behind the strange picture writings—the hieroglyphics—of Egypt. For no one in Egypt, nor anyone in the whole world, could decipher them.

Then in 1798, Napoleon led a military expedition into Egypt. With his 38,000 soldiers, Napoleon took a hundred artists, linguists, and scientists to help him better understand the history of that intriguing land.

Everywhere, they saw relics of the past—indecipherable inscriptions, decorated monuments and temple walls. Napoleon and his scholars wondered what secret messages those picture writings contained.

A year later, in 1799, the most significant of all archaeological discoveries up to that time occurred. One of Napoleon's soldiers unearthed a black stone—four feet long and two and a half feet wide—that would unlock the mystery of the picture writing and reveal secrets hidden for centuries.

Known as the Rosetta Stone, it is now housed in the British Museum. This rock slab, uncovered near the delta town of Rosetta, bore an ancient decree in three different scripts: hieroglyphic (picture writing), demotic Egyptian, and Greek. Of course, scholars could readily translate the Greek text, but the hieroglyphics were something else. However, twenty years later, in 1822, a brilliant young Frenchman by the name of Jean Francois Champollion startled the world by deciphering the hieroglyphics on the Rosetta Stone.

Thus, the vast treasures of Egypt's ancient past opened to the scholars of the world. But most important, the long-forgotten history of Egypt now stepped forward to confirm the pages of Scripture. The inscribed stones cried out to the whole world that what the Bible said was true!

The more the archaeologist digs, the more evidence he finds to confirm Bible history with historical records of past civilizations.

Recent discoveries at Tell Mardikh, the ancient city of Ebla in Syria—once a rich and sophisticated society of almost 300,000 people—have electrified the world of archaeology. Not since the discovery of the Dead Sea Scrolls have so many scholars in this field of study been so excited about a find. But it is even more exciting to the students of the Bible.

In a scribal school adjoining the city's palace, 14,000 inscribed clay tablets and fragments were found, dating back at least to 2300 B.C. The world's oldest discovered state archive contained the official records of the kingdom of Ebla for more than a century.

Some historians had questioned whether the Hebrews could have developed the art of writing by the time of Moses. Until the nineteenth century, no historical evidence existed to verify it. However, the Ebla tablets and other finds date back far beyond the lifetime of Moses. In fact, archaeologists have discovered whole libraries that date back centuries before Moses.

The Ebla tablets refer to a creation and a flood story. Also mentioned there are names and places which coincide with biblical ones: Esau, Abraham, Israel, Sinai, even Jerusalem. But, the real bombshell is the mention of the two "sin cities"—Sodom and Gomorrah.

Before the discovery of these tablets, no historical reference to these cities had been known except in the Bible. Therefore they were considered to be just mythical. However, many books will have to be rewritten, for these findings do indeed confirm many geographical names of that day. Some authors will have to concede that Genesis is more than just ancient shepherd songs and legends. The discoveries at Ebla and elsewhere have confirmed the authenticity of the Bible.

David said, "Thy word is true from the beginning." Psalm 119:160. And Isaiah agrees: "For thus saith the Lord that created the heavens; God himself that formed the earth and made it; . . . I the Lord speak righteousness, I declare things that are right." Isaiah 45:18, 19.

But how can we know that our Bible today speaks the same message it did thousands of years ago? No other book in history has survived so many perils. Yet miraculously, it has come down through the centuries intact. The text of the Bible has come to us practically unchanged, despite the fact that early volumes were laboriously hand copied.

In the summer of 1947, a Bedouin boy, looking for a lost goat near the northwest shores of the Dead Sea, idly tossed a stone through a hole in a cliff. He was startled to hear the sound of breaking pottery! At that moment began another of the most significant archaeological finds of all times. Muhammed ed-Dhib had stumbled upon the first of the treasures now known as the Dead Sea Scrolls. Other caves nearby revealed more pottery, more scrolls. Portions of every book of the Old Testament, except the book of Esther, were found.

Among the scrolls found in the caves was the Isaiah scroll—twenty-four feet in length, in an excellent state of preservation, and complete from verse one to the last. An extraordinary find—1,000 years older than any complete biblical Hebrew manuscript in existence!

The book of Isaiah mentions the name of Sargon, king of Assyria. Because this name had not been found in the list of kings who ruled during that time, the Bible was viewed by some as unreliable. Then, a Frenchman, Paul Botta, while excavating at Khorsabad, unearthed beautifully carved slabs of stone which later were discovered to be from the palace of none other than Sargon, the forgotten king! One of the cuneiform inscriptions deciphered contained Sargon's account of his conquests: "I beseiged and conquered Samaria and led away as a booty 27,290 inhabitants of it."

Sculptured lions, winged gods, human-headed bulls, and other priceless art objects were found at Khorsabad, along with a limestone relief of the head of Sargon II, king of Assyria. Again the spade of the archaeologist confirmed the Word of God.

Some scholars had believed that Isaiah had been written by several men over a long time period—that it was actually more than one book. However, the Dead Sea Scrolls provided excellent evidence that the book of Isaiah has always been one book with one author.

And how do the Dead Sea Scrolls of Isaiah compare with the Isaiah in our Bibles today? Professor Millar Burrows of Yale University says, "There are minor omissions and additions, but the remarkable fact is that there is nothing which can be called a major addition or omission."—*The Biblical Archaeologist,* vol. XI, no. 10, page 61. Scholars around the world were amazed to learn that the Old Testament has come down to us through so many centuries practically unchanged!

They say dead men do not tell tales. But they do! Tales more fascinating than fiction. Civilizations long dead are speaking from their dusty graves, confirming the accuracy and reliability of God's Word.

Until the nineteenth century, some scholars believed that Queen Semiramis built Babylon. Yet in the Bible, Daniel quoted Nebuchadnezzar as saying: "Is not this great Babylon, that I have built?" Daniel 4:30.

Who was right? In 1899, Robert Koldewey began excavating the old ruins of Babylon, unearthing tens of thousands of kiln-baked bricks, all bearing the stamp of King Nebuchadnezzar, all taken from the walls and temples of the city. A cuneiform tablet, recounting Nebuchadnezzar's achievements, was also found by the archaeologists of Babylon. On it Nebuchadnezzar asks, "Is not this Babylon the great which I have built?" The East India House inscription, now in London, devotes six columns of Babylonian writing to a description of the huge building projects of Nebuchadnezzar. The spade again stood by the Word of God.

Another mystery of secular history was the absence of the name of Belshazzar as a ruler of Babylon. The Bible named Belshazzar as the ruler of Babylon who witnessed the handwriting on the wall of the banquet hall. Was he only the invention of Daniel's fertile mind?

Nabonidus, successor of the great Nebuchadnezzar, had entrusted the kingship to his son Belshazzar, while he was away at Tema in Arabia for ten years. Tablets from archaeologists' finds state that the kingdom was indeed entrusted to Belshazzar, the crown prince.

"And as to Belshazzar the exalted son, the offspring of my body, do thou place the adoration of the great deity in his heart; may he not give way to sin; may he be satisfied with life's abundance; and may reverence for the great divinity dwell in the heart of Belshazzar, my first-born favorite son."—*God Speaks to Modern Man,* page 154.

Isn't it interesting that in the closing chapter of Daniel, we read: "But thou, O Daniel, shut up the words, and seal the book, even to the time of the end: many shall run to and fro, and knowledge shall be increased." Daniel 12:4.

Knowledge would be increased not only in the scientific world. Knowledge would also increase as to the accuracy of

God's Word. Bricks and cylinders, tablets and manuscripts—dug up by archaeologists in places where Bible characters walked in the ancient past—are proving that what the Bible says is true.

However, another compelling evidence that the Bible is God's inspired Word is its ability to foretell the future. "I am God, and there is none like me, declaring the end from the beginning, and from ancient times the things that are not yet done." Isaiah 46:9, 10.

Yes, as God pulls back the curtain of time, giving us a glimpse of the future, He demonstrates to the world that the Bible is not just a book. It is *His* Book.

Before Babylon reached its zenith of power and glory, God's Book foretold its fall: "And Babylon, the glory of kingdoms, the beauty of the Chaldees' excellency, shall be as when God overthrew Sodom and Gomorrah." Isaiah 13:19. The Bible even foretold the power that would overthrow this mighty kingdom:

"The Lord hath raised up the spirit of the kings of the Medes: for his device is against Babylon, to destroy it." Jeremiah 51:11.

The name of the man who would lead the armies against Babylon was prophesied 150 years before his birth, as was the very way he would do it. "Thus saith the Lord to his anointed, to Cyrus, . . . I will . . . open before him the two leaved gates." Isaiah 45:1.

Were the prophecies of the Bible fulfilled? Indeed they were! In the British Museum, in the Persian Hall, stands the Cyrus cylinder—discovered in the ruins of Babylon. On this clay cylinder, Cyrus tells of his conquest of Babylon.

The Bible not only foretold Babylon's destruction, it further stated: "And Babylon shall become heaps." Jeremiah 51:37. "It shall never be inhabited. . . . But wild beasts of the desert shall lie there; . . . and owls shall dwell there." Isaiah 13:20, 21. Only God could forsee the future and predict so accurately the fate of the mighty kingdom of Babylon.

Austen H. Layard, the explorer, describes the site of ancient Babylon: "Shapeless heaps of rubbish cover for many an acre the face of the land . . . a naked and hideous waste. Owls start from the scanty thickets, and the foul jackall skulks through the furrows."—*Discoveries Among the Ruins of Nineveh and Babylon,* page 413.

Of Babylon's former glory, nothing remains but its name on a signpost at the roadside. The vast heaps scattered over the ancient Babylonian ruins are monumental evidence to the inspiration and integrity of the Bible. We can but agree with the prophet of old: "The grass withereth, the flower fadeth: but the word of our God shall stand for ever." Isaiah 40:8.

And, friend, if God had the wisdom and ability to precisely foretell centuries in advance the future of ancient kingdoms past, can we doubt for a moment His ability and wisdom to predict accurately what our future holds for us? Hardly! In fact, Bible prophecy gives us the privilege of pulling up the blinds, looking into the future through God's eyes, and catching a glimpse of His solution to the problems threatening man's survival on Planet Earth.

The Bible is more than just authentic history, more than scientific facts, more than prophecies fulfilled. If it were not, it would not matter what men did with it. The theme of the Book, the heart of it all, is the account of what happened on a rugged hill outside of Jerusalem more than nineteen centuries ago. And it makes a difference what we believe about that! Either the Son of the living God died on that cross, or He did not. Either He was who the Bible says He was—or He was not. Was Calvary fantasy or fact? It makes a difference, and we need to know.

Perhaps the greatest evidence that the Bible is what it claims to be is the power in the Book to change lives. That power is wrapped up in one person—Jesus Christ! Jesus said, "Search the Scriptures; for in them ye think ye have eternal life: and they are they which testify of me." John 5:39.

Jesus was speaking of the Old Testament, for the New Testament had not yet been written. And as you turn the pages of the Old Testament, you will discover that they prophesy of a coming Messiah and tell of His mission of love and salvation.

Jesus told His disciples: "These are the words which I spake unto you, while I was yet with you, that all things must be fulfilled, which were written in the law of Moses, and in the prophets, and in the psalms, concerning me." Luke 24:44.

The Old Testament prophesied of Christ, and the New Testament is His life story. So you see, the entire Bible is a revelation of Jesus Christ, who came to demonstrate to a planet in rebellion what His Father was really like.

That is why the Bible is called the "Living Word of God." It carries a vitalizing power with it wherever it goes—a power that changes lives, transforms human character, gives strength to the weak, courage to the depressed, and hope to the dying. Jesus spent His time changing people—that is the heart of the Christian religion. And it is the heart of the Bible, the secret of its power. Jesus knew what power it was that changed men: "You shall know the truth, and the truth will set you free." John 8:32, NEB.

It is truth that sets men free, that changes men! It is the truth that makes a drunkard a sober and loving father. It is truth that frees the drug abuser. With so much deception being practiced in the world today, we ask, "What is truth?" Jesus gave the answer: "Thy word is truth." John 17:17.

The Bible, God's Word, is truth! The power of that Word can change the hearts of men and women. But God's Word can change only those who are willing to be changed. Those willing to accept the man in the Book—Jesus Christ. And millions of lives have been changed as they have studied the

Bible. No greater power exists in the world to touch hearts and change lives!

Sam Tannyhill is a dramatic example of the power of God's Word to change a man's life completely. Sam could never look back on a pleasant, carefree childhood. His parents were divorced when he was five years old, and Sam lived in a dozen different homes where his needs were not understood. Starved for love and affection, Sam did poorly in school, and his formal education ended in grade six.

Sam's criminal life really began when he was ten years old—small offenses, considered unimportant. No one took any positive action, feeling he would outgrow his "antisocial" behavior. Sam was never given any moral training; he never set foot inside a church. As time went on, instead of outgrowing his poor habits and attitudes, he became more involved in theft and crime. Finally he was convicted of forgery and sentenced to the Missouri State Penitentiary.

Two weeks after serving five and a half years there, Sam robbed a small restaurant in Ohio. At gunpoint he forced the waitress to accompany him. Later he said he had planned to let her out several miles from town. Unfortunately, the waitress recognized Sam and threatened to expose him. Her badly beaten body was found the next day.

Sam escaped into Kansas, and after several more robberies, was apprehended and confessed the whole affair. He stood trial and was sentenced to die in the electric chair in the Ohio State Penitentiary.

During Sam's time in prison, several Christians visited him. One visitor brought Sam a gift—a Bible belonging to the man's nine-year-old son. It was given to Sam only when he promised to read it. After he ran out of other books, Sam read the Bible to pass the time away. In his own words, he tells what happened as he read the Bible:

"I found a place where a man named Jesus sent some of His gang to bring Him a mule. For this I thought Him a horse thief. Then I ran across a place where He made wine. For this, I called Him a bootlegger. Then I found a place where He raised the dead, healed all manner of sickness, and cast out evil. Now I wondered, What manner of man is this? So I started at Matthew, and I read all the part called the New Testament. By that time I found Him, not a horse thief or bootlegger, but the Son of God. I knew of people who prayed and served that God and who lived up to His law, but that wasn't me. I was an ex-con, a murderer, but yet I read where people in the Bible were also outside of the law. Then I was troubled; I wanted that peace of mind this God was giving away, but how could I get word to Him? Can He really hear you when you pray? And will He answer a man who has never heard of Him?"

"So I tried praying. My prayers never got out of my cell. I prayed for help, but hung on to the world with both hands. . . . I decided . . . to give it one more try. . . . For three days there was no more miserable soul on this earth than I. I prayed, I cried, I prayed, and the longer it went on the more miserable I became.

"On November 4th I made one more try to reach that God who could give me that peace of mind. I got on my knees and truly confessed every wrong I could think of, and asked that God please help me. I told Him if I had forgotten any of my sins to have mercy on me and add them to the list, because I was guilty of them too.

"Let me tell you, I never had such a wonderful feeling in my life. I wanted to shout it to the world. Yes, I felt the Spirit of God as He truly brought His love into my heart. After I settled down to bed along about morning, I slept peacefully for the first time in my adult life. The next morning when I got up, I prayed my thanks to God before I even put on my clothes. That day I testified to my fellowmen here.

"I am in a cell in death row, but I am more free here than I ever was in the streets. I have no fear of death whatsoever. To me death is one step closer to my Jesus.

"I can truly say there is no sin too black that the blood of Jesus Christ can't wash as white as snow."—William A. Fagal, *Three Hours to Live,* pages 19-21.

From his cell on death row, Sam wrote Pastor William Fagal: "There are just four of us on death row at present, but I am glad to tell you that three of us are under the blood of Christ. Please pray that we will be able to get the fourth one before it is too late."—*Ibid.,* page 33.

Sam's last audible prayer was, "Lord, don't hold against these guards what they are about to do tonight. What I have done has forced them to do what they are about to do. If it is sin, Lord, then charge it up to my account, and forgive it just as You have forgiven all the rest of my sins. Amen."—*Ibid.,* page 45.

Sam's voice is still today, but the marvelous change the Word of God made in his life continues to be a witness drawing men and women to Jesus Christ. Never has there been a book that can so change the lives of men. That power can make all the difference in your life. As you personally read the Book, letting it speak to your mind and heart, you will be convinced that it comes from the heart of God—that it is God who speaks.

You see, friend, it makes a difference what we do with the Book. It is more than just a Book to carry to church. It is more than a Book to decorate coffee tables. It is more than helpful information or useful advice—it is God speaking to our hearts. It is His love letter to His children on Planet Earth. In it is the secret of survival, everlasting happiness, and peace of mind.

Yes, friend, it's not just the Book—it's the Author of the Book that makes the difference! And as we catch a glimpse of that Author, our faith will soar, for to know Him is to love and trust Him. The next chapter could change your life—forever!

Will There Ever Be Peace in the World?

Long before the sun glistened on the deep waters of the Euphrates River, the magnificent Babylonian palace bristled with excitement. From King Nebuchadnezzar's royal bedroom to the cobblestone courtyard, the very atmosphere seemed electrified. The king's advisers, clothed in their colorful robes of office, hurriedly stepped from their chariots and hastened to the palace. There was obviously a great urgency about something. Had war been declared? Was there a revolution?

Rumors quickly spread that the king had endured a very restless night. He had dreamed a dream that troubled him greatly, but he couldn't remember the particulars. The Babylonians placed great importance on dreams, and Nebuchadnezzar felt he had to know the dream and its interpretation. Despite the early hour, he had summoned the chief astrologers, magicians, and sorcerers to the court.

The story is recorded in the book of Daniel, chapter two: "In the second year of his reign, Nebuchadnezzar had dreams; his mind was troubled and he could not sleep. So the king summoned the magicians, enchanters, sorcerers and astrologers to tell him what he had dreamed. When they came in and stood before the king, he said to them, 'I have had a dream that troubles me and I want to know what it means.' " Daniel 2:1-3, NIV.

The wise men had anticipated something much more difficult. Only a dream! They were masters at interpreting dreams. This would be easy. How quickly they could relieve the king's anxiety! "Then the astrologers answered the king in Aramaic, 'O king, live forever! Tell your servants the dream, and we will interpret it.' " Daniel 2:4, NIV. By inventing explanations to people's dreams, these astrologers had risen to a high position in the court of Babylon. They felt confident that they could satisfy the king's concern.

But their self-confidence soon vanished as the proud monarch added, "This is what I have firmly decided: If you do not tell me what my dream was and interpret it, I will have you cut into pieces and your houses turned into piles of rubble." Daniel 2:5, NIV. The astrologers looked at each other in fear! How could they possibly know what the king had dreamed the night before? Dare they guess? The king might be testing them; maybe he did remember the dream! With their lives at stake, they tried to reason with the king. "There is not a man on earth who can do what the king asks! No king . . . has ever asked such a thing of any magician or enchanter or astrologer. What the king asks is too difficult. No one can reveal it to the king except the gods, and they do not live among men." Daniel 2:10, 11, NIV.

Rational though their plea was, the king had a point. For years he had supported these advisers lavishly. They claimed to have psychic powers and to be able to contact the gods. They claimed the ability to read the stars and foretell the future. Now it was up to them either to prove their claims or be exposed as deceivers. Desperately they stalled for time. However, their hesitant gestures soon indicated to the king that these men were frauds. Hot with anger, the king commanded: "Execute them! Execute all the wise men of Babylon." See Daniel 2:12.

Arioch, captain of the king's guard, hastened to obey the king's order. However, not all of the wise men had been summoned to the palace that morning. Perhaps the king had called for just the older, more experienced men. Daniel, Hananiah, Mishael, and Azariah were summoned from their quarters for the death decree. These four young Hebrews had been captured as prisoners by Nebuchadnezzar's army during his Palestinian campaign and had been been taken to the Babylonian palace to be educated. Instead of slaying all the officials of the conquered nations, it was customary for Babylonian kings to select the most talented and promising captives and to educate them as advisers.

When the soldiers came looking for Daniel and his friends to put them to death, Daniel spoke to Arioch and asked why the king had issued such a harsh decree. Arioch explained to Daniel what had happened. "At this, Daniel went in to the king and asked for time, so that he might interpret the dream for him." Daniel 2:16, NIV. In desperation the king agreed to give Daniel time. What a responsibility hung on Daniel's shoulders! Not only was his life and the lives of his three friends at stake, but the lives of all the wise men of Babylon. Much depended on what Daniel did the next few hours.

"Then Daniel returned to his house and explained the matter to his friends. . . . He urged them to plead for mercy from the God of heaven concerning this mystery, so that he and his friends might not be executed with the rest of the wise men of Babylon." Daniel 2:17, 18, NIV.

What a prayer meeting! Four young Hebrews praying that God would reveal to them the dream of a heathen king—and that before the deadline! The God of heaven did not fail to hear and honor those prayers. "During the night the mystery was revealed to Daniel in a vision. Then Daniel praised the God of heaven." Daniel 2:19, NIV. What excitement! God had revealed to this young Hebrew both the dream and the interpretation. Daniel hurried to Arioch, the chief executioner, and said, "Do not execute the wise men of

Babylon. Take me to the king, and I will interpret his dream for him." Daniel 2:24, NIV.

Arioch took Daniel to the king at once and said he had found a man among the exiles from Judah who could tell the king his dream. Nebuchadnezzar must have wondered whether such a novice from the ranks of his wise men could actually reveal his dream. Gazing intently at the young man before him, he asked, "Are you able to tell me what I saw in my dream and interpret it?" Daniel 2:26, NIV.

Without hesitation, Daniel replied, "The secret which the king hath demanded cannot the wise men, the astrologers, the magicians, the soothsayers, shew unto the king; but there is a God in heaven that revealeth secrets, and maketh known to the King Nebuchadnezzar what shall be in the latter days." Daniel 2:27, 28.

Daniel was humble, but bold, as he spoke for God. A knowledge of future events, he told the king, is not to be found in astrology or in the mystic arts of the occult. Only one dependable source of information about the future exists—the God of Heaven.

The king leaned forward, impatient to hear the dream and its interpretation.

"As you were lying there, O king, your mind turned to things to come, and the revealer of mysteries showed you what is going to happen. . . . You looked, O king, and there before you stood a large statue—an enormous, dazzling statue, awesome in appearance. The head of the statue was made of pure gold, its chest and arms of silver, its belly and thighs of bronze, its legs of iron, its feet partly of iron and partly of baked clay. While you were watching, a rock was cut out, but not by human hands. It struck the statue on its feet of iron and clay and smashed them. Then the iron, the clay, the bronze, the silver and the gold were broken to pieces . . . and became like chaff on a threshing floor. . . . The wind swept them away without leaving a trace. But the rock that struck the statue became a huge mountain and filled the whole earth." Daniel 2:29-35, NIV.

Overjoyed, the king declared, "Yes that's it! That's exactly what I saw in my dream."

"What could this strange dream possibly have to do with me?" you ask. Be assured that Nebuchadnezzar had similar thoughts, and he soon learned that this dream speaks in a very dramatic way to every human being from his time to the present. In just 150 words God sketched the main course of history from Babylon's time 600 years before Christ to the climax of Earth's history. He pulled back the curtain of history in advance. Nebuchadnezzar and Daniel looked down through the centuries to the end of time. Breathlessly the king waited for the interpretation. What could this dream mean?

Daniel said, "This is the dream, and now we will interpret it to the king." "You are that head of gold." Daniel 2:36, 38, NIV.

Babylon was the head! Babylon, a nation of pure gold! A smile of satisfaction must have crossed the king's face as he heard those words. The military conquests and the architectural splendor of Babylon were unsurpassed. Historians confirm that gold was a fitting symbol to represent the Babylonian kingdom. An abundance of gold was used in embellishing the buildings of Babylon. Notice one historian's description of the great ancient city:

"Situated in the garden of the east; laid out in perfect square . . . with a moat or ditch around . . . its gates of brass, its hanging gardens rising terrace above terrace . . . its two royal palaces . . . there, with the whole earth prostrate at her feet, a queen in peerless grandeur . . . stood this city, fit capital of that kingdom which was represented by the golden head."—Uriah Smith, *The Prophecies of Daniel and the Revelation,* pages 33, 34.

Had Daniel been just a clever politician trying to make

his way to the top in Babylon, he would have stopped the interpretation of the dream right there. But Daniel had a message that God wanted revealed to the world—a message not just for his time, but one that would be relevant to the end of Earth's history. And Daniel had the courage to present it. Boldly he declared, "After thee shall arise another kingdom inferior to thee." Daniel 2:39.

The king's smile of satisfaction must have quickly faded when he heard those words from Daniel. Babylon's proud monarch had probably given no thought to the idea that any other nation would ever rule the world. In fact, archaeologists have excavated clay tablets inscribed with these words by Nebuchadnezzar:

"For the astonishment of men I have built this house." "These portals for the astonishment of multitudes of people with beauty I adorned." "May it last forever."

However, God said that another power would arise, another kingdom would supersede the golden kingdom of Babylon. And Daniel lived to see this happen! He lived to see the silver kingdom replace the gold one. During the reign of Belshazzar, Nebuchadnezzar's proud and arrogant grandson, Cyrus the Mede, laid siege to Babylon, and on October 13, 539 B.C., the golden kingdom of Babylon came to an inglorious end.

It happened like this. Feeling recklessly secure in his capital and foolishly ignoring the Medo-Persian army, King Belshazzar arranged a great feast for a thousand of his nobles. To show his defiance of the God of heaven, he commanded that the golden vessels taken by his grandfather, Nebuchadnezzar, from the temple in Jerusalem be brought to his table. "And the king, and his princes, his wives, and his concubines, drank in them. They drank wine, and praised the gods of gold, and of silver, of brass, of iron, of wood, and of stone." Daniel 5:3, 4.

In the midst of this revelry, a bloodless hand emerged

from the dark. Slowly, the mystic fingers began to trace in fiery letters across the plastered wall words which no one could understand. Terrified, the people ceased their festivities. Silence gripped the great banquet hall.

"The king watched the hand as it wrote. His face turned pale and he was so frightened that his knees knocked together and his legs gave way." Daniel 5:5, 6, NIV.

Like his grandfather, Belshazzer summoned the enchanters, astrologers, and diviners, and said: "Whoever reads this writing and tells me what it means will be clothed in purple and have a gold chain placed around his neck, and he will be made the third highest ruler in the kingdom." Daniel 5:6, NIV.

However, in spite of the inducements, no one could read those fateful words. Finally, the queen mother appeared in the banquet hall and reminded Belshazzar of Daniel, who decades before had revealed the meaning of Nebuchadnezzar's dream. The prophet was summoned. Again the king made his offer of wealth and position. The aged Daniel quickly replied, "You may keep your gifts for yourself and give your rewards to someone else. Nevertheless, I will read the writing for the king and tell him what it means." Daniel 5:17, NIV.

Still trembling with fear, the king waited for Daniel's interpretation.

"MENE, MENE, TEKEL, UPHARSIN. This is the interpretation of the thing:

MENE; God hath numbered thy kingdom, and finished it.

TEKEL; Thou art weighed in the balances, and art found wanting.

PERES; Thy kingdom is divided, and given to the Medes and Persians." Daniel 5:25-28. (Peres is the singular form of Upharsin.)

Even as Daniel's solemn words reverberated around

the carved columns of the banquet hall, a messenger came
with the news that the city had been taken. The Euphrates
River bisected the city, and the Medes and Persians had di-
verted it out of its channel into a depression, making it possible for their soldiers to march down the riverbed under the
walls, and into the city. The massive brass gates along the
river's edge had been carelessly left unlocked. The city was
soon filled with enemy soldiers. The triumphant shouts of
Cyrus's army could be heard above the terrified cries of the
revelers.

Nearly 200 years earlier, God had described to the
prophet Isaiah the strategy by which Babylon was to be
taken, even naming the general who would accomplish it
150 years before he was born! "Thus saith the Lord to his
anointed, to Cyrus, whose right hand I have holden, to subdue nations before him; and I will loose the loins of kings, to
open before him the two leaved gates; and the gates shall
not be shut." Isaiah 45:1.

Daniel had predicted that after the golden empire of
Babylon, an inferior kingdom, represented by the chest and
arms of silver, would come to power. The coalition government of the Medes and Persians was certainly inferior to the
glorious Babylonian Empire. But it ruled the Middle East for
two centuries. However, Daniel also foretold the limitations
of that kingdom. Notice the next part of this moving prophecy: "Next, a third kingdom, one of bronze, will rule over the
whole earth." Daniel 2:39, NIV.

This prediction was fulfilled when the brilliant young
general, Alexander the Great, defeated Darius III of Persia, in
the battle of Arbela, 331 B.C. At the youthful age of 25,
young Alexander became ruler over the most extensive empire the world had known. The Greek historian Arian, writing
about Alexander, said, "I am persuaded there was no nation,
city, nor people . . . where his name did not reach. . . . There
seems to me to have been some divine hand presiding both

over his birth and actions." —*Historical Library,* book 16, chapter 12.

Fittingly, much of the armor worn by the Greek infantry was made of brass, the third metal in Nebuchadnezzar's image. The historian Herodotus described Greek pirates as "men of bronze coming from the sea." Amazing, isn't it!

King Nebuchadnezzar listened in awe as Daniel, continuing the interpretation, explained the legs of iron. "Finally, there will be a fourth kingdom, strong as iron—for iron breaks and smashes everything—and as iron breaks things to pieces, so it will crush and break all others." Daniel 2:40, NIV.

"On June 22, 168 B.C., at the battle of Pydna, perished the empire of Alexander the Great, 144 years after his death."—Theodor Mounsen's *History of Rome,* book 3, chapter 10.

The republic of Rome grasped the scepter of world control, crushing all opposition and subjecting whole nations to slavery. Even secular historians recognized Rome's fulfillment of the imagery of this famous prophecy. Edward Gibbon observed, "The images of gold, or silver, or brass, that might serve to represent the nations and their kings, were successively broken by the iron monarchy of Rome."—Edward Gibbon, *History of the Decline and Fall of the Roman Empire,* volume 3, page 634.

Hippolytus, a third-century theologian, wrote, "Rejoice blessed Daniel! Thou hast not been in error; all these things have come to pass. . . . Already the iron rules; already it subdues, and breaks in pieces."—*Ante-Nicene Fathers,* volume 5, page 210.

Rome was a ruthless nation, ruling with a "rod of iron." Her Caesars called themselves gods and demanded the worship and obedience of all men. She was the longest lived and most extensive of the four world empires.

But now the pattern of the prophecy changed. Daniel

predicted that no world empire would succeed Rome. "Just as you saw that the feet and toes were partly of baked clay and partly of iron, so this will be a divided kingdom; . . . so the people will be a mixture and will not remain united, any more than iron mixes with clay." Daniel 2:41-43, NIV.

Rome divided? The iron fibers of this giant empire which had ruled for 600 years disintegrated? Through luxury, political corruption, and moral decay, Rome lost its stability and strength, becoming an easy prey for barbarian tribes that began to invade the empire during the fourth century A.D. By 476, when Emperor Augustus was deposed, Rome had been divided into ten segments—listed here with their modern counterparts:

Alamanni (Germans)	Burgandians (Swiss)
Franks (French)	Lombards (Italians)
Anglo Saxons (English)	Suevi (Portuguese)
Visigoths (Spanish)	Heruli, Vandals, Ostrogoths (now extinct)

The nations of modern Europe developed from these tribes of the divided Roman Empire. Some were strong, some weak; some iron, some clay. But there is more to this prophetic interpretation. Now Daniel came to the most important part of the prophecy for us today: "And whereas thou sawest iron mixed with miry clay, they shall mingle themselves with the seed of men: but they shall not cleave one to another, even as iron is not mixed with clay." Daniel 2:43.

Many a world ruler has tried to weld these nations together by royal marriages—"mingling themselves with the seed of men." In fact, by the first decade of the twentieth century, virtually every crowned head of Europe was related. Yet this did not prevent World War I.

No plan to unite the world into one great empire, however

grand, can ever succeed. God has declared, **"They shall not cleave one to another."** Charlemagne, with the strength of the Holy Roman Empire behind him, failed. Charles V and Louis XIV tried and failed. Not even the great Napoleon Bonaparte could weld together the broken parts of the Roman Empire. At the age of 29, Napoleon overthrew the government of France and set out to conquer the world. He placed his relatives in power and had them intermarry, hoping to unite the nations. It appeared that nothing would stop him. However, just two small things spelled defeat for the great Bonaparte. On June 18, 1815, at Waterloo, his artillery became bogged down in the mud because of the heavy rains, and one of his generals misunderstood his orders.

Thirty years after Waterloo, Dr. Thomas Arnold said, "What was the principal adversary of this tremendous power? By whom was it checked, and resisted, and put down? By none and by nothing but the direct and manifest interposition of God."—*Lectures on Modern History,* page 3. Napoleon himself is reported to have said, "God almighty has been too much for me." Yes, God's prophecy stood fast!

Kaiser Wilhelm of Germany and later Hitler tried to marshal the world under one flag. Other moves have been made and will be made to bring about a united Europe, but no man, no group of men, or combinations of powers can ever bring unity for long; for God said, **"They shall not cleave one to another"**—a fitting epitaph for all these would-be world rulers!

King Nebuchadnezzar must have been puzzled by this turn of the prophecy. God foretold the doom of four great world empires. He predicted that Rome would be succeeded by ten nations, seven of which are represented in Western Europe today—some strong, some weak, but all hopelessly divided. What would happen next? With obvious joy and confidence, Daniel now came to the astounding climax of the interpretation of the great metallic image:

"In the time of those kings, the God of heaven will set up a kingdom that will never be destroyed, nor will it be left to another people. It will crush all those kingdoms and bring them to an end, but it will itself endure forever. This is the meaning of the vision of the rock cut out of a mountain, but not by human hands—a rock that broke the iron, the bronze, the clay, the silver and the gold to pieces. The great God has shown the king what will take place in the future. The dream is true and the interpretation is trustworthy." Daniel 2:44, 45, NIV.

There will never be another human world empire! God said that in the days of the kings represented by the ten toes (the nations of Europe today) He will set up a kingdom to end all earthly kingdoms—a kingdom that will last forever.

The next great event on the stage of human history will be the second coming of Jesus and the establishment of His kingdom, represented by the stone "cut out without hands." His will be a kingdom founded not by the hands of men, but by the mighty hand of God, a kingdom that will fill the whole Earth! Then will be fulfilled the prophecy, "The kingdoms of this world are become the kingdoms of our Lord . . . and he shall reign forever and ever." Revelation 11:15.

When Daniel finished telling the king his sensational vision and God's astounding interpretation, Nebuchadnezzar rose slowly from his throne and humbly prostrated himself before Daniel in honor of Daniel's great God, whose wisdom and power had been so impressively demonstrated. He acknowledged, "Surely your God is the God of gods and Lord of kings and a revealer of mysteries." Daniel 2:47, NIV.

By this giant metal image seen by Nebuchadnezzar in his dream six centuries before the birth of Christ, God unveiled the mysteries of centuries to come. The kingdoms represented by the gold, the silver, the brass, and the iron have all passed into history. Where are we living today? What will the next great glorious drama be?

Yes, the kingdom of Christ is coming soon. Sooner than we may think. As we look at the signs given in Scripture which are to precede Christ's return, it makes us wonder if we might even now be on the edge of tomorrow.

Yes, friend, "the dream is certain, and interpretation is sure"; the journey is almost over! The next great glorious drama will be Christ coming in the clouds of heaven to set up His kingdom—a kingdom that will never pass away. He has planned a beautiful tomorrow, and He wants you to be a part of that tomorrow—a tomorrow that has been made possible through Calvary. Won't you make a decision this very moment to be in God's eternal kingdom? Then you will hear from Christ's lips this invitation at His return: "Come, ye blessed of my father, inherit the kingdom prepared for you." Matthew 25:34.

Will there ever be peace in our world? Not until the kingdoms of Earth are finally and forever swept aside by the everlasting Kingdom ruled by Jesus Christ—the Prince of Peace.

But His reign of peace can begin in your heart and mine even now—if we will let Him be our king.

Is the World Coming to an End?

The story is told of a middle-aged man who clung precariously to the railing of a bridge while looking at the swift waters a hundred feet below. A policeman approached cautiously and gently tried to persuade the man not to jump. "Leave me alone!" the man shouted. "Life isn't worth living. It's too much for me."

"Well," replied the officer calmly, "you tell me why life isn't worth living, and I'll tell you why I think it is. If I can't convince you, then go ahead and jump."

At the end of the conversation, so the story goes, the policeman climbed over the railing, took the man's hand, and they both jumped!

The quality of life in the immediate future certainly is cause for concern. With the multiplied problems facing mankind today, many people are asking, "Is the world coming to an end? Is the future worth living for? Is there hope for a permanent solution to the crises facing us?"

If not, why not jump?

Does Planet Earth have a terminal illness, or can we prevent the projected doomsday? The future seems so fragile! Environmentalists hold out slim hope. The world's military leaders predict Armageddon. Politicians are trying to patch up our ailing planet—with band-aids. A spirit of pessimism and cynicism is sweeping the world. Is there no answer? Do we have to just sit and wait for the inevitable? People from all walks of life are asking, "How will it all end?"

World conditions have never been more grim, yet the vibrant, optimistic voice of our Lord rings with urgency and hope: "And when these things begin to come to pass, then look up, and lift up your heads; for your redemption draweth nigh." Luke 21:28. Along with the warning that time is running out for the earth as we know it, He brings us wonderful news: "And then shall they see the Son of man coming in a cloud with power and great glory." Luke 21:27. The return of Christ is the only permanent answer to this crisis hour.

Christ Himself gave an amazing series of prophetic insights concerning world history from His day to the end of time. One day as Jesus left the temple at Jerusalem, His disciples called His attention to its extraordinary beauty. Sadly, Jesus responded that the day would come when there would "not be left one stone upon another." Mark 13:2. The Jews fondly believed the temple would stand forever, and they were stunned by Jesus' prediction.

As soon as Jesus and the disciples reached the Mount of Olives, the disciples questioned Him about His statement. "Tell us, when shall these things be?" they said. "And what shall be the sign of thy coming, and of the end of the world?" Matthew 24:3. The disciples linked the destruction of the temple with the second coming of Jesus and the end of the world. They could not imagine the temple being destroyed, except at the end of the world.

Jesus' reply traced the events of world history to the end of time. He began by outlining the events that would take place during the thirty-nine years that remained before the destruction of Jerusalem. "For many shall come in my name, saying, I am Christ; and shall deceive many." Matthew 24:5. The Jewish historian Josephus recorded that several people appeared about that time claiming to be the Messiah.

Jesus further prophesied: "And ye shall hear of wars

and rumours of wars. . . . For nation shall rise against nation, and kingdom against kingdom: and there shall be famines, and pestilences, and earthquakes, in divers places." Matthew 24:6, 7. Jewish and Roman historians describe A.D. 31 to 70 as a time of great calamities. Wars broke out. There were four major famines and a series of major earthquakes. Yet Jesus said that "all these are the beginning of sorrows." Matthew 24:8.

Jesus warned that His followers would be persecuted, betrayed by their own relatives and friends. He also said, "This gospel of the kingdom shall be preached in all the world for a witness unto all nations; and then shall the end come." Matthew 24:14. The early Christian church, filled with the Holy Spirit, went forth to carry the gospel to the world. Thirty years later Paul declared that the gospel had been preached "to every creature which is under heaven." Colossians 1:23.

The fulfillment of each of these signs indicated that the destruction of Jerusalem was not far away. Speaking of the temple, Jesus said that the time would come when "enemies shall cast a trench about thee, . . . and shall lay thee even with the ground, and thy children within thee; and they shall not leave in thee one stone upon another." Luke 19: 43, 44.

But of equal importance, He gave the disciples a sign by which they would know when to escape the doomed city: "And when ye shall see Jerusalem compassed with armies, then know that the desolation thereof is nigh. Then let them which are in Judea flee to the mountains; and let them which are in the midst of it depart out." Luke 21:20, 21.

But how could those inside a besieged city ever get out? And why should those in Judea flee into the mountains? History gives the answer:

"After the Romans under Cestius had surrounded the city, they unexpectedly abandoned the siege when everything seemed favorable for an immediate attack. . . . The Roman general withdrew his forces without the least apparent reason. . . . Upon the retreat of Cestius, the Jews, sallying from Jerusalem, pursued after his retiring army; and while both forces were thus fully engaged, the Christians had an opportunity to leave the city. . . . Without delay they fled to a place of safety."—*The Great Controversy,* pages 30, 31.

When the seige resumed under the Roman general Titus, thousands of Jews perished. Both Josephus and Milman state that the famine was so severe that some parents ate their own children. Crimes perpetrated within the city walls were so gross that even hardened Roman soldiers were shocked. Despite an order from Titus to spare the temple, a torch strategically thrown through a window set the cedar-lined rooms of the temple ablaze. More than one million died in the destruction of the city, and the survivors were carried away as captives to be sold as slaves. Some were matched against wild animals in the circuses of Rome. Others escaped and wandered as homeless refugees.

And the temple stones? Josephus wrote that the temple walls crumbled so "there was left nothing to make those that come thither believe it had been inhabited." Not one stone "was left upon another." The soldiers plowed where the foundations had stood, trying to retrieve the gold that had melted and run down into the ground.

The prophecy given in A.D. 31 was fulfilled to the letter in A.D. 70. Yet historians record that not one Christian was destroyed. Recognizing the signs given by Christ, the Christians fled to safety before the destruction took place.

The fate of Jerusalem is a type, or example, of the destruction facing our planet. The signs given by Jesus that warned of approaching disaster for the city of Jerusalem also warn of the approaching destruction of this world. But between these two events lay dark centuries marked with blood, tears, and agony. Jesus said of those days, "For then

shall be great tribulation, such as was not since the beginning of the world to this time, no, nor ever shall be. And
except those days should be shortened, there should no
flesh be saved: but for the elect's sake those days shall be
shortened." Matthew 24:21, 22.

History confirms the accuracy of Jesus' prediction.
During the first and second centuries the circuses of Rome
were used as theaters in which Christians were slain by glad-
iators or fed to wild beasts. Other Christians were stripped of
their possessions and driven from their homes. During the
following centuries, referred to as the Dark Ages, historians
estimate that no less than 50 million people lost their lives. It
was an era of great tribulation.

This prophetic period ended at the close of the eighteenth century, cut short by the Protestant Reformation and
the discovery and settlement of America. Jesus said, "Immediately after the tribulation of those days shall the sun be
darkened, and the moon shall not give her light, and the
stars shall fall from heaven." Matthew 24:29. John the revelator was shown the same events:

"Lo, there was a great earthquake; and the sun became
black as sackcloth of hair, and the moon became as blood;
and the stars of heaven fell unto the earth." Revelation 6:
12, 13.

Historians give this account of the fulfillment of these
predictions:

"In the year 1755, on November 1, the most terrible
earthquake recorded up to that time occurred, commonly
called the 'Lisbon Earthquake.' It extended over four million square miles—reaching America and Greenland. The
most extreme violence mainifested by the shock was in
Spain and Portugal. Sir Charles Lyell gives this account of
the quake: A sound of thunder was heard underground,
and immediately afterward a violent shock threw down the
greater part of the city. In the course of about six minutes,

sixty thousand persons perished."—*Principles of Geology*, page 495.

The next event to take place in this sequence of signs in the natural world is described by John the revelator: "The sun became black as sackcloth of hair, and the moon became as blood." Revelation 6:12. This prophecy was fulfilled on May 19, 1780. The 1869 edition of Webster's dictionary gives the following account of the dark day: May 19, 1780—"so called on account of a remarkable darkness on that day extending over all New England. . . . Birds sang their evening songs, disappeared, and became silent; fowls went to roost; cattle sought the barnyard; and the candles were lighted in the houses."—Quoted in Arthur S. Maxwell, *Your Bible and You.*

An eyewitness gave this account:

"I could not help conceiving at the time, that if every luminous body in the universe had been shrouded in impenetrable shades, or struck out of existence, the darkness could not have been more complete. Though at nine o'clock that night the moon rose to the full, it had not the least effect to dispel the deathlike shadows."—Letter by Dr. Samuel Tenney, of Exeter, N.H. 1785, quoted in *Massachusetts Historical Society Collections.* Historians tell us that after midnight the darkness disappeared, and the moon, when first visible, had the appearance of blood.

The next sign to be seen in the heavens is described by Jesus: "The stars shall fall from heaven." Matthew 24:29. On November 13, 1833, Jesus' prediction concerning the falling of the stars was fulfilled. "The morning of November 13, 1833, was rendered memorable by the exhibition of the phenomenon called shooting stars, which was probably more extensive and magnificent than any similar one hitherto recorded. Probably no celestial phenomenon has ever occured in this country, since its first settlement, which was viewed with so much admiration and delight by one class of spectators, or with so much astonishment and fear by another class."—*American Journal of Science and Arts*, volume XXV, 1834.

According to a New York magazine, "No philosopher or scholar has told or recorded an event, I suppose, like that of yesterday morning. A prophet eighteen hundred years ago foretold it exactly."—*The New York Journal of Commerce*, November 14, 1833.

John described the events that would precede the second coming. Notice: "Lo, there was a great earthquake; and the sun became black as sackcloth of hair, and the moon became as blood; and the stars of heaven fell unto the earth." Revelation 6:12, 13.

Where are we living in relationship to these events? Let's take a look at the chronological order of these heavenly signs and their fulfillment."

The Great Earthquake	November 1, 1755
The Dark Day	May 19, 1780
The Falling Stars	November 13, 1833

The last of these signs took place about 150 years ago. The next events to take place are described in the next few verses of Revelation: "And the heaven departed as a scroll when it is rolled together; and every mountain and island were moved out of their places. And the kings of the earth, and the great men, and the rich men, and the chief captains, and the mighty men, . . . hid themselves in the dens and in the rocks of the mountains; . . . and said to the mountains and rocks, Fall on us, and hide us from the face of him that sitteth on the throne, . . . for the great day of his wrath is come; and who shall be able to stand?" Revelation 6:14-17.

The signs foretold have been fulfilled. The next event to

take place in this prophecy is the coming of Christ and the end of the world. Just as the people living at the time of the destruction of Jerusalem saw the armies encircle the city and knew that it was a sign of the end, so the people who see these signs in the heavens should recognize the handwriting of God on the wall of time. God is trying to tell us that we are living in the last hours of this world's history.

You would think that people would be preparing for Christ's soon coming. Instead, they are seeking their own pleasure—living for today, ignoring the catastrophic events scheduled for tomorrow.

Each year Americans spend 20 billion dollars on sports and entertainment, 70 billion on gambling, and more than 28 billion on alcohol and tobacco. American churches, on the other hand, report only 8 billion a year received in gifts and offerings. And we call ourselves a Christian nation! Paul said that in the last days men would be "lovers of pleasures more than lovers of God." 2 Timothy 3:4.

Paul continues his description of the last days: "People will be lovers of themselves, lovers of money, boastful, proud, abusive, disobedient to their parents, ungrateful, unholy, . . . without self-control, brutal." 2 Timothy 3:2, 3, NIV. That sounds like today's newspaper reports of happenings in Hometown, U.S.A.!

Public health departments report a serious upswing of venereal diseases, saying that the epidemic is a reflection of increasing promiscuity. And the aftermath is seen in soaring divorce rates and increasing numbers of alienated children. Statistics on marriage in America during the last century are alarming.

Jesus compared the conditions on Earth in the last days to the early biblical days of Sodom and Gomorrah: "Likewise also as it was in the days of Lot; . . . even thus shall it be in the day when the Son of man is revealed." Luke 17:28-30. Jude says, "Sodom and Gomorrah and the surrounding towns gave themselves up to sexual immorality and perversion." Jude 7, NIV.

Paul, speaking of the moral conditions that characterized these cities, said, "Even their women exchanged natural relations for unnatural ones. In the same way the men also abandoned natural relations with women and were inflamed with lust for one another. Men committed indecent acts with other men." Romans 1:26, 27, NIV.

Today, homosexuals are picketing, demonstrating, and campaigning to gain public acceptance of their way of life. According to *Time* magazine, "Television and movies are treating gay themes more openly and sympathetically. . . . Another sign of the times: Advice Columnist Ann Landers, a stalwart champion of traditional morality, now counsels parents not to be ashamed of their homosexual children."— *Time,* April 23, 1979.

Time is running out! The sins that called for the destruction of the antediluvian world exist today. Billy Graham is quoted as saying that if things are allowed to go on as they are much longer, God will have to apologize to Sodom and Gomorrah. Without Christ's prophecies about the end of the world and the setting up of God's eternal kingdom, man would have little or no hope for the future. He seems bent on his own destruction as evidenced by events now taking place.

By the year 2000, the world's population will have doubled. Seven billion people on Planet Earth! How can we survive a doubled population? What problems will these added billions produce? Can we cope with this challenge?

Informed sources tell us that when population passes food production, then worldwide famine, starvation, epidemics, and food wars are inevitable. How will we feed added billions when two thirds of the world's people are hungry now? How will we control violence and aggression in such an overcrowded world? With the diminishing natural resources and the rapid increase in population, man faces serious problems in surviving on Earth.

Where will energy and pure water come from? With a doubled population, how will we cope with contamination and pollution? More crowding means more waste and refuse, more garbage, more pollution of water, air, and land—more and more disease. Dr. W. H. Davis of the School of Biological Science, University of Kentucky, said, "Massive deaths among mankind in the near future are inevitable . . . as numbers of people continue to rise, pollution and other toxic products of our civilization will destroy the entire eco-system."

The more scientists learn about man-made chemicals in the environment, the greater the danger to public health seems to be. "Most specialists in the new field of environmental disease believe that 85 percent of all cancers are caused by exposure to substances in the air or water. These include everything from compounds in tobacco and automotive fumes to asbestos, vinyl chloride, the pesticide dieldrin, carbon tetrachloride and chloroform."—*Time,* November 25, 1974.

Now there is a new threat! Paradoxically, it involves chlorination, the process that most towns and cities use to kill disease-carrying bacteria in ordinary drinking water. When water from a polluted source enters the treatment plant, the chlorine apparently interacts with industrial and agricultural wastes to produce chemical compounds that are carcinogenic.

Everywhere we look, the increasing population, coupled with diminishing natural resources, seems to spell doom for mankind. Christ described the dilemma of Earth's last hour by saying that there would be "upon the earth distress of nations, with perplexity." Luke 21:25. Years ago, Sir Winston Churchill said: "We seem to be moving, drifting, steadily against our will, against the will of every race, and every people, and every class, toward some hideous catastrophe. Everyone wishes to stop it, but they do not know how."

The nations have stockpiled enough weapons and bacteria to destroy the whole world. Sir Charles Snow commented, "We know with the certainty of statistical truth that if enough of these weapons are made—by enough states—some of them are going to blow up through accident, folly, or madness." Who will pull the trigger first? When he does, the chain reaction will begin!

The relevance of Christ's prophecy concerning the end of the world is recognized by thinking men and women today in view of man's own plans to make this world uninhabitable.

That is why Christ said that men's hearts would fail them for fear as they looked at those things coming upon the earth. "The powers of heaven shall be shaken. And then shall they see the Son of man coming in a cloud with power and great glory." Luke 21:26, 27.

Christ is soon to come and write "finis" to Planet Earth's history as we know it. In fact, He said, "And when these things begin to come to pass, then look up, and lift up your heads; for your redemption draweth nigh." Luke 12:28.

The Bible warns of coming disaster and the end of the world, just as Noah warned the people living before the Flood. In fact, Jesus compared the conditions of Earth in the last days to those at the time of Noah: "But as the days of Noe were, so shall also the coming of the Son of man be. For as in the days that were before the flood they were eating and drinking, marrying and giving in marriage, until the day that Noe entered into the ark, and knew not until the flood came, and took them all away; so shall also the coming of the Son of man be." Matthew 24:37-39.

Before the flood, God sent Noah to warn the world of coming disaster. For 120 years Noah witnessed to the coming destruction by preaching and building an ark. Of the vast population then living, only eight persons survived—not because God failed to warn them, but because they failed to prepare for the day of destruction. Noah made his final appeal, the animals filed into the ark, followed by Noah and his family—and God shut the door. The destiny of the antediluvian world was sealed—forever! The flood followed, destroying every living person of that ancient civilization except Noah and his family, who believed God's warning and accepted His provision for salvation.

History is soon to repeat itself. The end is near. Jesus is coming, and the warning is being given. But everyone is so busy with sports events, dinner parties, packaged weekends, TV programs, and the cares of just making a living that God's warnings go unnoticed!

Jesus said, "Take heed to yourselves, lest at any time your hearts be overcharged with surfeiting, and drunkenness, and the cares of this life, and so that day come upon you unawares." Luke 21:34. God did not condemn the people living before the Flood because they ate, drank, and married. Their sin consisted in doing these things to excess—indulging without restraint, with no time for God in their lives.

Do you see the parallel? We have seen the handwriting of God in the skies telling us that we are living in Earth's last hour. The signs that Jesus predicted would precede His coming are being fulfilled. The last few grains of sand are trickling through the hourglass of time. Soon the Son of God will pierce the star-studded skies, attended by myriads of angels. Paul said, "The Lord himself will come down from heaven with a mighty shout and with the soul-stirring cry of the archangel and the great trumpet-call of God." 1 Thessalonians 4:16, LB.

God waits anxiously for that day, not that He may destroy a world, but that He may take His people home. That home is waiting! It's ready! Magnificent beyond description! Jesus said, "In my Father's house are many mansions: if it were not so, I would have told you. I go to prepare a place for you. And if I go and prepare a place for you, I will come again, and receive you unto myself; that where I am, there ye may be also." John 14:2, 3.

Friend, don't be satisfied with Earth's toys, while empty mansions wait! Nothing else really matters. The most important question to be settled is, Are you ready for Jesus to come?

The cost? Just a surrendered heart, a cleansed heart, pardoned by the blood of Jesus. The hour is late, and the stakes are high. There is not a moment to lose. Won't you lift your heart to God right now and ask Him to help you prepare for Christ's soon coming?

Will There Ever Be a World Ruler?

Halloween evening, 1938. As the nation's children dress up in sheets and shout, "Trick or treat!" a science fiction drama is airing on CBS radio. The drama is so fantastically real that a million Easterners panic!

In his resonant, convincing voice, Orson Welles narrates an adaptation of H. G. Wells' *War of the Worlds*. Though four or five times during the program it is announced that the program is fictional, not real, many people miss the announcements.

As if actually reporting on the spot, Welles tells of Martian cylinders falling over the country and of metal monsters as tall as skyscrapers walking in the cities, belching smoke while people die like flies around them. Welles reports that 7,000 soldiers have been trampled to death or burned to cinders by Martian heat rays! All this with sound effects so real it brings terror to those listening. Panic ensues.

In Newark, people run into the streets with wet towels over their faces for protection, anticipating a gas attack. In New York, people flee their apartments, carrying whatever possessions they can. In Harlem, a man stands terrified at his window, looking for "monsters wading across the Hudson River." In Pittsburgh, a woman grabs a bottle of poison and cries, "I'd rather die this way than that."

Several suicides are reported. In various Eastern cities,

people flock to churches to pray, thinking it is the end of the world.

Not only the uneducated and superstitious were scared out of their wits that Halloween night. Some educated scientists—whose faith in technology was so great that they believed it possible that an advanced civilization on Mars might indeed carry out such an invasion—even wrote "finish" to life on Planet Earth.

Now, four decades later, we find man still concerned with invasion from outer space, still concerned that flying saucers might arrive and end life on Earth. But military leaders and scientists warn that if man continues his arms race, it will not be necessary for this world to be invaded by Martians—earthlings are fully capable of destroying themselves!

In fact, the nations of Earth have amassed arsenals of unthinkable weapons—deadly beyond all imagining. The Soviet SS-18, one of the most powerful Soviet intercontinental ballistic missiles, is armed with up to ten warheads, each fifty times more powerful than the A-bomb dropped on Hiroshima.

Today any serious student of science can read in a major library how to build a nuclear bomb. And what will the nations do when terrorists use nuclear weapons for blackmail?

Devastating as bombs may be, a chemical assault is in some ways even more frightening. The Russian army now includes a chemical-warfare contingent of between 80,000 and 100,000 men training at forty sites in Eastern Europe. It would be naive in the extreme to think that they would go to all that expense and training if they did not intend someday to use their ghastly weapons.

At the same time, free and peace-loving America has become the chief arms merchant to the rest of the world. While nations plan, pray, and negotiate for peace, they are arming to the teeth! Is it any wonder that man is exploring space, probing the planets, hoping to find some place to escape it all?

Columnist Sidney J. Harris says we are "poised on the brink of the most calamitous conflict that can be imagined—indeed, it cannot be imagined!" Centuries ago, the prophets of the Bible predicted today's dangerous conditions. Even more distressing, they said that things will get worse before they get better: "And I saw three unclean spirits like frogs come out of the mouth of the dragon, and out of the mouth of the beast, and out of the mouth of the false prophet. For they are the spirits of devils, working miracles, which go forth unto the kings of the earth and of the whole world, to gather them to the battle of that great day of God Almighty. . . . And he gathered them together into a place called in the Hebrew tongue Armageddon." Revelation 16:13-16.

As one studies this great conflict, it quickly becomes obvious that this is more than just another war. It is the death knell of the world. A battle to end all battles! It is the final battle in the great controversy between good and evil—between a loving God and a traitor angel: Satan.

The prophet Joel wrote this description of events now transpiring on Earth: "Proclaim ye this among the Gentiles; Prepare war, wake up the mighty men, . . . let the weak say, I am strong. . . . Let the heathen be wakened." Joel 3: 9-12.

The Bible says that in the last days the slumbering, non-Christian nations will be awakened. Today, this is one of the most graphic signs of the end of the world.

Napoleon called China "the sleeping giant," advising the world to let her sleep, "for when this giant is awakened," he said, "her tread will shake the world."

China has awakened! Already she is a member of the nuclear club. With a population of one billion and her hand grasping a nuclear torch, her tread may well "shake the world."

And Africa, the angry young giant that demanded freedom, won it for nineteen of her countries in five years! No longer can she be ignored as simply a romantic paradise for wildlife photographers or hunting safaris.

The Middle East is smoldering! The nuclear clock is ticking! What madman will push the button, turn the key, drop the bomb! How will it all end? These questions can cause some sleepless nights for those who do not understand God's prophecies.

The prophet John said that spirits of devils would gather the whole world to that great battle of God Almighty. Armageddon is at our door! Satan himself is the power behind this great battle—the power behind the three unclean spirits.

Marvelous signs and unbelievable miracles will be used by the devil to maneuver the nations into the last great conflict. This battle takes place at the eleventh hour of Earth's history. Christ Himself will personally intervene and take charge of the battle.

"I saw heaven opened, and behold a white horse; and he that sat upon him was called Faithful and True." "And the armies which were in heaven followed him upon white horses. . . . And out of his mouth goeth a sharp sword, that with it he should smite the nations." Revelation 19:11, 14, 15.

At that critical moment, when the conflict is completely out of control, Christ will ride into battle with the armies of Heaven. He will call a halt to the affairs of a planet in rebellion.

When Christ comes to Earth the second time, He will not find a deserted world—an Earth whose inhabitants have slipped off to another planet. He will not find a world burned out by nuclear warfare—an orbiting mass of ashes! For the Bible declares: "The present heavens, and earth . . . have been kept in store for burning; they are being reserved until the day of judgement when the godless will be destroyed." 2 Peter 3:7, NEB.

Limited nuclear war may happen before Christ comes, but no wars of nations or men will destroy all life on Earth. We can be sure of that, because God Himself executes judgment at the coming of Christ. "See, the Lord is coming with thousands upon thousands of his holy ones to judge everyone, and to convict all the ungodly." Jude 14, 15, NIV. At that moment a great separation takes place. "The angels shall come forth, and sever the wicked from among the just." Matthew 13:49.

Both the just and the unjust will be living on Earth when Christ returns. Believers and unbelievers. Those who are ready to meet Him and those who are not. Riding at the head of the armies of heaven will be Jesus, King of kings and Lord of lords. Coming to put an end to sin and suffering. Coming to usher in the long-promised, everlasting kingdom.

During the closing days of Christ's ministry on Earth, He foretold His death to His disciples. Sensing their need for comfort and hope during those dark hours, He gave this most thrilling promise: "Let not your heart be troubled: ye believe in God, believe also in me. In my Father's house are many mansions. . . . I go to prepare a place for you. And if I go and prepare a place for you, I will come again, and receive you unto myself; that where I am, there ye may be also." John 14:1-3.

Over the centuries, whenever disappointment, hardship, or death have threatened Christ's followers, this star of hope—the promise of His return—has brought them courage and strength to endure. Jesus' followers eagerly looked forward to the fulfillment of this promise. The apostle Paul, writing from his prison cell, said he was "looking for that blessed hope, and the glorious appearing of the great God and our Saviour Jesus Christ." Titus 2:13.

Later, as the executioner stood but steps away, Paul tri-umphantly proclaimed: "I have fought a good fight, I have finished my course, I have kept the faith: Henceforth there is laid up for me a crown of righteousness, which the Lord, the righteous judge, shall give me at that day: and not to me only, but unto all them also that love his appearing." 2 Timo-thy 4:7, 8.

Paul could valiantly face the executioner's sword on that fateful day because he had faith in Christ's promise to return. As we face the approaching dark hours of Earth's history, it will be a great source of strength to remember that Jesus' promise to His disciples belongs to us as well. Jesus will return—that promise is the world's only hope!

All the prophets of the Old and New Testaments spoke of and looked forward to the second coming. In fact, one out of every twenty-five verses in the New Testament directly mentions some aspect of the second coming and the end of the world.

Jesus went to great lengths to give exact details of His second coming, because He knew Satan would attempt to confuse and mislead people on this subject. He said that in the last days we would be confronted with people claiming to be Christ. "For there shall arise false Christs, and false prophets, and shall show great signs and wonders." Matthew 24:24.

If we do not know how to tell the difference, how to spot the counterfeit, we may attach ourselves to an impostor, thinking him to be Christ. Jesus warned that it could hap-pen! And He was not talking about a few clumsy deceptions. Evidently He was talking about incredible impersonations—so carefully planned and executed that almost the whole world would be deceived! You see, these impostors will work miracles, heal the sick, and give supernatural demonstra-tions to back up their claims.

This will not be a matter of mistaking Christ for a counterfeit. No one could do that! But we may mistake the counterfeit for Christ and be fooled *before* Christ appears.

Suppose you turn on the TV some evening, and the newscaster reports that Christ has returned—that He is in Palm Springs, California, healing the sick, performing miracles, speaking words of love and peace and Christian unity. You watch thousands flocking to the desert to see Him. Huge crowds are kneeling before Him and receiving His blessing. What would you do? Hurriedly make a reservation on the next flight to Palm Springs? Rush out to see Him? Bow down and worship Him?

You might, if you do not know what the Bible teaches about Christ's coming. That is what Jesus said: "If they shall say unto you, Behold, he is the desert; go not forth: behold, he is in the secret chambers; believe it not." Matthew 24:26.

Jesus warned us not even to go see an impostor. Why? Because we could be deceived by his miracles and charisma. He may teach like Christ. He may heal like Christ. He may sound like Christ. He may look like Christ. And the temptation to doubt the Scriptures may be overwhelming, for Jesus said, "If it were possible, they shall deceive the very elect." Matthew 24:24.

Someday soon, the whole world will be made new, and its citizens will be united under one Ruler—Jesus Christ. But before that happens, we must beware of any impostor who would arrive and attempt to bring the world under his rulership.

We dare not trust even our own senses! What we see. What we hear. What we feel. How can we spot an impostor? The Bible is our only safe guide in making that decision. Consider a few unmistakable signs or features unique to Christ's second coming.

His coming will be visible. "As the lightning comes from the east and flashes to the west, so will be the coming of the Son of Man." Matthew 24:27, NIV. You will not have to be told when Christ comes. Everyone will know about it! You will *see* Him coming. "Behold, he cometh with clouds; and every eye shall see him." Revelation 1:7.

Every eye shall see Him! The eyes of the old. The eyes of the young. The eyes of the saint. The eyes of the sinner. Even the eyes of the blind! *Every* eye shall see Him coming. There will be nothing regional or exclusive about His coming.

We are even told *how* He will come: "And then shall appear the sign of the Son of man in heaven: and then shall all the tribes of the earth mourn, and they shall see the Son of man coming in the clouds of heaven with power and great glory." Matthew 24:30.

Christ is not going to appear suddenly in some distant city or quietly step out of a flying saucer. He is coming back with power and great glory, and every eye will see Him!

What will He be like when He comes the second time? We need to know. Two angels thought so too. After the Lord's resurrection, He spent some time with His disciples sharing His final instructions with them—assuring them of His love and presence with them "even unto the end of the world." Matthew 28:20. The time had come for Christ to ascend to His Father's throne, and as He stood with hands outstretched in blessing, He slowly ascended heavenward. The disciples stood gazing upward, straining their eyes for a last glimpse of their Lord.

"Suddenly two men dressed in white stood beside them. 'Men of Galilee,' they said, 'why do you stand here looking into the sky? This same Jesus, who has been taken from you into heaven, will come back in the same way you have seen him go into heaven.' " Acts 1:10, 11, NIV.

The same Jesus! Jesus with flesh and bones. Jesus with nail prints in His hands and feet. Jesus with a wound in His side. The same Jesus who talked and walked and prayed with the disciples. The same Jesus who went away in the clouds will return the same way!

That would be difficult for an impostor to do, don't you think? But the hardest part to duplicate is yet to come, for the Bible says: "<u>The Son of man shall come in his glory, and all the holy angels with him</u>." Matthew 25:31.

He is <u>not coming back by Himself</u>! When He comes, He will be accompanied by all the holy angels, filling the skies with glory indescribable! When just one angel rolled back the stone from Christ's tomb, the Roman guards fell down in a daze. And that was the glory of just one angel! Think of the glory of the "ten thousand times ten thousand, and thousands of thousands" of angels who will accompany Jesus. We will know it is an impostor if he doesn't come in the clouds of the sky with all the holy angels and with every eye watching!

But there is more! You see, it is easier to spot an impostor if we are well acquainted with the genuine, and God has not taken any chances by leaving us without sufficient knowledge to tell the difference. Actually, Satan would have to have the cooperation of all nature to duplicate Christ's coming: "And there were voices, and thunders, and lightnings; and <u>there was a great earthquak</u>e, such as was not since men were upon the earth, so mighty an earthquake, and so great." "<u>And every island fled away, and the mountains were not found</u>." Revelation 16:18, 20.

You cannot keep an earthquake secret—at least not one like that! One that levels all the mountains and causes every island to disappear! But wait, there is even more! "According to the Lord's own word, we tell you <u>that we who are still alive, who are left till the coming of the Lord, will certainly not precede those who have fallen asleep</u>. For the Lord himself will come down from heaven, with a loud command, with the voice of the archangel and with the trumpet call of God, <u>and the dead in Christ will rise first</u>." <u>1 Thessalonians 4:15, 16, NIV.</u>

Not only will Christ's coming be visible, <u>it will be audi</u>-

ble—heard by everyone! So penetrating will be the call of God and the fanfare of the trumpet that the dead in Christ will be awakened and come forth from their graves. Do you see how impossible it would be for Satan to counterfeit the real coming of Christ?

Notice also that the text says "that we who are still alive, . . . will certainly not precede those who have fallen asleep." In other words, the living righteous will not be caught up to meet the Lord before the righteous dead are resurrected.

Notice what happens to the righteous living at Christ's second coming: "Then we which are alive and remain shall be caught up together with them in the clouds, to meet the Lord in the air." 1 Thessalonians 4:17.

The faithful followers of Jesus are caught up with the resurrected dead to meet the Lord in the air. What a happy reunion that will be for many families.

Paul tells us of something else that will happen when Christ comes: "Behold, I shew you a mystery; . . . we shall all be changed, in a moment, in the twinkling of an eye, at the last trump: for the trumpet shall sound, and the dead shall be raised incorruptible, and we shall be changed. For this corruptible must put on incorruption, and this mortal must put on immortality." 1 Corinthians 15:51-53.

God will give every follower of Jesus His gift of love— life everlasting. All other gifts are meaningless without this gift of immortality. And there is something else that God will give His people: "We look for the Saviour, the Lord Jesus Christ: who shall change our vile body, that it may be fashioned like unto his glorious body." Philippians 3:20, 21.

A body like Christ's! No more aches. No more pain. No more disease. What news could be more welcome?

You see, God has given so many distinguishing characteristics of the genuine coming of Christ that no one need be deceived. The tragedy is that millions will bow down and worship an impostor simply because they did not bother to read and remember what the Bible says about the second coming.

Some people even believe that it really is not important how or when Christ will come, because they think everyone will be taken to heaven anyway. But nothing could be farther from the truth. John the revelator described the fate of those who have been deceived:

"The heaven departed as a scroll when it is rolled together; and every mountain and island were moved out of their places. And the kings of the earth, and the great men, and the rich men, . . . and the mighty men, . . . hid themselves in the dens and in the rocks of the mountains; and said to the mountains and rocks, Fall on us, and hide us from the face of him that sitteth on the throne. . . For the great day of his wrath is come; and who shall be able to stand?" Revelation 6:14-17.

They are lost, and they know it! What a sad picture, when it could have been so different. Friend, that day will be real! There will be no waking up to find it only an Orson Welles dramatization!

What a traumatic experience it was for millions of Americans that Halloween night who were deceived into believing that fiction was reality. But it is far more dangerous to believe that something which is real is fiction! Treating God's prophecies, God's reality, as fantasy is tampering with our own destiny.

If we are deceived or are not prepared for Christ's coming, we lose everything. Nothing is really more important on Earth than being ready to meet Jesus when He comes.

How fragile the earthly treasures we prize so greatly! One earthquake, one tornado, one nuclear bomb, one doctor's diagnosis, one threatening phone call from a stranger in the night, and our security is shattered. That is why Paul said: "Set your affections on things above, not on the things on the earth." Colossians 3:2.

Today we can still decide. Today we can still choose. And in choosing Jesus, we are choosing everything that matters.

Where will you be—and what will you be doing—when Jesus comes? When the earth shakes, mountains and islands disappear, cities topple? When a small cloud appears on the horizon, growing in size, getting brighter every moment until everyone in the world is aware of this dazzling object in the skies?

As He draws nearer to Earth, every eye beholds Christ, not as a man of sorrows but as a mighty conqueror! No mortal mind is adequate to conceive its splendor: "His glory covered the heavens." Habakkuk 3:3. "And he hath on his vesture and on his thigh a name written, KING OF KINGS, AND LORD OF LORDS." Revelation 19:16.

The clash of arms and the tumult of battle are stilled. The wicked pray for the rocks to fall on them rather than look upon the face of Him whom they have rejected or neglected. A loud shout pierces the air, and a trumpet sounds. Graves open, and the righteous dead rise out of those graves. The righteous living are caught up together with them to meet the Lord in the air and are taken to those mansions prepared by our Lord for a vacation lasting 1,000 years! Could anything be more thrilling—if we are prepared? Can't you feel the excitement? You can be a part of that joyful number who proclaim, "Lo, this is our God; we have waited for him, and he will save us." Isaiah 25:9.

How Can I Ever Find Time to Rest?

Vacation! What pleasant fantasies race through the mind at the mere mention of the word!

Vacations are times of fun, of relaxation, of togetherness, of excitement. TV and radio commericals, magazine ads, travel brochures, and billboards beckon vacationers to "fly the friendly skies" to some exotic paradise. Jammed airports, backed-up freeways, crowded beaches—all spell vacation time. There is no end of unusual places or packaged tours to tantalize the vacation bound.

Of course, there is always the lure of "Blue Hawaii"—an island paradise where tourists in aloha shirts and muumuus really "go Hawaiian."

Some people prefer camping in one of the national parks, such as Glacier, Yosemite, or Yellowstone, where the fascination of the "mud pots" or Old Faithful keeps cameras clicking. Others like nothing more than canoeing on a remote lake or skiing the slopes at Sun Valley or Aspen.

Others explore the museums and ancient castles, capturing everything on film to relive and retell another day.

Whatever and wherever, vacations are a change of pace and place. Almost everyone enjoys a break.

That is how Sam Brown felt. Sam was a workaholic who punched a time clock ten to twelve hours a day, six days a week. He was considered the most productive man in his organization. He never took time off, never found time for anything but work. But once a year Sam loaded his family and camping gear into his old station wagon and headed for a remote lake in Montana.

Anyone who knew Sam would tell you that he deserved that vacation. Sam always felt that the two weeks slipped by too quickly, that he would really enjoy staying a little longer. "Maybe three weeks next year," he mused. "That wouldn't be too long."

We would certainly have to agree! But what would you think about a vacation that lasted not for a few weeks or a few months, but for a <u>thousand years</u>? Incredible? So it seems! Yet the Bible tells of such a vacation for someone who really needs it. "And I saw an angel come down from heaven, having the key of the bottomless pit and a great chain in his hand. And he laid hold on the dragon, that old serpent, which is the Devil, and Satan, and <u>bound him a thousand years</u>." Revelation 20:1, 2.

Talk about a workaholic! Satan never punches a time clock. He has been on the job around the clock, seven days a week, month in and month out for thousands of years. No coffee breaks. No holidays. No sick time. And no vacations—ever!

And talk about production! Everywhere, every day, we see the diabolical accomplishments of this fallen angel. We see it in hospitals and nursing homes, prisons and refugee camps, earthquakes and tornadoes, crime and war. If anyone ever earned a vacation, Satan has. Yet strange as it may seem, he is not anxious for one. He has to be forced to take it.

After his rebellion, Satan and his angels were cast out of Heaven. The Bible says, "There was war in heaven. . . . The great dragon was cast out, that old serpent, called the Devil, and Satan, which deceiveth the whole world: he was cast out into the earth, and his angels were cast out with him." Revelation 12:7-9.

Planet Earth, fresh from the Creator's hand, became Satan's headquarters. By deceit he wrested control from Adam and Eve, and for 6,000 years he has shown how he would run the world. Earth is a theater in the universe that illustrates what happens when God's commands are ignored, when man chooses to do his own thing, to go his own way!

Christ came and died on Calvary to ransom this hijacked planet and its inhabitants from Satan's control. The crucifixion of Christ demonstrated to the universe how far this sinister angel will go in his attempt to destroy God and His kingdom. But when Christ returned to heaven, the victor over death and sin, Satan knew his time was running out. That is why Peter cautioned, "Be alert, be on watch! Your enemy, the Devil, roams around like a roaring lion, looking for someone to devour." 1 Peter 5:8, TEV.

The war that began in heaven will end on Earth after Satan's forced vacation—a vacation lasting 1,000 years. This time period is often referred to as the millennium, which comes from two Latin words, *milli* and *annum,* that mean "a thousand years."

When will this millennium, or Satan's vacation, begin? Can we know? Indeed we can! Let's take a look at the events surrounding Christ's second coming. Paul describes that coming: "The Lord himself shall descend from heaven with a shout, with a voice of the archangel, and with the trump of God." 1 Thessalonians 4:16.

Notice what John says: "Marvel not at this: for the hour is coming, in the which all that are in the graves shall hear his voice, and shall come forth; they that have done good, unto the resurrection of life; and they that have done evil, unto the resurrection of damnation." John 5:28, 29. So there are two great resurrections: (1) the resurrection of life for those who have done good, and (2) the resurrection of damnation for those who have done evil. And as we study the Bible, we discover that one resurrection takes place at the beginning of the thousand years and the other at the end.

The apostle John makes it clear which resurrection takes place first. "Blessed and holy is he that hath part in the first resurrection." Revelation 20:6. Notice that only the righteous, or holy, will have any part in the first resurrection. Paul describes the details of this resurrection: "The Lord himself will come down from heaven, with a loud command, with the voice of the archangel and with the trumpet call of God, and the dead in Christ will *rise first.*" 1 Thessalonians 4:16, NIV, emphasis supplied.

On that day will be fulfilled the promise made by Jesus, "He that believeth in me, though he were dead, yet shall he live." John 11:25. Yes, the righteous dead will be raised from their graves when Christ returns. Isaiah describes this joyous event: "Awake and sing, ye that dwell in dust: . . . and the earth shall cast out the dead." Isaiah 26:19.

Immediately another thrilling event takes place. "Then we which are alive and remain shall be caught up together with them in the clouds, to meet the Lord in the air: and so shall we ever be with the Lord." 1 Thessalonians 4:17. At that same moment the saved will be changed. The Bible says, "We shall all be changed, in a moment, in the twinkling of an eye, . . . for the trumpet shall sound, and the dead shall be raised incorruptible, and we shall be changed. For this corruptible must put on incorruption, and this mortal must put on immortality." 1 Corinthians 15:51-53. The righteous will have perfect bodies, never again subject to disease or death. That seems almost too good to be true!

It is interesting to note that the righteous living will not be taken to heaven before Christ's second coming and the resurrection of the righteous dead, for we read, "According to the Lord's own word, we tell you that we who are still alive, who are left till the coming of the Lord, will certainly *not pre-*

cede those who have fallen asleep. For the Lord himself will come down from heaven, . . . and the dead in Christ will rise first." 1 Thessalonians 4:15, 16, NIV, emphasis supplied.

All the righteous, both the living and those resurrected at Christ's coming, will be taken to heaven at the same time. "So shall we ever be with the Lord." 1 Thessalonians 4:17. John said, "They shall be priests of God and of Christ, and shall reign with him a thousand years." Revelation 20:6.

What a vacation! A thousand years with our Lord and loved ones in the New Jerusalem.

Are you wondering what the righteous could possibly find to do in heaven for a thousand years? Well, aside from the unspeakable joy of fellowship with Christ and His followers, John gives us this insight: "And I saw thrones, and they sat upon them, and judgment was given unto them." Revelation 20:4. The righteous will participate in the solemn task of judging the fallen angels and the unsaved. Paul said, "Do you not know that the saints will judge the world? . . . Do you not know that we will judge angels?" 1 Corinthians 6: 2, 3, NIV.

"But why have a judgment after everyone's fate has been decided?" you ask. Have you ever thought what your reaction might be if you looked for someone in Heaven that you expected would be there and you could not find him? You would certainly wonder what caused him to be lost. During the millennium the records of the lost will be opened. The most carefully guarded secrets and purposes will be exposed. That is what the Bible says:

"Therefore judge nothing before the appointed time; wait till the Lord comes. He will bring to light what is hidden in darkness and will expose the motives of men's hearts." 1 Corinthians 4:5, NIV.

After the saved examine the records of the lost, they will understand why God could not save them. God's love and justice will be fully revealed. The saved will agree with John, the disciple, "Even so, Lord God Almighty, true and right-eous are thy judgments." Revelation 16:7.

"Well, that's very interesting," you say, "but what happens to the wicked?" The Bible says that the wicked "hid themselves in the dens and in the rocks of the mountains; and said to the mountains and rocks, Fall on us, and hide us from the face of him that sitteth on the throne, and from the wrath of the Lamb: for the great day of his wrath is come; and who shall be able to stand?" Revelation 6:15-17.

What an awesome picture! The prophet Jeremiah adds these vivid details: "At that time those slain by the Lord will be everywhere—from one end of the earth to the other. They will not be mourned or gathered up or buried." Jeremiah 25:33, NIV. It is quite obvious that there will be no one to mourn or bury the wicked slain at Christ's coming, for the righteous will have been taken to heaven.

But will that be the end for the sinner? Not at all! The righteous dead will be raised in the first resurrection, but the Bible clearly states that Christ's second coming will not disturb the wicked dead. "The rest of the dead lived not again until the thousand years were finished." Revelation 20:5.

Now let's focus our attention on the events that take place on the earth during the millennium. The righteous who are alive when Christ comes, along with those raised from the grave, all go to heaven together. On the other hand, the wicked who are still living will be slain by the glory of Christ's coming, while those in the grave will remain there.

The prophet Jeremiah describes the earth after Christ's return: "I beheld the earth, and, lo, it was without form, and void; and the heavens, and they had no light. I beheld the mountains, and, lo, they trembled, and all the hills moved lightly. I beheld, and, lo, there was no man, and all the birds of the heavens were fled. . . . All the cities thereof were broken down at the presence of the Lord, and by his fierce anger." Jeremiah 4:23-26.

What chaos! The desolation and ruined condition of the earth at that time will be unimaginable. It certainly would not be a very desirable vacation spot! And yet John says, "I saw an angel come down from heaven, having the key of the bottomless pit and a great chain in his hand. And he laid hold on the dragon, that old serpent, which is the Devil, and Satan, and bound him a thousand years." Revelation 20:1, 2.

This is a symbolic vision. The bottomless pit describes the earth in its chaotic condition. The Greek word for bottomless pit is *abussos*. This same Greek word is used in the Septuagint to describe the chaotic condition that existed on the first day of creation. Genesis 1:2 says that the earth at that time was "without form, and void." So Satan and his angels spend a forced vacation on a devastated planet. They deserve what they receive!

And what better symbolism could God use to describe Satan's condition during the 1,000 years than being "chained" or "bound"? Think for a moment. The righteous are in heaven. The wicked are dead. Everyone is gone. Everywhere there is ruin. The great chain with which Satan is bound is a chain of circumstances. There is no one to deceive. There are no lives to twist or destroy. No longer does he have access to human beings.

We use the same figure of speech today. If you want to do something that circumstances will not permit, you say, "My hands are tied." So it is with Satan. He would love to continue his sinister work, but there is no one around. His hands are tied. He is "bound." He has nothing to do but wander to and fro on the earth and reflect on the results of his rebellion against God.

But even this thousand-year vacation will end. Let's look at the events that will transpire at the close of the millennium. John said, "I John saw the holy city, new Jerusalem, coming down from God out of heaven." Revelation 21:2. What a sight! A city about the size of Oregon coming down from heaven in all its splendor and settling upon the earth! And John wrote, "The nations of them which are saved shall walk in the light of it." Revelation 21:24.

Almost simultaneously, as the city descends with Christ and His followers, another dramatic event takes place: "As for the rest of the dead, they did not come to life until the thousand years were completed." Revelation 20:5, Moffatt.

What a sight it will be to see the wicked dead raised to life—a vast number, all the wicked from Adam's day to the second advent. John says, "The number of whom is as the sand of the sea." Revelation 20:8.

At the same moment another event takes place. John says that "when the thousand years are expired, Satan shall be loosed out of his prison. And shall go out to deceive the nations." Revelation 20:7, 8. His vacation is over. The chain of circumstances that bound him is removed, for now he has people to deceive again! As soon as he has a chance, he is back to his old tricks, deluding and deceiving.

Once again the unsaved choose Satan as their leader. The devil marshals them into one vast army bent on taking the New Jerusalem by force. This is Earth's last great battle. The mighty army under the rebel angel's leadership advances.

John describes what happens: "They went up on the breadth of the earth, and compassed the camp of the saints about, and the beloved city." Revelation 20:9. The archenemy of God grasps his last opportunity to attempt to seize world dominion by capturing the city of God.

However, John makes it clear that this desperate attempt will be totally abortive. In what is called His "strange act" (see Isaiah 28:21), God will finish the battle before Satan can destroy anything more. "Fire came down from God out of heaven, and devoured them." Revelation 20:9. Peter saw this fire in vision and wrote: "The heavens shall pass away with a great noise, and the elements shall melt with fervent heat, the earth also and the works that are therein shall be burned up." 2 Peter 3:10.

Satan, his angels, and sinners will then be forever gone! "This is the second death." Revelation 20:14. Now let's summarize the world-shattering events that take place before, during, and after the thousand-year period.

Events at the beginning of the millennium:
1. Christ comes again.
2. The righteous dead are raised.
3. The righteous are taken to heaven.
4. The living wicked are slain.

Events during the millennium:
1. The earth is desolate.
2. All the wicked are dead.
3. Satan is on vacation—he is "bound."
4. The saints are reigning.

Events at the close of the millennium:
1. The wicked dead are resurrected.
2. Satan is loosed; his vacation ends.
3. Christ, the saints, and city come to Earth.
4. As Satan and his army advance to take the city, fire comes down and devours the wicked.
5. The earth is purified and recreated.

Notice that the first three events at the close of the millennium occur almost simultaneously.

John says, "I saw a new heaven and a new earth: for the first heaven and the first earth were passed away." Revelation 21:1. Out of the ashes of a charred world cleansed from the deadly virus of sin, God recreates a new world.

God gave Isaiah a picture of that new Earth: "Behold, I create new heavens and a new earth: and the former shall not be remembered, nor come into mind." "The voice of weeping shall be no more heard in her." "They shall build houses, and inhabit them; and they shall plant vineyards, and eat the fruit of them." "Mine elect shall long enjoy the work of their hands." Isaiah 65:17, 19, 21, 22.

What a glorious eternity God promises the saved! The human mind cannot comprehend the glory and the beauty of the paradise God is preparing for those who love Him so much that they are willing to follow Him. "Eye hath not seen, nor ear heard, neither have entered into the heart of man, the things which God hath prepared for them that love him." 1 Corinthians 2:9. The most glorious vacation spot on Earth will be nothing compared to the vacationland God has prepared for the saved in the earth made new.

And to think that all of this the wicked could have enjoyed, but the price tag seemed too high! They were unwilling to choose Christ as their Saviour and Lord. They exchanged eternal life in paradise for the "pleasures of sin for a season." Hebrews 11:25. What an exchange! So much for so little! As John says, "What is a man profited, if he shall gain the whole world, and lose his own soul? or what shall a man give in exchange for his soul?" Matthew 16:26.

Regardless of the price, friend, eternal life in God's beautiful new Earth will be worth it all. Could you use an extended vacation? Does it seem you never can find time to rest and relax? Why not begin planning now for a never-ending vacation in the new Earth?

Will This World Ever Get Better?

As the golden desert sun sank behind the ancient Egyptian pyramids, a secret perfectly kept for 3,265 years was about to be unfolded!

On November 26, 1922, the eight-year search by Howard Carter for the missing Pharaoh in the Valley of the Kings was drawing to a close. With his wealthy patron, Lord Carnarvon, Carter broke the time-honored seal of the tomb, and the fabulous treasures of the boy king, Tutankhamen, lay strewn before them!

Here in Carter's own words is what he saw when he first peered into the chamber through a small hole in the door: "I inserted the candle and peered in. . . . At first I could see nothing. . . . But presently, as my eyes grew accustomed to the light, details of the room within emerged slowly from the mist, strange animals, statues and gold—everywhere the glint of gold. For the moment—an eternity it must have been to the others standing by—I was struck dumb with amazement, and when Lord Carnarvon, unable to stand the suspense any longer, inquired anxiously, 'Can you see anything?' it was all I could do to get out the words, 'Yes, wonderful things.'"—*Reader's Digest*, January 1979, page 198.

What Carter saw in his initial glimpse was only the contents of the antechamber, which centuries before had been entered by thieves and left in disarray. Soon, however, additional rooms were discovered—opened for the first time since the death of the boy king Tutankhamen.

No one could possibly have comprehended the staggering wealth, the dazzling art, or the glory of the past until this moment of discovery. King Tut's tomb yielded undreamed-of treasure. No royal sepulchres had ever been found intact in the burial grounds of the kings.

His death mask of beaten gold reveals the handsome features of the boy-king who ruled only nine years and died under mysterious circumstances at the age of 19 in 1350 B.C. The beard under his chin identified King Tut as one with Osiris—the Egyptian god of the dead.

Egyptians believed that when a man died, he was rowed by a ferryman across the water to the West, where he was received by Osiris. King Tut had his boat in the tomb, ready for his trip. Tut was buried in a nest of seven coffins, one being solid 22-carat gold and weighing 296 pounds. More than 143 jewels were distributed over his body. Effigies of gods and goddesses, jewels, chests, vases of ivory, furniture, and other items of beauty were found within the tomb.

More than 5,000 priceless treasures were found there. It took Carter more than nine years to remove the last objects and supervise their transfer to the Egyptian Museum in Cairo. However, King Tut was one of the poorer pharaohs of Egypt: he had ruled only nine years. The wealth and glory of the former pharaohs will forever be shrouded with mystery and intrigue.

Centuries before King Tut, the pharaohs built massive pyramids in an effort to preserve their bodies and immense wealth. Great pains were taken to insure the safety of the pharaoh's body and possessions. Within the pyramid, secret passages, false tunnels, and concealed doors were all part of the plan contrived to keep the tombs secret.

But the crypts rimming the Nile Valley failed to keep

their secrets. Grave robbers successfully entered every other tomb found in Egypt—even the secret, old resting places craftily hidden in the heart of these ancient pyramids. And the gold and jeweled treasures of the pharaohs had been stolen away by bandits. So a little more than 1,000 years from the time the first pyramid was built, Thutmose I, instead of building a pyramid for his future tomb, turned his eye to the desolate hills across the Nile from Thebes, to the place now known as the Valley of the Kings—where his tomb could be guarded more easily.

Here all the pharaohs of the next few dynasties followed in the footsteps of Thutmose I by constructing hidden burial chambers in the desert rock at the foot of the great cliff towering over the Valley of the Kings.

However, even these burial chambers failed to hold their secrets. These tombs, too, were plundered for their wealth. Only the carved drawings and wall paintings remain within the excavated chambers and passages. Except for King Tut's tomb, the former glory of Egypt's pharaohs was lost.

Two hundred years before King Tut ruled, the Israelites were slaves in Egypt, pressed into servitude by a new line of pharaohs. In fact, it was probably Thutmose I, the same pharaoh who built the first hidden tomb in the Valley of the Kings, who became alarmed by the strength of the Hebrews in spite of their bitter life of slavery and commanded that every male born to the Hebrews should be thrown into the Nile River. During the time this cruel decree was in force, a son was born to two slaves, Amram and Jochebed. Determined that their little son should not die, Jochebed succeeded in hiding the child for three months.

Then, fearing for his safety, she wove a basket, made it watertight, carefully placed her precious baby inside, and carried it to the river, where she and her daughter, Miriam, hid it among the rushes at the water's edge.

Miriam hid herself a short distance away to watch what would happen. Soon, she heard someone coming. It was Princess Hatshepsut, daughter of the pharaoh, coming to the river to bathe with her servants. The princess soon spotted the little basket boat floating among the bulrushes. She instructed her maid to bring the basket to her.

As she opened the basket's lid, she read the story at a glance. Some unknown mother had resorted to this means to save her baby's life. Quickly determining to save the infant, she decided to adopt him. Since she had no male heir, this baby would become ruler when her father, Thutmose I, died. The princess named the child Moses, which means "drawn out of the water."

When Miriam, watching from her hiding place, saw how tenderly Hatshepsut held her baby brother, she came running and asked if she could get a nurse for the baby. Miriam was instructed to find a nurse at once. Naturally, she ran to summon her mother, and for nearly twelve years Hatshepsut paid Jochebed, Moses' own mother, to care for him.

During that time, Moses was taught to obey and trust in the God of heaven. Then, from his humble home Moses was taken to the royal palace, where he became the son of the princess.

At the court of pharaoh, Moses received the highest civil and military training, for Thutmose I was determined to make his adopted grandson his successor on the throne—and he saw to it that Moses was educated for his high station. He became a part of that fantastic civilization.

Eventually he would occupy the royal throne. All the wealth, influence, and power of the then civilized world lay at Moses' feet. It was his for the taking if he would cast his lot with the Egyptians and forget the God of heaven. The palace of pharaoh would be his home; the Valley of the Kings would be his final resting place. His body would be wrapped in a hundred yards of fine linen. He could have been a mummy!

But no one has ever found the underground burial chamber of Moses. There is no mummy—no golden death mask. No temple statues bear his likeness. No tomb was ever built. He never became the pharaoh of Egypt. Moses chose something better. For while the relics of Egypt's past are impressive, they cannot compare with the future Moses chose.

"By faith Moses, when he was come to years, refused to be called the son of Pharaoh's daughter; choosing rather to suffer affliction with the people of God, than to enjoy the pleasures of sin for a season." Hebrews 11:24, 25.

Moses, groomed to be the future monarch of fabulous Egypt, cast his lot with a nation of slaves, for he was looking beyond the palaces, beyond the pleasures of earthly wealth and ease, to a future that made Egypt's fortunes fade into insignificance. He chose to become the son of the mighty King—the son of the God of Heaven!

For the next forty years, after fleeing the court of Thutmose I, Moses—the educated philosopher, historian, military general, and royal Egyptian son—herded sheep. The last forty years of his life were spent leading the Hebrew people, whom God had rescued from slavery.

Moses died alone atop Mount Nebo, without royal fanfare, without an elaborate funeral marker. An unfair exchange, you say? This life for the one he could have enjoyed at the royal palaces in Egypt? Not so, my friend. For Moses knew that "eye hath not seen, nor ear heard, neither have entered into the heart of man, the things which God hath prepared for them that love him." 1 Corinthians 2:9.

He wanted to be among the faithful who would enter the City of God. He longed to hear the voice of Jesus, richer than any music, saying, "Come, ye blessed of my Father, inherit the kingdom prepared for you from the foundation of the world." Matthew 25:34. Like Abraham, Moses had his eyes firmly fixed on a city "which hath foundations, whose builder and maker is God." Hebrews 11:10.

Can we be sure that this city to which the ancient patriarchs looked with such longing is a real city—and not just a symbol or a figment of their imagination? Jesus gives the answer: "Let not your heart be troubled. . . . In my Father's house are many mansions. . . . I go to prepare a place for you. And if I go and prepare a place for you, I will come again, and receive you unto myself; that where I am, there ye may be also." John 14:1-3.

While John was exiled on the little island of Patmos off the coast of Turkey, God showed the disciple His city in vision. Afterward John wrote: "And I John saw the holy city, new Jerusalem, coming down from God out of heaven, prepared as a bride adorned for her husband." Revelation 21:2. Few illustrations present such happiness and beauty as that of a bride preparing for her wedding day.

John had difficulty describing the unimaginable beauties he saw on the "other side." He had to keep saying, "It was like this," or, "It was like that," and in spite of the limitations of human language, his description leaves us breathless!

"The wall of the city had twelve foundations, and in them the names of the twelve apostles of the Lamb." "The foundations of the wall of the city were garnished with all manner of precious stones." Revelation 21:14, 19.

The color arrangement of the foundation stones has the appearance of a giant rainbow. This will be a constant reminder to the citizens of the great city that God will never again destroy the earth, for it will stand forever.

But we should take a closer look. John adds: "The city lieth foursquare, and the length is as large as the breadth: and he measured the city with the reed, twelve thousand furlongs." Revelation 21:16.

The city is square and 1,500 miles in circumference—

or 375 miles on each side. The state of Oregon is approximately 375 miles square, so this gives us some idea of the size of God's New Jerusalem.

If you are wondering if the city is big enough for the saved, remember that greater New York houses nineteen million people. One mathematician has estimated that the New Jerusalem could house two billion people. In other words, there will be room enough for every person who wants to be a citizen.

The city itself is built of pure gold. "The twelve gates were twelve pearls: . . . and the street of the city was pure gold, as it were transparent glass." Revelation 21:21.

If such a city existed on Planet Earth today, everyone would be packing up and trying to get reservations on the next plane, regardless of the cost! But there is good news! Soon that city will be the capital of this Earth made new, a home that will one day descend from heaven. John saw it "coming down from God out of heaven" to a new and perfect Earth where sin no longer exists, "for the first heaven and the first earth were passed away." Revelation 21:2, 1.

It may surprise you that Planet Earth is to be the future home of the saved, but it should not. Jesus said, "Blessed are the meek: for they shall inherit the earth." Matthew 5:5.

He did not say they would inherit a place on a cloud or that they would inherit another planet. He said they would inherit the earth. This is in keeping with the promise to Abraham that his seed should inherit the earth.

Perhaps you are thinking that you are not sure you want to live on Earth forever. There is so much violence, corruption, pollution, so much disease, suffering, and heartache. In its present state, this world would not be much of a gift! God's gifts are always good, always perfect. And He is going to give us a perfect Earth! A new Earth!

Peter gives us further insight as to how God will accomplish this: "But the day of the Lord will come as a thief in the night; in the which the heavens shall pass away with a great noise, and the elements shall melt with fervent heat, the earth also and the works that are therein shall be burned up." " Nevertheless we, according to his promise, look for new heavens and a new earth, wherein dwelleth righteousness." 2 Peter 3:10, 13.

The prophet Isaiah described the new earth that God will prepare for us in these words: "The wilderness and the solitary place shall be glad for them; and the desert shall rejoice, and blossom as the rose." Isaiah 35:1.

What flower could better describe the beauty and perfection of the earth made new than the rose? Not only will the earth itself be made new, but God will also remove the blight of sin and suffering from His children who inhabit Planet Earth.

It will be a home where pain cannot exist. There will be no cancer, no heart attacks, no arthritis, no colds, no illness—forever! "And the inhabitant shall not say, I am sick." Isaiah 33:24.

"Then the eyes of the blind shall be opened, and the ears of the deaf shall be unstopped. Then shall the lame man leap as an hart, and the tongue of the dumb sing: for in the wilderness shall waters break out, and streams in the desert." Isaiah 35:5, 6.

Yes, everyone will have a perfect body—and eternal youth! Man's relentless search for the fountain of youth will finally be over! We will be able to drink from the pure water of the river of life and eat from the tree of life.

"And he shewed me a pure river of water of life, clear as crystal, proceeding out of the throne of God and of the Lamb. In the midst of the street of it, and on either side of the river, was there the tree of life, which bare twelve manner of fruits, and yielded her fruit every month: and the leaves of the tree were for the healing of the nations." Revelation 22: 1, 2.

Isaiah tells us more good news about our future home: "Violence shall no more be heard in thy land, wasting nor destruction within thy borders." Isaiah 60:18.

No violence! Just peace and harmony and love! It almost seems too good to be true. Yet God's promises never fail. "They shall not hurt nor destroy in all my holy mountain: for the earth shall be full of the knowledge of the Lord, as the waters cover the sea." Isaiah 11:9. "The wolf also shall dwell with the lamb, and the leopard shall lie down with the kid." Isaiah 11:6.

Nothing will hurt or destroy! No need for burglar alarms. No need for locks and bolts on doors and windows. No need for safe-deposit boxes. But the promise that means the most is found in the book of Revelation: "And God shall wipe away all tears from their eyes; and there shall be no more death, neither sorrow, nor crying, neither shall there be any more pain: for the former things are passed away." Revelation 21:4.

The inhabitants of the new earth will never fear death. How many of us have had loved ones snatched away by man's great enemy—death? But on the earth made new, we will not even get weary, much less become ill or die: "They shall run, and not be weary; and they shall walk, and not faint." Isaiah 40:31.

As we study the history of Planet Earth in relation to the rest of God's creation, we find that this Earth is the prodigal world in the universe—the one world where the ugly plague of sin has spread for 6,000 years. You would think that our world would be the outcast of the universe, but God has promised that one day soon this Earth will be the center, or the capital, of God's universe!

"And I heard a great voice out of heaven saying, Behold, the tabernacle of God is with men, and he will dwell with them, and they shall be his people, and God himself shall be with them, and be their God." Revelation 21:3. "And they shall see his face." Revelation 22:4.

Think of taking hold of a hand—and
  finding it God's hand!
Think of feeling invigorated—and
  finding it immortality!
Think of waking up—and
  finding it home!
                    —Anonymous

A home away from the tenements and tempers, out of the smog and traffic and pollution, in a land where a "pure river of life, clear as crystal" proceeds "out of the throne of God and of the Lamb." Revelation 22:1.

But what will keep us busy in such a place of peace and tranquility? Without crime and sickness to worry about, without the rent to pay and gas to buy and groceries to bag? What will the inhabitants of God's city do? It will be a place where every faculty will be developed, every capacity increased. The scientist who has studied atoms and nuclei and the mysteries of life can talk to the Creator of all things. The secrets of the universe will be open to him.

Have you ever had visions of a dream house you wanted to build? Isaiah says: "They shall build houses, and inhabit them; and they shall plant vineyards, and eat the fruit of them. They shall not build, and another inhabit; they shall not plant, and another eat: for as the days of a tree are the days of my people, and mine elect shall long enjoy the work of their hands." Isaiah 65:21, 22.

So you will be able to build to your own specifications without regard to cost or type of material. And you will have no taxes or finance companies to worry about. Perhaps you enjoy gardening. Just think—no potato bugs or corn borers, no blight, no drought. Just paradise from pole to pole!

We will each have two homes—a city home and a country home. The mansion Jesus is preparing in the New Jerusalem and the country home we will build. The city home will surely come in handy, because the Bible says, "For as the new heavens and the new earth, which I will make, shall remain before me, saith the Lord, so shall your seed and your name remain. And it shall come to pass, that . . . from one sabbath to another, shall all flesh come to worship before me, saith the Lord." Isaiah 66:22, 23.

God promises that there will be special times of worship and communion with our Creator, Redeemer, and King. Everyone will come to worship before God—before His throne in the New Jerusalem. What an exciting time that will be, getting together to sing praises and rejoice in the city each Sabbath! The new earth will be a happy place, a joyful place for God and for His people: "And the ransomed of the Lord shall return, and come to Zion with songs and everlasting joy upon their heads: they shall obtain joy and gladness, and sorrow and sighing shall flee away." Isaiah 35:10.

How can we make certain we are citizens of the earth made new? How can we make the necessary preparations and secure the necessary reservations? How can we know our name is on one of those mansions in the New Jerusalem? The answer is so simple—yet so many people try to make it so complex!

God's promise to Abraham, given so many years ago, will be fulfilled. Abraham dwelt on the earth as a stranger, or pilgrim: "For he looked for a city which hath foundations, whose builder and maker is God." Hebrews 11:10. Jesus said He is preparing that city, and soon it will be the capital of the earth recreated by God. The citizens of that land will be the seed of Abraham—just as God promised so long ago.

"Wait a minute," you say. "I'm not a Jew. What will happen to me?" The Bible gives the answer: "If ye be Christ's, then are ye Abraham's seed, and heirs according to the promise." Galatians 3:29.

You see, if you belong to Christ—if you have accepted Him—then you are Abraham's seed. An heir of that promised land! Of the posterity of Abraham it is written: "These all died in faith, not having received the promises, but having seen them afar off, and were persuaded of them, and embraced them, and confessed that they were strangers and pilgrims on the earth." Hebrews 11:13.

We, too, are strangers and sojourners on this Earth, but we can be a part of God's beautiful tomorrow if we reach out and accept the gift that God has promised every person through Jesus, His Son. There is no other way. Will you reach out by faith right now and invite Him into your heart as the Saviour and Lord of your life? Then heaven will be your home!

Who Am I and Where Did I Come From?

Driven on by a relentless dream to trace his family to its "deepest roots," Alex Haley, a black American, spent more than a decade in a search which carried him to three continents. He patched together bits and pieces of his family's history passed down the centuries by word of mouth, catching snatches here and there from plantation and census records or family wills. By 1967, seven generations of Haley's "roots" had been documented on the United States side. However, the riddle of the past, the African side, remained a mystery.

Haley excitedly turned his search for roots to black West Africa. According to geneologies passed down through the centuries by old men of the Mandingo tribe in Gambia, Haley's great-grandfather, four times removed, had been kidnapped and shipped away to America on a slave boat in 1767. Further investigation in England revealed that the *Lord Ligonier,* a slave ship, had indeed picked up slaves on the Gambia River in 1767 and sailed on to Annapolis, Maryland, where the slaves were sold.

Legal records disclosed that Haley's ancestor had been sold in 1768 to John Waller of Richmond, Virginia. Alex Haley had traced his heritage back to its African roots. His spectacular book, and a subsequent televised version of it, touched off a national craze—a search for personal identity, a movement that had been gaining momentum during the previous decade. But Africa was not Alex Haley's deepest roots. God has made the matter of man's origin a vital part of His last warning message to a dying world. Using the symbolism of an angel—a messenger streaking through the heavens—He reminds man of his origin, his deepest roots.

"I saw another angel fly in the midst of heaven, having the everlasting gospel to preach unto them that dwell on the earth, and to every nation, and kindred, and tongue, and people, saying with a loud voice, Fear God, and give glory to him; for the hour of his judgment is come: and worship him that made heaven, and earth, and the sea, and the fountains of waters." Revelation 14:6, 7.

In these verses, modern man is called to worship the Judge of all mankind, God his Creator. This message is to go to the whole world just before the second coming of Jesus, reminding man of his Creator and his origin. Evidently, looking over the centuries, God saw that man would forget his roots. Yet in the Bible God has clearly shared with us the story of our origin. Isn't that logical? God was the only one there! Who else could know of our beginning?

The very first book in the Bible is called Genesis, meaning "the book of beginnings." Could there be a better place to start? "In the beginning God created the heaven and the earth." Genesis 1:1. That is how the world began. And one of the most amazing truths of the New Testament is that Jesus, the Son of God who existed from all eternity, created the universe. The Bible speaks one clear, consistent message on this point:

"In the beginning was the Word, and the Word was with God, and the Word was God. The same was in the beginning with God. All things were made by him; and without him was not any thing made that was made." "And the Word was made flesh, and dwelt among us, (and we beheld his glory, the glory as of the only begotten of the Father,) full of grace and truth. John 1:1-3, 14.

So you see, the Creator of this world is none other than the One who gave His life for the world on Calvary! The apostle Paul clearly shows how God the Father and His Son worked together in the creation of this world.

"God . . . created all things by Jesus Christ." Ephesians 3:9. "God . . . hath in these last days spoken unto us by his Son, whom he hath appointed heir of all things, by whom also he made the worlds." Hebrews 1:1, 2. Yes, the gentle Jesus who died on Calvary created the world and all the creatures in it.

Let's go to the book of beginnings, to Genesis, and re-live Creation week. The Bible tells us that in the beginning the earth was without form or shape, a mass of matter in space. Then, on the first day of Earth's history, out of the darkness and chaos the voice of God commanded, "Let there be light." Genesis 1:3. Instantly, the darkness vanished! "God divided the light from the darkness. And God called the light Day, and the darkness he called Night. And the evening and the morning were the first day." Genesis 1:4, 5. The very first day, the beginning of everything on Planet Earth!

And on the second day God said, " 'Let there be an expanse between the waters to separate water from water.' . . . And it was so. God called the expanse 'sky.' " Genesis 1:6-8, NIV. So God created the atmosphere, and Earth's second day ended. All that could be seen was the restless, rolling water and a heavy mist enveloping the earth.

On the third day God spoke again: " 'Let the water under the sky be gathered to one place, and let dry ground appear.' And it was so." Genesis 1:9, NIV. What a spectacle! Instantly continents, islands, and beaches took shape, rising mysteriously out of the restless waters. And God called the dry ground "land" and the waters He called "seas."

But God was not finished with His work on that third day of creation. Yet another divine command was given: " 'Let the land produce vegetation: seed-bearing plants and trees on the land that bear fruit . . . according to their various kinds.' And it was so." Genesis 1:11, NIV. What a transformation! Immediately the barren hills and valleys were covered with living grass, flowers, shrubs, and trees. The Bible tells us that all things were created for God's pleasure. See Revelation 4:11. What a joy that must have been to Him, designing thousands of intricate flowers, ferns, and trees, all indescribably beautiful. Then He gave them power to reproduce "each after his kind" through all time to come. God must have been pleased with His work, for the Bible states, "God saw that it was good." Genesis 1:12, NIV.

As darkness covered the earth, ending the third day and beginning the fourth, God said, " 'Let there be lights in the expanse of the sky to separate the day from the night, and let them serve as signs to mark seasons and days and years, and let them be lights in the expanse of the sky to give light on the earth.' And it was so. God made two great lights—the greater light to govern the day and the lesser light to govern the night. He also made the stars." Genesis 1:14-16, NIV.

The clouds broke up. The mist enveloping the earth disappeared as the rays of the warm sun filtered through to the earth that was ablaze in vibrant colors. For the first time the beauty of the newborn world was open to full view. In just four days the dark, empty, water-covered globe of chaos was transformed by God, the Creator, into a paradise.

"God saw that it was good. And the evening and morning were the fourth day." Genesis 1:18, 19. And what a day it had been! As Earth's fourth day ended, a robe of brilliant golds, oranges, and reds slowly vanished into darkness. The moon rose and shone on the lakes and beaches, and the heavens glowed with millions of tiny stars. A gentle breeze rustled in the treetops, and the rhythmic waves splashed on the beaches. Never has an earthly night been more magnificent!

But God did not plan a silent world, an empty planet! "He created it not in vain, he formed it to be inhabited." Isaiah 45:18. In fact, God used the first four days of creation to prepare a home for a host of living creatures. On the fifth day God said, "Let the waters bring forth abundantly the moving creature that hath life, and fowl that may fly above the earth . . . after their kind." Genesis 1:20, 21. Instantly the seas and lakes burst with new life! Great whales surged through the waters. Salmon, goldfish, playful porpoise, and thousands more moved underwater. And at last the silence on Earth was broken. The air was filled with the songs of the birds—birds of every size and color, marvelously designed for flight. What a God!

However, God did not create the world just for the fish and the birds. The Bible says that on the sixth day, God spoke again: "Let the earth bring forth the living creature after his kind, cattle, and creeping thing, and beast of the earth after his kind: and it was so." Genesis 1:24. Soon the roaring of the lion, the bleating of sheep, and the barking of dogs was heard, along with hundreds of other animals and insects. "God saw that it was good." Genesis 1:25.

God was pleased with His work. But the best He saved until last. All week He had been preparing Planet Earth for this. The Creator said, "Let us make man in our image. . . . In the image of God created he him; male and female created he them." Genesis 1:26, 27. God could have said, "Let's make man like a dog." Or He could have said, "Let's make man in the image of a monkey." But He did not. Instead, He made man like Himself! God could have shown no greater love. Man could receive no greater honor.

Here is clearly set forth the origin of the human race, roots that extend far deeper than the seven generations of Alex Haley. One New Testament genealogical record traces

Adam's roots, our ancestors' roots, with these words: "Which was the son of Enos, which was the son of Seth, which was the son of Adam, which was the son of God." Luke 3:38.

The author of the book of Acts tells us that God "hath made of one blood all nations of men." Acts 17:26.

Malachi puts it another way: "Have we not all one father?" Malachi 2:10. Yes, the genealogy of the human race begins, not with germs, mollusks, and quadrupeds, but with a Creator—a Creator who made man like Himself, with the ability to see and feel, smell and hear, think and choose, understand and love, and to remember where he came from.

The Bible describes the inhabitants of Planet Earth with these words: "Thou hast made him a little lower than the angels, and hast crowned him with glory and honour." Psalm 8:5. The human race is God's masterpiece of creation! The object of His supreme love, a love to be shared, for God said, "Be fruitful, and multiply, and replenish the earth, . . . and have dominion over . . . every living thing that moveth upon the earth." Genesis 1:28. Man was to be the ruler, or governor, of the earth.

God prepared a garden home especially for Adam and Eve somewhere amid the wonder and beauty of the newborn world. "The Lord God planted a garden eastward in Eden; and there he put the man whom he had formed." Genesis 2:8.

After the creation of Adam and Eve on the sixth day, the Bible says, "Thus the heavens and earth were finished, and all the host of them." Genesis 2:1. As God took inventory of everything He had made, the Bible says He concluded, "It was very good." Genesis 1:31, NIV. Such a short time, just six days of work, and creation was done. The Bible says, "He spake, and it was done; he commanded, and it stood fast." Psalm 33:9.

Adam and Eve must have gazed in wide-eyed wonder

as the blazing sun, in all its glory, began to slip over the western horizon, ending the sixth day of creation. But wait, the Genesis account of creation is not ended! The Bible record continues: "On the seventh day God ended his work which he had made; and he rested on the seventh day from all his work which he had made." Genesis 2:2. God rested! Not because He was weary, for Isaiah tells us that God never gets weary. He rested because He was finished. As one pleased with His accomplishments He looked with satisfaction upon the work of His hands!

But God did something else besides rest: "God blessed the seventh day, and sanctified it: because that in it he had rested from all his work which God created and made." Genesis 2:3. First God blessed the seventh day. He made it an object of divine favor, a day that would be a blessing to His creatures. Next, He sanctified it. He set it apart as a holy day. In other words, God proclaimed the seventh day to be a special day to continually remind man of his beginning, his roots! As long as you and I set aside the seventh day to worship our Creator, we will never lose sight of who we are, where we came from, or what our destiny can be. We will be forever linked with our Creator.

God knew that it was essential for man, even in Eden, to set aside the seventh day as a day of rest and worship. He appointed this special segment of time for fellowship with His creatures. Each week Adam and Eve celebrated the birthday of the world on the seventh day with their Creator.

However, sin broke this close communion and separated man from his God. By the time of Moses God's people, the Israelites, who were in cruel bondage, had forgotten their roots and God's special day of fellowship. But God had a plan to remind them of it. God called Moses to lead His people out of Egypt into the promised land of Palestine. On their way through the Sinai wilderness, the Israelites ran out of food, and God miraculously provided bread for them from heaven, called manna, for forty years.

There was something amazing about the manna. It appeared on the ground only the first six days each week, never on the seventh. Why? God wanted His people to know that the One who led them out of Egypt was also their Creator. God wanted to point them back to their roots by having them honor His holy day, the birthday of the world.

God gave instruction regarding the manna: "Six days ye shall gather it; but on the seventh day, which is the sabbath, in it there shall be none." Exodus 16:26. A double portion fell on the sixth day so they would not have to gather it on the seventh day. Some of the people disregarded God's instructions and went out on the Sabbath to gather manna, but they did not find any. The Lord asked, "How long refuse ye to keep my commandments and my laws?" Exodus 16:28.

You see, the Sabbath was instituted at creation and was observed by God's people long before the Exodus. God's laws and commandments were given to man before Sinai, for it was not until several weeks later that God, on Mount Sinai, etched the Ten Commandments on tables of stone with His own finger.

One of those commandments was given to make certain that His people would never forget their relationship to their Creator. In fact, it begins with the word *remember*. "Remember the sabbath day, to keep it holy. Six days shalt thou labour, and do all thy work: But the seventh day is the sabbath of the Lord thy God: in it thou shalt not do any work, ... for in six days the Lord made heaven and earth, the sea and all that in them is, and rested the seventh day: wherefore the Lord blessed the sabbath day, and hallowed it." Exodus 20:8-11.

God asked man to remember the seventh-day Sabbath as a memorial of creation. The Sabbath is a memorial as old as the world itself. To remember the Sabbath is to remember the Creator. God promises His people many blessings if they obey Him and remember His memorial of creation. "If you cease to tread the Sabbath underfoot, and keep my holy day free from your own affairs, . . . if you honour it by not plying your trade, not seeking your own interest or attending to your own affairs, then you shall find your joy in the Lord." Isaiah 58:13, 14, NEB.

Had man always remembered that memorial of God's creation, the problems he faces today—a forgotten God, a meaningless life, an identity crises—would all be solved. There would be no evolutionists, no skeptics, no agnostics! But sad to say, as we trace the history of God's people through the centuries, we discover that they quickly forgot what God asked them to remember. They forgot to worship Him on His holy day and, strange as it may seem, before long they began to worship gods of sticks and stones. They lost sight of their roots!

However, there were revivals of Sabbath observance during the centuries as God's prophets brought man's attention back to God their Creator. Isaiah emphasized that God never intended to confine the Sabbath to Israel, or the Jewish people. Far from it! It was instituted thousands of years before the Jewish race. God did not restrict such a blessing to just one people. He invites everyone to remember and keep the Sabbath with Him. Through Isaiah He said, "Every one that keepeth the sabbath . . . will I bring to my holy mountain, and make them joyful in my house of prayer: . . . for mine house shall be called an house of prayer for all people." Isaiah 56:6, 7.

Nowhere in the Bible is the seventh day called "the Sabbath of the Jews." Jesus made it clear that it was a day for all mankind when He said, "The sabbath was made for man, and not man for the sabbath." Mark 2:27. God said, "The seventh day is the sabbath of the Lord, thy God." Exodus 20:10. No wonder God spoke of it through Isaiah as "my holy day." Isaiah 58:13. Jesus also said that he is "Lord even of the sabbath day" (Matthew 12:8) because He made it! That is why John the revelator called it "the Lord's day." Revelation 1:10.

The Sabbath is more than a memorial of creation and the Creator. It is a sign between God and man. "Moreover also I gave them my sabbaths, to be a sign between me and them, that they might know that I am the Lord that sanctify them." Ezekiel 20:12. The One who made the Sabbath holy during creation week is the same One who makes sinful people holy. This also requires creative power. Our Creator is also our Saviour. The invitation is given, "And hallow my sabbaths; and they shall be a sign between me and you, that ye may know that I am the Lord your God." Ezekiel 20:20. By observing the Sabbath we tell the world that the Lord is our Creator and God.

The Sabbath was instituted and celebrated before sin reared its head on Planet Earth, and the Sabbath will also be celebrated after sin is forever banished from Earth. "As the new heavens and the new earth, which I will make, shall remain before me, saith the Lord, so shall your seed and your name remain. And it shall come to pass, that from one new moon to another, and from one sabbath to another, shall all flesh come to worship before me, saith the Lord." Isaiah 66:22, 23. Throughout all eternity God's people will celebrate the Sabbath to honor Him as their Creator and Redeemer. Does it not seem reasonable that if the Sabbath was celebrated before sin came to Earth, and it will be celebrated when the earth is made new, that God's people should celebrate it now?

If we have any question about God and the Sabbath, it can be settled by discovering what Jesus' relationship was to the Sabbath while He was here on Earth. Luke tells us what Jesus did on the Sabbath. "He came to Nazareth, where he had been brought up: and, as his custom was, he went into the synagogue on the sabbath day, and stood up for to read." Luke 4:16. The Bible says it was Jesus' custom to go to the synagogue on Sabbath.

But which day is the Sabbath, you ask? How can we be certain which is the seventh day? Webster says, "**Sabbath:** the seventh day of the week (Saturday)."—*Webster's New World Dictionary,* second college edition. The same day that was Sabbath at creation is the seventh day of the week today.

Had the day been changed or forgotten between the time of Adam and Moses, God would have rectified it when He wrote the Ten Commandments at Sinai. Had the day been lost between the time of Moses and Jesus, Christ would surely have set the record straight. And of course the Jews, who keep strict record of time, still worship on the seventh day, or Saturday.

The identity of the day of rest was never questioned during Jesus' life on Earth. The only controversy arose over how He kept it. The rabbis had distorted Sabbath observance by instituting austere, cumbersome regulations. Jesus tried to eliminate their man-made requirements and show the true beauty and meaning of Sabbath observance. When they accused Jesus of breaking the Sabbath because He healed people on that day, He answered, "It is lawful to do well on the sabbath days." Matthew 12:12.

The Bible says that Jesus healed men and ministered to their needs on the Sabbath. This is what the Sabbath is all about—making us whole people, setting us free from guilt, prejudice, and selfishness, and giving us peace of mind; restoring us to the image of God and pointing us back to our Creator. This was the work Jesus came to do, and it was the work the disciples did after He left them.

The true meaning of Sabbath observance was demonstrated by the devoted followers of Jesus at the time of His death. In the very shadow of the world's greatest crisis, we catch a glimpse of Jesus' friends resting according to God's command, leaving the work of anointing Jesus' body until after the Sabbath hours. "And that day was the preparation, and the sabbath drew on. And the women also, which came with him from Galilee, followed after, and beheld the sepulchre, and how his body was laid. And they returned, and prepared spices and ointments; and rested the sabbath day according to the commandment." Luke 23:54-56.

The day before the Sabbath, their hope in Jesus had been crushed. They witnessed Him dying a cruel death on the cross. Their dreams and hopes lay in a darkened tomb. As a last act of devotion, they wanted to anoint His dead body. The Bible tells us that "upon the first day of the week, very early in the morning, they came unto the sepulchre, bringing the spices which they had prepared." Luke 24:1.

Let's take another look at the events of those three memorable days. On the preparation day (now called Friday) Jesus died, and the women prepared spices and ointments. On the Sabbath (now called Saturday), the women rested according to the commandment, and Jesus rested in the tomb. On the first day of the week (now called Sunday), the women came to anoint Jesus, but found the tomb empty because Christ had risen!

The Bible speaks of three consecutive days. The preparation day, or Good Friday; the first day of the week, or Easter Sunday; and the day in between, or Saturday, which the Bible calls the Sabbath. Do you see that there can be no possible doubt as to which day was the Sabbath at Jesus' death?

Jesus hung on the cross on the preparation day and cried, "It is finished." John 19:30. His work of redemption completed, He rested in the tomb over the Sabbath and rose on Sunday, the first day of the week. Even in death Jesus kept the Sabbath!

As we stand near the cross, we get the feeling that any

day in the seven will not do! For to tamper with the Sabbath would be to tamper with creation, with Sinai, and with Calvary itself! Yes, it matters which day in seven we celebrate. George Vandeman wrote, "How can we see His followers refusing to desecrate the sacred hours even with their labor of love, how can we see Him dying on the cross because the law could not be compromised even to save His own life—how can we stand in the blazing light of Calvary and say it doesn't matter?"—George E. Vandeman, *A Day to Remember,* page 40.

The Creator said "remember," yet so many forget. But that was not God's intention. Jesus expected that Christians would keep the Sabbath for all time. Notice His words of instruction: "Pray ye that your flight be not in winter, neither on the sabbath day." Matthew 24:20. Jesus expected that Christians in A.D. 70, when Jerusalem was destroyed, would still be keeping the Sabbath.

The New Testament records that Jesus' followers kept the Sabbath after the resurrection: "They came to Thessalonica, where was a synagogue of the Jews: And Paul, as his manner was, went in unto them, and three sabbath days reasoned with them out of the scriptures." Acts 17:1, 2. Another Sabbath when Paul was preaching in the synagogue, some visitors asked him to preach to them the next Sabbath: "The Gentiles besought that these words might be preached to them the next sabbath." "And the next sabbath day came almost the whole city together to hear the word of God." Acts 13:42, 44. In fact, the book of Acts records 84 meetings that Paul held on the Sabbath.

The Sabbath runs like a golden thread from Genesis to Revelation. The book of Revelation describes those who are prepared to meet Jesus when He comes: "Here is the patience of the saints: here are they that keep the commandments of God, and the faith of Jesus." Revelation 14:12. Jesus said, "If ye love me, keep my commandments" (John

14:15), and one of those commandments tells us to "remember the Sabbath day," a sign between man and God forever!

The same Jesus who asked you to "remember," stretches out His hands—hands once nailed to the cross of Calvary for your sins—and gently calls, "Follow Me."

Won't you decide today to follow your Saviour wherever He leads you?

What Is History's Greatest Religious Secret?

In an age when satellites streak around the world in an hour and a half, it is difficult to imagine how limited man's knowledge of the world must have been a few thousand years ago. Then it was unthinkable to sail beyond the sight of land, because dark mystery and intrigue haunted the open seas. In fact, men of old believed that the Earth was a flat platform at the center of the universe. As late as the fifteenth century, old sailors ridiculed Columbus when he tried recruiting a crew for the voyage that brought him to America. They said his ship would fall off the edge of the earth!

As far back as 250 B.C., the Greek astronomer Eratosthenes described the earth as a sphere, Yet, people still clung to that old belief passed along from generation to generation. It was not until centuries later, after the research of Galileo and Copernicus and the explorations of Magellan, that the idea of a globe became generally accepted.

Strange, isn't it, how we accept fiction as fact without investigating to see for ourselves! Take the spider as an example. For nearly twenty centuries people commonly believed that spiders had six legs. Incredible? But that's the way it was! About 350 B.C. the ancient Greek philosopher Aristotle had said that a spider had six legs, and no one questioned the wisdom of the great Aristotle. If he said spiders had six legs, then spiders had six legs!

161

Some twenty centuries later the biologist Lamarck closely examined a spider. What a surprise! He found that spiders had eight legs, and that they were not insects but arachnids!

Unbelievable? Wait until you hear the next commonly held belief—and the rest of that story!

Thousands of Christians are aware of another belief passed along from generation to generation that will not bear the close scrutiny of history or Scripture. Surprising as the thought may seem, millions of sincere Christians observe Sunday, the first day of the week, thinking that they are doing what God has instructed them to do. They are totally unaware that they are keeping a day God never set aside as a day of rest or worship.

As we turn to biblical history, we discover that God designated a specific time as a weekly appointment for Himself and mankind. Let's go back in time before Lamarck, before Galileo and Aristotle, to creation week. In the first book of the Bible we read, "By the seventh day God had finished the work he had been doing; so on the seventh day he rested from all his work. And God blessed the seventh day and made it holy, because on it he rested from all the work of creating that he had done." Genesis 2:2, 3, NIV.

Before sin was known to man, God appointed this day as a memorial of creation. The birthday of the world! A day God said to remember. His exact words are, "Remember the sabbath day, to keep it holy. Six days shalt thou labour, and do all thy work: but the seventh day is the sabbath of the Lord thy God." Exodus 20:8-10.

Look at a calendar. It is easy to see that the seventh day of the week is *Saturday,* not Sunday. Little wonder God instructed mankind to "remember." He must have known how man would forget!

Maybe you are asking, "How can we know for sure which day is the seventh? Hasn't the calendar been changed? Hasn't the weekly cycle been altered?" Yes, the calendar has been changed, but the weekly cycle has never been altered. The Julian calendar, adopted in 46 B.C., was in use from the life of Christ until A.D. 1582. At that time Pope Gregory XIII introduced the Gregorian calendar that is in use in most countries of the world today. In order to bring the calendar into harmony with the seasons, Friday the fifth of October was changed to Friday the fifteenth, but this in no way affected the weekly cycle.

Of course, had the weekly cycle been altered between the time of Adam and the time of Moses, God would surely have rectified it when He wrote the Ten Commandments which identify the Sabbath as the seventh day. God certainly would not ask mankind to worship on the seventh day of the week if man did not know which day it was.

However, it is obvious that the children of Israel kept the seventh-day Sabbath even before God spoke the Ten Commandments at Sinai. God gave these instruction concerning the gathering of manna: "Six days ye shall gather it; but on the seventh day, which is the sabbath, in it there shall be none." "So the people rested on the seventh day." Exodus 16:26, 30. Had the weekly cycle been altered between Moses and the time of Christ, Jesus surely would have set the record straight. But we read this about Jesus: "As his custom was, he went into the synagogue on the sabbath day." Luke 4:16.

Astronomers and historians confirm that time has not been lost and that no change has been made in the weekly cycle since before the days of Christ. James Robertson, Director American Ephemeris, United States Naval Observatory, wrote, "We have had occasion to investigate the results of the works of specialists in chronology and we have never . . . had the slightest doubt about the continuity of the weekly cycle since long before the Christian era. . . . There has been no change in our calendar in past centur-

ies that has affected in any way the cycle of the week."—
Ref. No. EN23/H5 (14) (1)

Orthodox Jews have worshiped on the seventh day
since the Exodus, more than 3,500 years ago. Wherever
they are in the world they still recognize Saturday, the seventh day of the week, as the day God set aside for worship.

Even if the Bible were our only source of information,
we would still be able to determine which day is the seventh
day, or the Sabbath. As we turn to the account of the crucifixion, the book of Luke summarizes the events of that weekend. After Christ died on the cross on Friday, the Bible com-
ments: "It was Preparation Day, and the Sabbath was about
to begin. The women who had come with Jesus from Galilee followed Joseph and saw the tomb and how his body
was laid in it. Then they went home and prepared spices and
perfumes. But they rested on the Sabbath in obedience to
the commandment. On the first day of the week, very early
in the morning, the women took the spices they had prepared and went to the tomb." Luke 23:54-56; 24:1, NIV.

Most of the Christian world celebrates what is called
Good Friday in memory of Christ's death. They celebrate
Easter Sunday in memory of Christ's resurrection. The Bible
tells us that the day in between is the Sabbath, "according to
the commandments." Even though Luke wrote these words
many years after the cross, he still referred to Sunday as "the
first day" of the week, and he still called the seventh day
"Sabbath." The biblical record carefully distinguishes these
two days.

In fact, the apostles continued to worship and preach
on the seventh-day Sabbath for many years after the cross.
The Bible speaks of Paul and his companions when they
visited Antioch: "They . . . went into the synagogue on the
sabbath day, and sat down." Acts 13:14. Later, "When the
Jews were gone out of the synagogue, the Gentiles besought that these words might be preached to them the next

sabbath." "And the next sabbath day came almost the whole city together to hear the word of God." Acts 13:42, 44.

It was Paul's custom to worship in the synagogue every Sabbath, for we read: "He reasoned in the synagogue every sabbath." Acts 18:4. From these biblical facts one can easily see that there is no evidence that Christ or His disciples changed the day of worship. There is no record in the Bible commanding such a change.

Scholars from the various Sunday-keeping groups acknowledge this. Catholic Cardinal James Gibbons once wrote, "You may read the Bible from Genesis to Revelation, and you will not find a single line authorizing the sanctification of Sunday. The Scriptures enforce the religious observance of Saturday."—*The Faith of Our Fathers,* pages 111, 112.

Clovis G. Chappell, a Methodist, concedes the same point, when he says, "The reason we observe the first day instead of the seventh is based on no positive command. One will search the Scriptures in vain for authority for changing from the seventh day to the first."—*Ten Rules for Living,* p. 61.

There is no biblical record that Christ or His disciples kept any other day or instructed others to do so! "Then how did Sunday keeping get started?" you ask.

We learn from Socrates Scholasticus, a fifth-century historian: "Almost all churches throughout the world celebrate the sacred mysteries [the Lord's Supper] on the Sabbath of every week, yet the Christians of Alexandria and at Rome, on account of some ancient tradition, have ceased to do this." —*Ecclesiastical History,* as quoted in Carlyle B. Haynes, *From Sabbath to Sunday,* page 35.

Other historians record that the Waldenses, Albigenses, and Celts observed the seventh-day Sabbath during the Middle Ages, and the practice is well documented in modern times by Christians around the world.

Many church historians place the beginning of a gradual change of days sometime between A.D. 70 and 135, the dates when two bitter and bloody insurrections by the Jews were crushed by the Romans. To understand the causes for this change of days, we need to consider briefly the relationship between the Roman Empire and the Jews during this time. Dr. Samuele Bacchiocchi states, "Beginning with the First Jewish Revolt against Rome (66 to 70), various repressive measures—military, political and fiscal—were imposed by the Romans upon the Jews, on account of the Jewish resurgent nationalism which exploded in violent uprisings."—*Divine Rest for Human Restlessness,* page 238.

In A.D. 135 the Jewish revolt led by Bar-Kokkba was crushed by the armies of Emperor Hadrian. Outraged, "Hadrian at this time prohibited the practice of the Jewish religion throughout the empire, condemning especially Sabbath observance."—*Ibid.,* page 237.

The mounting hostility of the Romans against the Jews, coupled with the conflict between Jews and Christians, encouraged a rash of anti-Jewish literature, which, in turn, created strong anti-Jewish sentiment throughout the Roman Empire. Christians became increasingly sensitive about identification with the Jews. Since Sabbath keeping tended to identify them with the Jews, many Christians began minimizing its obligations.

"Impressive indications [suggest] that Sunday observance was introduced at this time in conjunction with Easter-Sunday, as an attempt to clarify to the Roman authorities the Christian distinction from Judaism."—*Ibid.,* page 237. With this in mind, it is easy to see how Christians living in the capital city of the Roman Empire led the way in dissociating themselves from Sabbath keeping. They were located at the center where hostility was the strongest!

It is especially understandable that they might shy away

from Sabbath keeping, which was held in contempt by the Romans, in view of the fact that the church at Rome was composed predominantly of Gentiles, who were converts from paganism. It is interesting to note how Paul addressed the church in Rome: "I am talking to you Gentiles." Romans 11:13, NIV. These Christians, recently converted from paganism, were not as well established in Sabbath keeping as were Jewish Christians, who had always practiced Sabbath keeping.

But why was Sunday chosen rather than some other day of the week? That's a good question! The pagans in the Roman Empire had been sun worshipers for many years, celebrating Sunday as the sun's day. The Roman emperors had even represented themselves as sun gods, stamping the emblem of the sun on their coins and buildings and demanding worship from their subjects.

Some theologians believe that the church saw an advantage in compromise with paganism. By adopting a few pagan customs, the pagans would convert to Christianity more quickly and feel more at home. It would also benefit the empire by uniting its subjects into one great religion.

For centuries Sunday was celebrated, not as a holy day, but as a holiday. Then both days were kept as holy days. We read the following from *Apostolic Constitutions:* "Keep the Sabbath [Saturday], and the Lord's day [Sunday] festival; because the former is the memorial of creation, and the latter of the resurrection."—*Apostolic Constitutions,* book 7, chapter 23. Roman Christians were not the only ones who became careless and gradually compromised their faith. The erosion of the purity of the church spread throughout the Christian world. The centuries tell their story.

As long as the apostles were alive, the church stood firm and pure, but when the second- and third-generation Christians came along, we see evidence of compromise and apostasy.

Dr. W. D. Killen wrote: "Between the days of the apostles and the conversion of Constantine . . . rites and ceremonies, of which neither Paul nor Peter ever heard, crept silently into use, and then claimed the rank of Divine institutions."—*The Ancient Church,* pages xv, xvi.

This drift into compromise was accented by the first civil Sunday law passed by the Roman Emperor Constantine on March 7, A.D. 321. While still a pagan, he legislated: "On the venerable Day of the Sun let the magistrates and people residing in the cities rest, and let all workshops be closed. In the country, however, persons engaged in agriculture may freely and lawfully continue their pursuits." —*History of the Christian Church,* 1902 edition, volume 3, page 380.

The next step in making Sunday keeping an integral part of Christianity was taken by the church at Rome in the Council of Laodicea. It made the first religious law concerning the keeping of Sunday. "In the year 325, Sylvester, Bishop of Rome . . . officially changed the title of the first day, calling it the Lord's day."—*Historia Ecclesiastica,* page 739.

At another Council of Laodicea, held in 364, the following law was made: "Christians shall not Judaize [keep Sabbath] and be idle on Saturday . . . , but shall work on that day; but the Lord's day they shall especially honour, and, as being Christians, shall, if possible, do no work on that day. If, however, they are found Judaizing, they shall be shut out . . . from Christ."—*A History of the Councils of the Church,* volume 2, page 316.

In spite of this, Christians were still observing the Sabbath in the sixth century, for Pope Gregory denounced "as the prophets of Antichrist those who maintained that work ought not to be done on the seventh day."—*The Law of Sunday,* quoted in Carlyle B. Haynes, *From Sabbath to Sunday,* page 43.

It is important to keep in mind that the Bible was not available to everyone at that time as it is now. Doctrines were passed along by word of mouth until the laymen could scarcely distinguish between Scripture and tradition. Few really knew the truth as it was taught by Christ and His disciples.

Centuries passed, and the Protestant Reformation came, questioning many rites and traditions that had supplanted the teachings of God's Word. The cry of the reformers was, "The Bible and the Bible only as our rule of faith." Many, like Huss and Jerome, paid for their fidelity to the Bible by being burned at the stake.

However, after the sixth century the Sabbath truth lay almost dormant, hidden under centuries of tradition. Few closely examined to find out what the Scriptures taught. They accepted what had been passed along through generations, never questioning whether it was fact or fiction.

The following statements are by Roman Catholic authors, whose church led the way in the change from Sabbath to Sunday. "The Catholic Church for over one thousand years before the existence of a Protestant, by virtue of her Divine mission, changed the day from Saturday to Sunday."—*The Christian Sabbath,* page 16.

From the *Convert's Catechism* we read:

Q. *Which is the Sabbath day?*

A. Saturday is the Sabbath day.

Q. *Why do we observe Sunday instead of Saturday?*

A. We observe Sunday instead of Saturday because the Catholic Church, in the Council of Laodicea (A.D. 336), transferred the solemnity from Saturday to Sunday.—*The Convert's Catechism of Catholic Doctrine,* page 50.

Why, some may ask, did the Catholic Church—by its own free and open admission—institute this change? The answer lies, at least in part, in the place of authority accorded by the Roman church to *tradition.*

"Like two sacred rivers flowing from paradise, the Bible and divine Tradition contain the Word of God. . . . Though these two divine streams are . . . of equal sacredness, . . . still, of the two, TRADITION is to us more clear and safe."—Joseph Faa di Bruno, *Catholic Belief*, page 33.

One of the main points of difference between Protestants and Catholics during the early days of the Reformation was over the authority of tradition in the church. When Martin Luther declared that he must follow the Bible and the Bible only, he challenged many of the institutions of the Catholic Church that were based solely on tradition. In fact, the Council of Trent was convened to decide exactly what position the Catholic Church should take on tradition and its relationship to the Bible. The question was finally settled. Notice the summary given of the speech that turned the tide, as recorded by H. J. Holtzman:

"Finally, at the last opening on the eighteenth of January, 1562, all hesitation was set aside: the Archbishop of Reggio made a speech in which he openly declared that tradition stood above Scripture. The authority of the church could therefore not be bound to the authority of the Scriptures, because the Church had changed . . . the Sabbath into Sunday, not by command of Christ, but by its own authority."—*Canon and Tradition*, page 263.

What swung the pendulum when all seemed at a standstill? It was the fact that the church had, in effect, changed one of God's commandments on the authority of tradition! Protestants may be more surprised than Catholics over this revelation. Roman Catholics have long taken pride in what they believe to be the authority of their church to interpret Scripture in the light of tradition.

And just what is this "tradition"—upon which the change of the Sabbath from Saturday to Sunday was largely based?

"Romanism," writes Loraine Boettner, "holds that the

the Bible must be supplemented by a great body of tradition consisting of 14 or 15 apocryphal books or portions of books equivalent to about two-thirds the volume of the New Testament, the voluminous writings of the Greek and Latin church fathers, and a huge collection of church council pronouncements and papal decrees as of equal value and authority—a veritable library in itself. . . .

"Roman Catholics hold that there are two sources of authority: Scripture, and developing tradition, with the church being the judge of Scripture and therefore able to say authoritatively what the right interpretation of Scripture is. This, in effect, gives three authorities: the Bible, tradition, and the church. The primacy is in the hands of the church since it controls both tradition and the interpretation of Scripture. . . .

"Rome. . . . maintains that alongside of the written Word there is also an unwritten Word, an oral tradition, which was taught by Christ and the apostles but which is not in the Bible, which rather was handed down generation after generation by word of mouth. This unwritten Word of God, it is said, comes to expression in the pronouncements of the church councils and in papal decrees. It takes precedence over the written Word and interprets it. The pope, as God's personal representative on earth, can legislate for things additional to the Bible as new situations arise."—*Roman Catholicism,* pages 75-77.

The Bible, taken by itself, does not support the idea of an authoritative, extra-biblical tradition. Do you remember the question Jesus asked the religious leaders of His day? He asked: "Why do ye also transgress the commandment of God by your tradition?" And He added, "But in vain they do worship me, teaching for doctrines the commandments of men." Matthew 15:3, 9.

Do you see the issue? Will you follow Christ and the Bible, or human traditions? It is not merely a matter of days and numbers. It is a matter of masters! That is the real issue!

God asks us to remember Him as our Creator by keeping the Sabbath day. To do as He asks means we show our loyalty to Him. When a person keeps a man-made Sabbath, he is obeying man's traditions. When we discover God's will, it is our joy to follow it. That is why Jesus once said in sadness, "These people honor me with their lips, but their hearts are far from me. They worship me in vain; their teachings are but rules taught by men." "He said to them: 'You have a fine way of setting aside the commands of God in order to observe your own traditions!' " Mark 7:6, 7, 9, NIV.

Jesus said, "Their hearts are far from me." You see, it is really a matter of the heart. A matter of love. The Bible says, "This is love for God: to obey his commands. And his commands are not burdensome." 1 John 5:3, NIV.

The way we show our love for God is by our willingness to obey Him. It is easy to love Him when we consider His great love for us. No amount of love on our part can ever compare with the love God has for us.

"This is how God showed his love among us: He sent his one and only Son into the world that we might live through him. This is love: not that we loved God, but that he loved us and sent his Son as an atoning sacrifice for our sins." 1 John 4:9, 10, NIV.

Why Is Morality Declining?

"The nice thing about crime," some have said, "is that it usually happens to someone else."

Perhaps Vicky Mabley of Sylvania, Georgia, also held this wishful view until her two-year-old son, Freddie, was kidnapped and held for $225,000 ransom. Or maybe Dr. Eleanor Banks of Chicago felt that way until she was shot in the leg as she tried to beat off two armed assailants with her purse. Possibly Walter and Mabel Nelson of Berrien Springs, Michigan, also held that view until a gang of toughs broke into their home one night, tied them up, and drove off with their automobile.

Unpleasant as the fact may be, crime is out of control. No longer can we sigh apathetically or blithely shrug our shoulders and say that crime is something that happens to someone else.

Every time the clock ticks, another crime has been committed. Crime and violence are everywhere, and some night soon, who knows—it may stalk your own darkened hallway! Statisticians claim we stand better than one chance in four of becoming the victim of a mugger, rapist, burglar, embezzler, or some other criminal.

Yes, crime is big business. But don't think for a moment that all crimes are committed by the Mafia or other hardened criminals. President Johnson's blue-ribbon Crime

Commission reported in 1967 that 91 percent of Americans surveyed admitted to committing acts for which they could have been sent to prison. These Americans were not simply the criminal element, but so-called honest, respected citizens of our land!

Yet Americans are pledged by culture and constitution to support law and order, peace and safety. But the past two decades have brought anything *but* law and order, peace and safety. The sixties were heydays for criminals, not only in the United States, but in most Western countries. Race riots, political assassinations, hijackings, cult murders, terrorist kidnappings, student sit-ins, and government corruption shocked the world.

The seventies brought an increasing acceptance of the so-called new morality and of situation ethics. The prevailing philosophy was "Do your own thing." And that could mean anything from smoking pot to streaking naked in public places or aborting an unwanted baby. It was a time when neon signs blatantly beckoned the man on the street into topless bars and porno movies. When gays and lesbians came out of their closets, and live-in roommates unabashedly proclaimed their unmarried status.

The sixties and seventies were shocking, but some predict that they may seem like child's play compared with what will likely occur in the eighties and nineties. President Johnson's commission listed some 200 factors responsible for lawlessness and outlined ways to correct the upward swing in crime. However, some twenty years later we discover that crime has increased, not decreased, despite the implementation of many of the recommendations.

Like many physicians, we seem to be treating symptoms, not diseases. Many authorities believe that the soaring crime rates and immorality found in society today are the ugly products of permissive teachings and faulty role-models in our homes, schools, and churches.

From the home a new generation of children has emerged—children who are questioning, skeptical, and challenging. Children love to imitate, yet who will be their ethical, moral, and spiritual role-models? Fathers fudge on income-tax forms, mothers seek abortions, and both parents cheat on each other. The children see it all. And the broken homes are leaving ugly scars.

Who is to instill a sense of right and wrong if parents cannot or will not? Surely, parents cannot leave so great a responsibility to the schools!

Relativism and permissiveness are being modeled or taught in most educational institutions. And a general feeling exists that we have outgrown the Bible's moral standards. *Christianity Today* reported a lecture given at a youth conference at Elmhurst College:

"Professor Fletcher told a group of young people, most of high school age, that neither rape, nor incest, nor any other sexual act, nor indeed the denial of one's Lord or the violation of the First Commandment by having another god, is necessarily and always wrong. He urged that when the situation is right, any of these is morally right."—*Christianity Today,* October 8, 1965.

But the question we must ask is, Who determines when a situation is right? Is not the judgment of even good people often impaired at times? If there is no standard of right and wrong outside of ourselves, we can justify almost anything. We may steal for a "fix," commit adultery if we are attracted to someone, or shoot a person we dislike. The Bible reminds us we are not good judges of what is right and what is wrong: "There is a way that seems right to a man but in the end it leads to death." Proverbs 16:25, NIV.

The apostle Paul predicted: "The time will come when people will not listen to sound doctrine, but will follow their own desires and will collect for themselves more and more teachers who will tell them what they are itching to hear.

They will turn away from listening to the truth and give their attention to legends." 2 Timothy 4:3, 4, TEV.

Many congregations today are being told that God's standard of right and wrong, His commandments, have been abolished, that they are no longer relevant, or that they are impossible to keep. As a result, many people are following their own desires, "doing their own thing," and society is reaping a bumper crop of broken homes, juvenile delinquency, and violent crimes. The Bible says "They sow the wind, and they shall reap the whirlwind." Hosea 8:7, Amplified.

Yes, sad to say, we are discovering that we do not get freedom by throwing out the rules. Remove the standard of right and wrong, and chaos follows. Roland R. Hegstad, editor of *Liberty* magazine, wrote: "Twenty centuries ago the apostle Paul wrote a crime report. Directed to the Christian church in Rome, a city where dissipation, crime, and moral rot were foreshadowing decline of the empire, . . . the apostle laid it on the line: 'Thus, because they have not seen fit to acknowledge God, he has given them up to their own depraved reason. This leads them to break all rules of conduct.'" Romans 1:28, NEB—*How to Stop Crime*, page 11.

What are the rules? Can we know what is right or wrong? Is anything black or white anymore, or does most behavior fall into the fuzzy gray area in between?

A long time ago God gave us a formula for a crime-free society. And had it always been followed, crime would never have existed! Everyone would be safe and happy any place on Earth. When the children of Israel camped at Mount Sinai, the Lord came down to meet them and said, "I am the Lord thy God, which have brought thee out of the land of Egypt, out of the house of bondage." Exodus 20:2.

First the Lord identified Himself as their deliverer from slavery. He was the One who had opened up the Red Sea before them. He was their protector. In other words, He was saying, "I care for you. You can trust Me." Then He spoke His divine law so man could know how to live in peace and safety—so he would know what was right and what was wrong. God spoke these words:

Thou shalt have no other gods before me.

Thou shalt not make unto thee any graven image, . . .

Thou shalt not take the name of the Lord thy God in vain. . . .

Remember the sabbath day, to keep it holy. Six days shalt thou labour, and do all thy work: But the seventh day is the sabbath of the Lord thy God. . . .

Honour thy father and thy mother. . . .

Thou shalt not kill.

Thou shalt not commit adultery.

Thou shalt not steal.

Thou shalt not bear false witness against thy neighbour.

Thou shalt not covet. Exodus 20:3-17.

As the people of Israel listened, they were greatly moved. If that was God's will, they determined to do it! But then, knowing how forgetful we humans can be and not wanting to trust the exact wording to the frail memory of man, God wrote it all on two tables of stone with His own finger. "When the Lord finished speaking to Moses on Mount Sinai, he gave him the two tables of the Testimony, the tablets of stone inscribed by the finger of God." Exodus 31:18, NIV.

Even though this was the first time God had given His law in written form, it had existed from all eternity. Long before Sinai, or even before Adam and Eve, the eternal, unchangeable standard of right had been the basis of God's heavenly government.

In fact, even the angels were governed by it. They could

choose to follow God's law or choose to ignore it and rebel against it. Satan and his angels chose to "do their own thing"—to make their own rules. And this rebellion led to their expulsion from heaven. "There was war in heaven. The great dragon was cast out, that old serpent, called the Devil, and Satan, which deceiveth the whole world: he was cast out into the earth, and his angels were cast out with him." Revelation 12:7, 9. But there were angels who chose to follow God and remain loyal to His law. "Bless the Lord, ye his angels, that excel in strength, that do his commandments." Psalm 103:20.

Adam and Eve had a knowledge of God's law in Eden, for they felt the emotions of shame and guilt after wrongdoing. They recognized they had disobeyed God by taking something that did not belong to them and by choosing to follow another god.

When Cain became angry because God accepted Abel's offering and not his, the Lord asked him, "Why are you angry? Why is your face downcast? If you do what is right, will you not be accepted? But if you do not do what is right, sin is crouching at your door." Genesis 4:6, 7, NIV.

God's law had to be in effect at the time, for we are told, "Where no law is, there is no transgression." Romans 4:15. Webster says, "Transgression . . . the breaking or violation of any law."—*Webster's New Twentieth Century Dictionary*, 1973 edition.

Abraham knew and obeyed the law of God long before the law was spoken at Sinai. God said He would bless Abraham and his descendants. "Because that Abraham obeyed my voice, and kept my charge, my commandments, my statutes, and my laws." Genesis 26:5. And, of course, long before Sinai, Joseph's sensitive conscience led him to meet the temptation of Potiphar's wife by saying, "My master has withheld nothing from me except you, because you are his wife. How could I do such a wicked thing and sin against

God?" Genesis 39:9, NIV. Joseph knew that adultery was sin; he knew God's standard of right and wrong. He had firmly determined not to transgress God's law.

The children of Israel had been instructed to serve and obey God, but during their cruel captivity in Egypt, the knowledge of God's law gradually dimmed. After the Exodus, just a few weeks before they reached Sinai, the Lord rebuked Moses because the Israelites were violating His law by attempting to gather manna on the Sabbath. "And the Lord said unto Moses, How long refuse ye to keep my commandments and my laws?" "So the people rested on the seventh day." Exodus 16:28, 30.

So you see, the fourth commandment was recognized *before* Sinai. Yes, God's law is the eternal standard of right for the universe. And really, should it surprise us that God has a law governing His kingdom? The apostle Paul wrote: "God is not the author of confusion." "Let all things be done decently and in order." 1 Corinthians 14:33, 40.

No orderly government can exist without laws. No harmonious, happy, safe society can function without rules. Nature itself has laws. Even children cannot play games without rules.

The laws of our land are based on God's divine law. In the chambers of the Supreme Court of the United States, towering above the heads of the justices appear two great figures carved in stone. One represents Majesty of Government and one Majesty of Law. Between the two appear the two tables of the Ten Commandments.

Impressive as this may be, commandments etched in stone or attached to chamber walls are not enough. The Bible says, "It is not those who hear the law who are righteous in God's sight, but it is those who obey the law who will be declared righteous." Romans 2:13, NIV.

You see, not only is it important to know the commands of God, we must also respond. Jesus said, "If ye love me, keep my commandments." John 14:15. In fact, Jesus, quoting from the Old Testament, pointed out that love is the basis for keeping all the commandments. "Thou shalt love the Lord thy God with all thy heart, and with all thy soul, and with all thy mind. This is the first and great commandment." Matthew 22:37, 38. Then He said, "The second is like unto it, Thou shalt love thy neighbour as thyself. On these two commandments hang all the law and the prophets." Matthew 22:39, 40.

If we really love God with all our hearts, minds, and souls, we certainly will express that love by keeping the first four commandments.

1. God will be number one in our lives.
2. Our worship will be reserved for Him alone.
3. We will respect and reverence His holy name.
4. We will be anxious to keep our appointment with Him each Sabbath.

And if we really love our fellow men as we love ourselves, we will surely

5. Respect and honor our parents.
6. Value life.
7. Preserve morality.
8. Respect the property of others.
9. Be honest in our relationships with each other.
10. Not covet that which belongs to another.

Estimates indicate that more than 35 million laws have been drafted by man to control behavior, but in just 297 words God drafted a code of conduct that in essence covers all human behavior. What a God! But more important, unlike the defective or unwise laws that men make and remake, "The law of the Lord is perfect." Psalm 19:7.

Theologian Augustus Strong wrote: "Law is only the transcript of God's nature." Today we would say, the Ten Commandments are but a profile of God's character—character that is unchangeable! "I am the Lord, I change not." Malachi 3:6.

You see, any change in the law of God would make it less than perfect. Being a perfect law, it can never be altered. That is the truth Jesus spoke when He said: "It is easier for heaven and earth to disappear than for the least stroke of a pen to drop out of the Law." Luke 16:17, NIV.

But you say, "I've always felt that the Ten Commandments restricted my happiness, sort of fenced me in." God never meant His law to be a burden to man or to restrict his happiness. On the contrary, God intended it to be a wall of protection shielding us from sorrow and guilt. He intended that His law would ensure everyone's freedom and safety everywhere. "O that there were such an heart in them, that they would fear me, and keep all my commandments always, that it might be well with them, and with their children for ever!" Deuteronomy 5:29.

Just as we build guardrails on bridges and mountain roads to keep us from plunging off the road, God gave us His law to protect and guard us on the road of life. But there is another reason God gave man His law: "By the law is the knowledge of sin." Romans 3:20. As Paul said, "I had not known sin, but by the law: for I had not known lust, except the law had said, Thou shalt not covet." Romans 7:7.

Dr. Arthur Bietz tells of an African princess who had been led to believe by her subjects that her beauty was unsurpassed. However, one day a trader came to her village and sold her a mirror. When she looked into the mirror she was horrified by her ugliness and smashed the mirror to pieces!

God's law is like a mirror, and as we look into it, like the African princess, we may not be pleased with what we see, for the law points out sin in our lives. Destroying the law or ignoring it will not change our condition. The imperfection is still there! That is what James meant when he wrote: "Anyone who listens to the word but does not do what it says is like a man who looks at his face in a mirror and, after looking at himself, goes away and immediately forgets what he looks like. But the man who looks intently into the perfect law that gives freedom, . . . not forgetting what he has heard, but doing it—he will be blessed in what he does." James 1:23-25, NIV.

Perfect as the law is, it cannot ensure man's obedience. The children of Israel promised sincerely, "All that the Lord hath spoken we will do." Exodus 19:8. But a few days later they made a golden calf and worshiped it! They broke God's law. And there was a consequence to that disobedience. Paul wrote: "The wages of sin is death." Romans 6:23.

The law points out sin, but no amount of good that we do in the future will erase sin committed in the past. How can we be forgiven? How can we be saved from the penalty of a broken law, which is death?

At the very gates of the Garden of Eden, God instituted a graphic reminder that disobedience brings death—either to the disobedient or to an innocent substitute. He instructed Adam to bring an innocent lamb and take its life. This was God's way of helping Adam understand how the innocent Son of God must die to satisfy the claims of a broken law. Christ, the Lamb of God, would take man's punishment, suffer his death!

You see, the law could not atone for man's sin; it could not save. The apostle Paul said, "If there had been a law given which could have given life, verily righteousness should have been by the law." Galatians 3:21. It is not the law that brings forgiveness and salvation—it is God's grace! Only through Christ's sacrifice can man have eternal life. "The wages of sin is death; but the gift of God is eternal life through Jesus Christ our Lord." Romans 6:23.

Salvation cannot be earned by keeping the law: "By grace are ye saved through faith; and that not of yourselves: it is the gift of God: not of works, lest any man should boast." Ephesians 2:8, 9. If we are saved by grace, are we free then to live a life of disobedience? Never! Paul wrote: "What shall we say then? Shall we continue in sin, that grace may abound? God forbid. How shall we, that are dead to sin, live any longer therein?" Romans 6:1, 2. Salvation is offered to those who want to join God's family, to be part of His kingdom, and to live by His rules.

Perhaps this can best be illustrated by the story of a young man who killed someone in a fit of anger. He was apprehended and taken to prison. As he contemplated what he had done, he recognized he had broken the law. He felt a surge of guilt and fear. He was sentenced to die, but just before the execution, the warden handed him a pardon which read, "Pardoned by the grace of Governor Brown."

Tell me, does this mean that the prisoner is now free to live a lawless life? To do his own thing? Not at all! Because he was pardoned by a gracious governor, the young man should feel more than ever his obligation to uphold the laws of the land.

Most important, God's law points out our sins and helps us feel the need of a Saviour. As we accept Christ as our Saviour, He provides forgiveness and also the power to keep His commandments, for He promised: "I will put my laws into their mind, and write them in their heart." Hebrews 8:10.

It is easy to do something you love to do, isn't it? And that is what the Lord promised to those who choose to follow Him. He will write His law in their hearts so they will love to do it. That is the only way man will be able to obey and follow God. It was because of His love for His Father that Christ was able to keep the commandments: "I have kept my Father's commandments, and abide in his love." John

15:10. And Jesus asks us to show our love for Him by keeping His commandments: "If ye love me, keep my commandments." John 14:15.

The greatest demonstration of love and obedience to the will of God was vividly portrayed one cold, dark night under an old olive tree in a garden. With drops of blood trickling down His face, the Son of God prayed, "O my Father, if it be possible, let this cup pass from me: nevertheless not as I will, but as thou wilt." Matthew 26:39.

The fate of the human race hung in the balance—a guilty world was to be saved or lost. Would this young Galilean put all desire for life and human fulfillment aside and die at Calvary? He could wipe the sweat from His brow and say, "Let the sinner suffer the consequence of his own sins." Or He could let wicked men nail Him to a cross so man could be pardoned. In that awful crisis when everything was at stake, Jesus dipped His pen of love in the crimson ink drained from his own veins and wrote "pardoned" across your record and mine!

The old rugged cross on a hill called Mount Calvary is an eternal memorial of the price God was willing to pay to satisfy the claims of the broken law and to save guilty man.

If the law could have been abolished or changed, Jesus would not have needed to die. Calvary would have been unnecessary. But God could not ignore man's guilt. He could not just sweep sin under the rug. He could not change His law. So sinful man needed a Saviour. And thank God for His love in consenting to give His only-begotten Son to die as our substitute! "God so loved the world, that he gave his only begotten Son." John 3:16.

Yes, He gave His Son to die on the cross. And we are told that "by his own blood he . . . obtained eternal redemption for us." Hebrews 9:12.

Is not that good news, my friend?

How Can I Have Financial Security?

Planet Earth had just come from the Creator's hands in all its splendor and perfection, glorious beyond description! The stroke of a Master Artist greeted the eye at every turn. Magnificent sunrises were rivaled only by breathtaking sunsets. Peaceful lakes nestled between the hills. Gorgeous flowers of every hue and blossoming vines delighted the senses. Majestic trees swayed in the gentle breeze, and the branches of fruit trees drooped under their load of tempting fruit.

Birds of every description filled the air with their happy songs. The streams and lakes were alive with beautiful fish. Animals roamed unafraid in the lush meadows. What a paradise Adam and Eve enjoyed!

But God wanted to demonstrate His love in another special way for Adam and Eve. "The Lord God planted a garden . . . and there he put the man whom he had formed." Genesis 2:8.

Just think! Somewhere amid the wonder and beauty of the newborn world God designed a garden home for Adam and Eve. The most lavish home on Earth cannot begin to compare with the world's original garden home! There were no supermarkets, no checkout counters in Eden, for God supplied their food. God said to Adam and Eve, "I give you every seed-bearing plant on the face of the whole earth and every tree that has fruit with seed in it. They will be yours for food." Genesis 1:29, NIV.

They had no rent or taxes, no locks and keys, no threat of vandals or burglars. In fact, there were no hospitals, drugstores, or whining dental drills in Eden. Adam and Eve enjoyed perfect health and endless youth. They also had perfect love for each other and a boundless love for God. And God wanted them to share that love, for He said, "Be fruitful, and multiply, and replenish the earth." Genesis 1:28.

You see, God intended that Planet Earth should be inhabited by one big, happy, healthy family. God also had something else in mind for Adam and Eve. He wanted to give them a position of responsibility. And isn't that important for man's well-being? Don't we all need a challenge? Don't we all enjoy the feeling of a job well done? A sense of accomplishment? God told them: "Have dominion over the fish of the sea, and over the fowl of the air, and over every living thing that moveth upon the earth." Genesis 1:28. In other words, God entrusted them with the management of His world. As David says, "The earth is the Lord's, and the fulness thereof; the world, and they that dwell therein." Psalm 24:1.

In the book of Haggai we read, "The silver is mine, and the gold is mine, saith the Lord of hosts." Haggai 2:8. And, in Psalms we find this statement: "Every beast of the forest is mine, and the cattle upon a thousand hills." "If I were hungry, I would not tell thee: for the world is mine, and the fulness thereof." Psalm 50:10, 12.

"Well," you say, "I work and earn my salary. That belongs to me, doesn't it?"

In a sense it does, yet without God's blessings of health, strength, and intellect, you could not earn anything. The Bible says, "Remember the Lord your God, for it is he who gives you the ability to produce wealth." Deuteronomy 8:18, NIV.

We really do not own anything! God has a prior claim on us and our possessions. We are just stewards of God. The *Concise Oxford Dictionary* defines a steward as "a person entrusted with the management of another's property."

Today when a person agrees to manage another person's property he wants to know what the owner expects of him. God had an understanding with Adam, for the Bible states, "You are free to eat from any tree in the garden; but you must not eat from the tree of the knowledge of good and evil, for when you eat of it you will surely die." Genesis 2:16, 17, NIV.

God tested man's love and loyalty through this one restriction. Adam and Eve could eat from all the other trees in the garden, but they were not to touch this specific tree. By obeying God they would show their recognition of His ownership. If they were faithful stewards and chose to maintain their allegiance to God, they would live forever in a world that was paradise from pole to pole!

But that is only the beginning of the story. Eve listened to the serpent and ate the forbidden fruit. Then, "she also gave some to her husband, . . . and he ate it." Genesis 3:6, NIV. They failed the test. They were unfaithful stewards, and they lost everything: happiness, love, their garden home, and the dominion of Earth. In fact, they became slaves! "Don't you know that when you offer yourselves to someone to obey him . . . you are slaves to the one whom you obey?" Romans 6:16, NIV.

Satan hijacked the world from God. He took Adam and Eve's dominion! Later, when Christ came to Earth to recover the stolen world, Satan attempted unsuccessfully to bribe Him into sinning. He wanted to be the ruler of this world forever! After Jesus had fasted in the wilderness for forty days, Satan came to tempt him. The Bible gives this record of that encounter: "The devil taketh him up into an exceeding high mountain, and sheweth him all the kingdoms of the world, . . . and saith unto him, All these things will I give thee, if thou wilt fall down and worship me." Matthew 4:8, 9.

Satan did not deceive Christ. The things Satan promised to give Christ were not really his to give. They had been obtained by fraud and deceit. Adam had sold out to the devil, so Satan claimed to be the prince of this world.

However, Satan's fate was sealed forever at Calvary. By His death, Christ paid the price to purchase back a lost world and the right to offer fallen man his original dominion. So everything we are or have comes stamped with the cross, bought by Christ's blood. Whether we love and serve Him or not, all we have, and we ourselves, are His property, created by Him and redeemed by Him. And just like Adam and Eve, we are stewards of what God entrusts to us.

This was the message Jesus shared with His disciples on the Mount of Olives after He had given certain signs which would announce His second coming. He said that the kingdom of Heaven is like a man traveling to a far country who called his servants and gave them his possessions to manage while he was away: "Unto one he gave five talents, to another two, and to another one; to every man according to his several ability; and straightway took his journey." Matthew 25:15.

Jesus said that after a long period of time the master returned and called in his servants to give an account of the talents he had given them. Notice carefully what these servants did with the talents given them. The first one, who had been given five talents, said, "Lord, thou deliveredst unto me five talents: behold, I have gained beside them five talents more." Matthew 25:20.

Delighted with the faithfulness of this man, the master said, "Well done, thou good and faithful servant: thou hast been faithful over a few things, I will make thee ruler over many things: enter thou into the joy of thy lord." Matthew 25:21.

Similarly, the servant with the two talents doubled them and also received the praise of his master.

Then, the servant with one talent came and said, "Lord, I knew thee that thou art an hard man, reaping where thou hast not sown, . . . and I was afraid, and went and hid thy talent in the earth: lo, there thou hast that is thine." Matthew 25:24, 25. And the master said to take the talent from the wicked servant: "Cast ye the unprofitable servant into outer darkness: there shall be weeping and gnashing of teeth." Matthew 25:30.

This servant had buried his talent. He never used what he had to bless others. He was lazy and selfish. He was not faithful. And Paul wrote, "It is required in stewards, that a man be found faithful." 1 Corinthians 4:2.

"Well," you ask, "what are the specific talents for which we are responsible as God's stewards? I don't think I have any talents."

Today the word *talent* means the ability to sing or play an instrument, paint a picture, sew a dress, write, or organize. But these were not necessarily the talents God had in mind. As God's stewards we are responsible for everything He gives us, including life, time, abilities, and possessions. God will ask us whether we have used these talents to enrich ourselves and satisfy our whims and pleasures or to bless others.

The greatest of all talents we possess is life! Paul wrote, "God that made the world and all things therein, . . . giveth to all life, and breath, and all things." Acts 17:24, 25. Our life originated with God, and He sustains it. Every heartbeat, every breath of air, even the food we eat, are gifts from God. And Paul urges us: "I beseech you therefore, brethren, by the mercies of God, that ye present your bodies a living sacrifice, holy, acceptable unto God, which is your reasonable service." Romans 12:1.

A "living sacrifice" means unreserved commitment

and submission to Christ's leadership in our lives. He is our example. We are to follow Him. He lived unselfishly. The Bible says that Jesus "went about doing good." Acts 10:38. Most of us seem to be content to just go about! But we are not to bury our talents as the lazy servant did. We are to use them to glorify God. Our talents are not to be used to get the praise of men or to earn merit with God. They are loaned us to bless others.

"What are you so puffed up about? What do you have that God hasn't given you? And if all you have is from God, why act as though you are so great, and as though you have accomplished something on your own?" 1 Corinthians 4:7, LB.

Every man is also a steward of time. Really, time is just another way of viewing life. Benjamin Franklin said that "time is the stuff life is made of." The Bible says, "So teach us to number our days, that we may apply our hearts unto wisdom." Psalm 90:12.

To waste time is to waste life, and we will have to account to God for that. Every person has the same number of hours in a day and the same number of minutes in each hour. It is up to us to choose how we spend our talent of time. Of course, God set aside a specific time period, the Sabbath, as a means of expressing our belief in Him as our Creator. This day is a time of fellowship with God and His family, as well as a time for us to rest and be refreshed. God asks that one seventh of our time be used in this very special way.

Maybe you are wondering how you can possibly find time in your busy schedule to rest on the Sabbath. Jesus gives the answer: "Seek ye first the kingdom of God, and his righteousness; and all these things shall be added unto you." Matthew 6:33. You see, it is a matter of showing appreciation to God for all His blessings. And more than that, it is a matter of faithful stewardship—a matter of using our time, talents, possessions, and life for the glory of God.

When the Elamites invaded and overthrew Sodom, Abraham's nephew, Lot, was taken captive. When the news reached Abraham, he determined to rescue Lot. He prayed for God to be with him and give him success. Not only did he secure the release of Lot and his family, but all the captives, as well as their treasures. When Abraham returned, the King of Sodom came out to meet him and urged him to keep the treasures he had recovered and just return the captives. But Abraham refused to enrich himself that way.

Next, Melchizedek, a priest of God, brought Abraham a meal and blessed him. Then the Bible says that Abraham "gave him tithes of all." Genesis 14:20. Abraham wanted to express his appreciation for God's help in securing the release of Lot. He wanted to acknowledge God's ownership and blessings. More than 150 years later Abraham's grandson expressed his gratitude to God in the same way. While fleeing from his angry brother, Jacob felt utterly alone and afraid. He wanted so much the protection of his God, but he felt so guilty about robbing his brother, Esau, that he was afraid God had forsaken him and would not forgive him. With a great sense of remorse, Jacob confessed his wrongs to God and then wearily lay down on the ground and slept. The Bible tells the rest of the story:

"He dreamed, and behold a ladder set up on the earth, and the top of it reached to heaven: and behold the angels of God ascending and descending on it." Genesis 28:12. In his dream, Jacob saw the Lord standing above the ladder and heard God say, "I am with thee, and will keep thee in all places whither thou goest, and will bring thee again into this land." Genesis 28:15.

When Jacob awakened, he knew God had spoken and promised guidance and protection. He was deeply touched, and gratefully promised, "Of all that thou shalt give me I will surely give the tenth unto thee." Genesis 28:22.

David felt the same way when he wrote:

"What shall I render unto the Lord for all his benefits toward me?" Psalm 116:12. David longed to show his appreciation to God for all the blessings He had given him. In other words, David was saying, "Sometimes I wonder how to thank Him."

Have you every wondered how to thank Him? Do you sometimes wonder if "thank You" is enough? That is where stewardship comes in. It is a tangible way of expressing our appreciation to God for all His benefits.

Jacob said he would return to God a tenth, or a tithe, of all he received, just like his grandfather, Abraham. The first written instruction regarding tithing, or returning a tenth to the Lord, is recorded in the book of Leviticus: "All the tithe of the land, whether of the seed of the land, or of the fruit of the tree, is the Lord's: it is holy unto the Lord." Leviticus 27:30.

To return a tenth impresses the mind with the truth that God is Creator and the source of every blessing. In the book of Numbers we are given an explanation as to the use of the tithe: "I have given the children of Levi all the tenth in Israel for an inheritance, for their service which they serve, even the service of the tabernacle of the congregation." Numbers 18:21. In the Old Testament the tithe was used to support God's work. In the New Testament, Paul wrote, "Do ye not know that they which minister about holy things live of the things of the temple? and they which wait at the altar are partakers with the altar? Even so hath the Lord ordained that they which preach the gospel should live of the gospel." 1 Corinthians 9:13, 14.

Jesus commended the tithing system when He rebuked the scribes and Pharisees: "Ye pay tithe of mint and anise and cummin, and have omitted the weightier matters of the law, judgment, mercy, and faith: these ought ye to have done, and not to leave the other undone." Matthew 23:23.

There are some who say, "Isn't that only for the Jews?" Perhaps that is best answered by asking another question. Are the blessings of heaven only for Jews? Hardly! The Bible says, "All the tithe of the land . . . is holy unto the Lord." Leviticus 27:30.

The Lord says that the tenth of everything is holy unto Him. So you see, the tithe is not a gift that we give to God, for it belongs to Him. He just gives us the privilege of returning it to Him, to test our stewardship, to see if we will honor and acknowledge His ownership. In fact, the Bible asks: "Will a man rob God?" Malachi 3:8. The possibility of robbing God seems incredible! Who would dare to rob Him? The Bible says it is possible. In fact, it accused some people of that offense: "Ye have robbed me. But ye say, Wherein have we robbed thee? In tithes and offerings." Malachi 3:8.

God promises blessings to those who honor Him with tithes and offerings. "Bring ye all the tithes into the storehouse, that there may be meat in mine house, and prove me now herewith, saith the Lord of hosts, if I will not open you the windows of heaven, and pour you out a blessing, that there shall not be room enough to receive it." Malachi 3:10.

Obviously, heaven doesn't have plate glass windows to open. This is a graphic illustration of God's willingness to reward our faithfulness. Malachi just used a common experience from his day as an example. In his day it was a custom on feast days for the rich to open the shutters of their windows and toss out gold or silver coins to passers-by. However, God did not promise to toss out just a few small coins. He said He would pour out so many blessings we would not find room to contain them!

God also promised: "And I will rebuke the devourer for your sakes, and he shall not destroy the fruits of your ground; neither shall your vine cast her fruit before the time in the field." Malachi 3:11.

The tithe, or tenth part of our income, belongs to God,

so when we return it to Him, we are not really giving Him anything. It is already His. With offerings, it is left up to each of us to decide what we will give. Yet even here the Bible has guidelines. Jesus said, "Give, and it shall be given unto you; good measure, pressed down, and shaken together, and running over." Luke 6:38.

Perhaps you are thinking, if God owns everything—the gold, silver, cattle, and land—why does He need my money? That is God's plan for financing His work on Earth. He never intended the church to be financed by lotteries, bingo games, or raffles. And isn't tithing a responsible way to finance the ministry? Each person gives according to what he receives. If you earn a thousand dollars you return a hundred to God. If you earn a hundred you return ten. Could anything be more fair?

But, perhaps more important than financing God's work is the benefit the giver receives. As we return the tithe to God we express our appreciation for what He has done for us, and we become less selfish and greedy. We become more concerned for the poor, the sick, the orphans, and the widows. And as we share our blessings with them, we grow in love and compassion, becoming more and more like our Saviour.

Jesus once told of a rich farmer who had a tremendous crop one year. The harvest was so great that his barns could not contain it. Finally he made a decision: "This will I do: I will pull down my barns, and build greater; and there will I bestow all my fruits and my goods." Luke 12:18. Then this man made a most remarkable statement: "Soul, thou hast much goods laid up for many years; take thine ease, eat, drink, and be merry." Luke 12:19. He did not acknowledge where his blessings came from. He did not recognize his Creator or his obligation as a steward. He utterly forgot the poor, the orphans, the widows. He thought only of himself. Notice what God said unto him: "Thou fool, this night thy soul shall be required of thee: then whose shall those things be?" Luke 12:20.

Matthew wrote: "What is a man profited, if he shall gain the whole world, and lose his own soul?" Matthew 16:26.

God wants us to give to Him because we love Him. He does not want our gifts if they are given grudgingly or out of a sense of duty. "He which soweth sparingly shall reap also sparingly; and he which soweth bountifully shall reap also bountifully. Every man according as he purposeth in his heart, so let him give; not grudgingly, or of necessity: for God loveth a cheerful giver." 2 Corinthains 9:6, 7.

God says that our money and our hearts are closely associated: "But lay up for yourselves treasures in heaven, where neither moth nor rust doth corrupt, and where thieves do not break through nor steal: for where your treasure is, there will your heart be also." Matthew 6:20, 21.

The problem with modern man is that his life has become so complex and his schedule so busy that he either forgets or does not take time to remember where all his blessings come from. He fails to consider the price that was paid to redeem him from sin. As a result, he neglects to honor God with his time, his talents, and his treasure. Each of us needs to be reminded daily that

> The things that we love and hold dear to our hearts
> Are just borrowed; they're not ours at all.
> Jesus only lets us use them to brighten our lives,
> So remind us, remind us, dear Lord.
> —adapted from Dottie Rambo,
> "Remind Me, Dear Lord"

How Can I Face Death Without Fear?

It was Labor Day, 1969. While American families dashed off to auto races or crammed in a last weekend of camping before the start of school, halfway around the world Bishop James Pike and his wife, Diane, started out on what proved to be their last journey together. Two days later the religious world was stunned by headlines announcing that the former Episcopal Bishop of California was missing in Palestine, lost in the barren Judean desert bordering the Dead Sea!

The bishop had been no stranger to headlines over the years. He had caused some embarrassment to his church, as well as alarm to many conservative Christians, by his highly unorthodox beliefs and his candor in publicizing them. The church welcomed his resignation.

Shortly before his disappearance Pike had provoked another controversy in the religious community by his avid interest and enthusiastic endorsement of spiritualism. Early in his ministry he had rejected portions of the Bible, choosing to follow what he called "empirical evidence" in determining biblical accuracy. At one time he even said that he did not believe in life after death. However, that conviction was uprooted by a series of events triggered by the suicide of his son, Jim, on February 4, 1966.

Not long after this tragedy, strange things began to

happen. When Pike returned to the Cambridge apartment he had earlier shared with his son, postcards appeared by his bed, tilted at 140-degree angles.

Open safety pins showed up on bathroom and kitchen counters, all positioned at 140-degree angles. Books with tantalizing titles were placed before the bishop's nightstand, tilted at the same 140-degree angle. Bishop Pike concluded that the 140-degree angle would be the 8:20 clock position, the very time his son took his life!

Other mysterious things occurred. Pike opened his closet and found half of his clothes thrown in a heap on the floor. The others were in perfect order. A mirror slid slowly off the wall as Pike and two friends sat watching spellbound.

Unable to explain these supernatural happenings, Pike decided that death does not end all, that his son was still trying to communicate with him. He could have quieted his troubled heart and questioning mind had he believed what God's Word teaches concerning the dead. Regardless of how much we may probe the mysteries of life and death, we do not know what is on the other side of the grave except as the Bible reveals it to us.

Pike was deceived by what the Bible calls "familiar spirits." See Isaiah 8:19. The Bible declares that the dead do not return to their homes. "As a cloud vanishes and is gone, so he who goes down to the grave does not return. He will never come to his home again." Job 7:9, 10, NIV.

If this is true, what power caused those supernatural events in the bishop's apartment? The Bible teaches that not every supernatural event comes from God. Another power is at work in the unseen psychic world. John the revelator identified it when he wrote, "They are the spirits of devils, working miracles." Revelation 16:14.

Do you see how important it is not to depend upon your senses? Our only safety is found in the Word of the Living God, but this was not the source Pike sought for information and guidance. Mediums contacted Pike, claiming to have talked to his son. Pike arranged séances in an effort to communicate with his dead son; the most widely publicized was with medium Arthur Ford. This séance was televised from Toronto, Canada.

An apparition claiming to be Pike's son appeared at the séance. Pike said he "sensed" Jim's presence, and the conversation which took place revealed intimate events known only to Pike and his son—or so Pike thought! From that moment the bishop was committed to spiritualism and psychic phenomena. He failed to let the Bible be his ultimate authority, so there was nothing to keep him from believing these supernatural manifestations. He leaned on feeling and trusted his unreliable senses of sight and sound.

How sad that Bishop Pike ignored the words of Isaiah, "When they shall say unto you, Seek unto them that have familiar spirits, and unto wizards that peep, and that mutter: should not a people seek unto their God? for the living to the dead?" Isaiah 8:19.

God says we must trust in Him and His Word for information about the unknown, for the next verse says, "To the law and to the testimony: if they speak not according to this word, it is because there is no light in them." Isaiah 8:20. Whatever the teaching may be, if it is not in harmony with the inspired writings of Scripture, it is unreliable—false!

Bishop Pike and his new bride, Diane, left Jerusalem with a group of tourists. After visiting Bethlehem they struck out into the desert by themselves. A day later they were lost. Their car broke down, and they started out on foot to locate help, but after a couple of hours in the desert heat Pike collapsed. They agreed that Diane should go for help alone. The next day Diane found her way to safety, but Pike died in the desert and was not found for several days.

While the search was being conducted to locate Bishop Pike in the desert, Diane told the press that Arthur Ford and other mediums reported that her husband was alive and well! After his body was recovered from the desert, Diane claimed she saw her husband ascend to heaven and that he was greeted there by his son and his old friend, Paul Tillich.

What a strange trio that would be in heaven: A bishop who rejected the divinity of Christ, a son reported to have said he did not want a religion that forced God and Jesus down his throat, and Paul Tillich, the well-known theologian known as the father of the "death-of-God" school.

Did Pike talk with his son? Did the bishop really go to heaven? Where did Diane receive her information? Who sends supposed messages to the living from those who have died?

We need to know! We can know!

Death, like the chill of the arctic night, is an unwelcome, depressing fact of life. No sooner are we born than we begin to die. Whether we like it or not, death is an uninvited, unwanted guest that inevitably knocks at everyone's door.

But, where does man go at death—if anywhere? Isn't it a little frightening to take a journey, not knowing what the destination may be or whether we will ever come back? When Henry Ward Beecher was dying, he said, "Now comes the mystery." As Socrates prepared to drink his cup of hemlock poison, he exclaimed, "Farewell, I go the way of all flesh, but whether to life or oblivion, I know not."

What a sad, uncertain way to end one's life! The most frightening thing about death is the unknown, the uncertainty about what lies beyond. An epitaph on a tombstone in Richmond, Virginia, reads:

> Stop, my friend, as you go by.
> As you are now, so once was I.
> As I am now, you soon shall be.
> So, prepare yourself to follow me.

After reading the inscription, a schoolboy took a crayon and added these lines:

> To follow you I'm not content,
> Until I know just where you went.

That's pretty good thinking! Where does a man go when he dies? To heaven? Hell? Purgatory? Oblivion? Is death a great new adventure, or just endless silence? Are our goodbyes the final act, or is death just a pause between two eternities? Where are our beloved dead? Centuries ago Job asked the question that every person asks himself at some time in his life, "If a man dies, will he live again?" Job 14:14, NIV. Isn't that the most important question to be answered about death?

Let us turn to our only dependable source of information for the answer. The Bible's teaching on death is consistent, not confusing. You may discover some surprises, but the Bible's answers are reasonable and satisfying, and best of all, comforting!

The prophet Isaiah wrote, "Thy dead men shall live, together with my dead body shall they arise. . . . And the earth shall cast out the dead." Isaiah 26:19. Yes, there is a life beyond death. Our beloved dead will live again! But when? At the moment of death or some later time? What happens when a man dies?

One of the most frequently quoted passages of Scripture concerning death is found in Ecclesiastes 12, which describes what happens to a man when he dies: "Then shall the dust return to the earth as it was: and the spirit shall return unto God who gave it." Ecclesiastes 12:7. In other words, when a man dies, his body, made up of the elements of the earth, returns to dust, and his spirit returns to God.

To fully understand what the "spirit" is, we need to look at creation and discover how God made man in the beginning: "The Lord God formed man of the dust of the ground, and breathed into his nostrils the breath of life; and man became a living soul." Genesis 2:7.

God took the elements of the earth—hydrogen, oxygen, calcium, iron, phosphorous, sodium—and formed the human body. Adam had a brain, but he was not thinking. He had a heart in his chest, but it was not beating. He had blood in his arteries and veins, but it was not circulating. He had strong biceps, but they were not flexing. He was ready to live, but he was not alive—not yet!

Then God breathed into his nostrils the breath, or spark of life, and "man became a living soul." The New International Version says, "Man became a living being."

What was this spark of life that God breathed into Adam's nostrils? Job said, "All the while my breath is in me, and the spirit of God is in my nostrils." Job 27:3. The "spirit," or breath, is what keeps the body alive. James says, "The body without the spirit is dead." James 2:26. We might illustrate it this way:

DUST + SPIRIT = A LIVING SOUL

Or, more simply,

ELEMENTS OF EARTH + BREATH = A LIVING BEING

Then, what happens at death? Just the reverse:

DUST − SPIRIT = A CORPSE

Or, more simply:

ELEMENTS OF EARTH − BREATH = A CORPSE

We can best understand this truth with an illustration.

Connect a light bulb to electricity. What happens? You get light! No one puts the light in the bulb. The light comes by uniting two components: the bulb plus electricity. When you disconnect the electricity the light goes out. So it is with life and death.

When God puts His breath into that special combination of earthly elements, man's life turns on—he lives. When the breath, or spark of life, goes back to the Creator, man dies. All that is left is the body, composed of the elements of Earth, which returns to dust. The living soul, or living being, simply ceases to exist. It surrenders its consciousness at death. The Bible states that when the breath of life, or spirit, leaves the body, consciousness ceases. "Put not your trust in princes, nor in the son of man, in whom there is no help. His breath goeth forth, he returneth to his earth; in that very day his thoughts perish." Psalm 146:3, 4.

Then where do the dead spend their time between death and their resurrection? Job tells us: "If I wait, the grave is mine house." Job 17:13. According to the Bible, when a man dies, he does not go to heaven or to hell. Neither does he go to purgatory. In fact, he does not live at all, anywhere! Death is a cessation of life until the resurrection morning, when body and breath are united again.

Bishop Pike did not talk with his dead son. The Bible says, "The living know that they will die, but the dead know nothing." Ecclesiastes 9:5, NIV. However comforting it may have been to Bishop Pike to think that he was talking with his loved one, however convincing the information given in the séances, God says, "The dead know nothing."

Nothing? Nothing!

Evidently the dead do not even know what the living are doing, for the Bible says of the man who has died, "His sons come to honour, and he knoweth it not; and they are brought low, but he perceiveth it not of them." Job 14:21.

And isn't that the best way, after all? Think for a moment. Suppose that a young mother died and went to heaven, leaving her husband with several small children. Imagine that she was able to see all that happened back on Earth. In time her husband remarries, and a stepmother comes into that home who neglects those small children. Day after day she sees what is going on, yet she is helpless to do anything about it. Would that be heaven or hell for that young mother?

One of the most comforting truths in God's Word is that when a person dies he or she rests quietly, undisturbed by the problems of life until the call of the Lifegiver. Is it any wonder that the Bible likens death to a sleep? The prophet Nathan told King David, "When thy days be fulfilled, . . . thou shalt sleep with thy fathers." 2 Samuel 7:12.

Jesus Himself called death a sleep. He told His disciples, "Our friend Lazarus sleepeth; but I go, that I may awake him out of sleep." John 11:11.

The disciples were confused by this statement. They knew Lazarus had been ill for some time, so they replied, "Lord, if he sleep, he shall do well. Howbeit Jesus spake of his death: but they thought he had spoken of taking of rest in sleep. Then said Jesus unto them plainly, Lazarus is dead." John 11:12-14.

As Jesus and the disciples made their way to Bethany, Martha, the sister of Lazarus, rushed out to meet Christ and cried, "Lord, if thou hadst been here, my brother had not died." John 11:21. No doubt she was right!

Confidently, Jesus answered her, "Thy brother shall rise again." John 11:23.

Notice carefully Martha's response: "I know that he shall rise again in the resurrection at the last day." John 11:24. Martha was a close friend and follower of Jesus. She thought He was speaking of the resurrection at the end of the world. She had listened to Jesus teach. She may have been in the crowd when He said, "Marvel not at this: for the hour is coming, in the which all that are in the graves shall hear his voice, and shall come forth." John 5:28, 29.

Martha assured Jesus that she expected to see Lazarus in the resurrection at the end of the world. However, Jesus was about to give a dramatic preview of that event. Coming to the cave where Lazarus's tomb was, Jesus asked that the stone sealing the entrance be taken away. Concerned by such a request, Martha objected: "But, Lord, . . . by this time there is a bad odor, for he has been there four days." John 11:39, NIV.

But the stone was rolled away, and Jesus cried out in a loud voice, "Lazarus, come forth." John 11:43. And Lazarus came forth!

Someone has said it was well that Jesus specified He was speaking only to Lazarus; otherwise, every grave on Earth would have opened!

Lazarus came to life, but he was still wrapped in grave clothes, just the way he was laid in the tomb. Although he had been dead for four days, we have no record of Lazarus recounting his experiences during death. This is in keeping with the biblical teaching that "the dead know nothing." Jesus simply called him forth from the sleep of death—a sleep that can be broken only by the call of the Lifegiver Himself! This is the call that Job anticipated: "Thou shalt call, and I will answer thee." Job 14:15.

Martin Luther said the same thing in the sixteenth century: "We shall sleep until He comes and knocks on the little grave and says, Doctor Martin, get up! Then I shall rise in a moment and be happy with Him forever."—*The Christian Hope,* page 37.

What a wonderful hope Christians have of a life beyond the grave! In the catacombs of Rome are inscriptions on the tombs of those who died in pagan hopelessness. Over and over again are inscribed these words of sorrow and finality: "Goodbye for all eternity." "Goodbye forever." Yet, on the tombs of the Christians are found these words of hope and courage: "Goodbye until we meet again." "Good night until the morning."

Don't you like that? Isn't it comforting to have the Christian hope—to know that our goodbyes are not final? That there is a great resurrection morning coming after the dark night of death? That Christ will call and our beloved dead will answer? The Christian need not sorrow and grieve in utter despair like those who have no hope.

This is the message of comfort that the apostle Paul shared with the early Christians: "But I would not have you to be ignorant, brethren, concerning them which are asleep, that ye sorrow not, even as others which have no hope." 1 Thessalonians 4:13.

The real hope, the real comfort for sorrowing, grieving hearts is not in the séance chamber or in confused messages from the spirit world. It is in the Lord Jesus Christ!

The message of Christianity that shook the pagan Roman Empire was the good news of the resurrection. The pagans had lost confidence in their religion, and death seemed like a dark pit from which there was no hope of escape. Paul and the early Christians pointed to the resurrection as God's answer to death, the grim enemy of all mankind.

By Christ's death on the cross, His burial in the tomb, and His glorious resurrection, He gained the victory not only over sin, but over death itself! Jesus proclaimed triumphantly, "I am the resurrection, and the life: he that believeth in me, though he were dead, yet shall he live." John 11:25. The resurrection of Christ's followers is as certain as the resurrection of Christ Himself!

When will this happy occasion take place? When will God's sleeping children live again? The apostle Paul gives us the answer: "Now is Christ risen from the dead, and become the firstfruits of them that slept." "For as in Adam all die, even so in Christ shall all be made alive." "Christ the firstfruits; afterward they that are Christ's at his coming." 1 Corinthians 15:20, 22, 23.

The dead will live again at Christ's second coming! Later Paul declares, "Behold, I shew you a mystery; We shall not all sleep, but we shall all be changed, in a moment, in the twinkling of an eye, at the last trump: for the trumpet shall sound, and dead shall be raised incorruptible, and we shall be changed." 1 Corinthians 15:51, 52.

Then Paul tells how we will be changed: "This corruptible must put on incorruption, and this mortal must put on immortality." 1 Corinthians 15:53. Our bodies will be changed when Christ returns: "Our conversation is in heaven; from whence also we look for the Saviour, the Lord Jesus Christ: who shall change our vile body, that it may be fashioned like unto his glorious body." Philippians 3:20, 21.

David said he would be satisfied when he awakes from the sleep of death: "I shall be satisfied, when I awake, with thy likeness." Psalm 17:15. We may not know exactly how our bodies will be changed, but we shall be satisfied! We will have a body like Christ's.

But what about the reunion with our beloved dead? The apostle Paul describes it beautifully: "According to the Lord's own word, we tell you that we who are still alive, who are left till the coming of the Lord, will certainly not precede those who have fallen asleep. For the Lord himself will come down from heaven, with a loud command, with the voice of the archangel and with the trumpet call of God, and the dead in Christ will rise first. After that, we who are still alive and are left will be caught up with them in the clouds to meet the Lord in the air. And so we will be with the Lord forever. Therefore enourage each other with these words." 1 Thessalonians 4:15-18, NIV.

Could any words be more encouraging? What a glorious hope! When Jesus bursts through the blue and looks upon the dusty graves of His sleeping followers, His mighty voice will call out, just as He called to Lazarus: "Come forth!" And the graves on a thousand hillsides around the earth will burst open. The dead will hear His voice and come forth! Families and friends will be united, never to part again. What a day that will be! No pen can describe it!

This is the future that Calvary has made possible: Seeing our Lord face to face, joining our loved ones who have fallen asleep in Jesus. What hope this message brings!

But the most important question to be answered is, How can we be certain today that we can have victory over death and the grave? God's promise of eternal life is clear: "He that hath the Son hath life; and he that hath not the Son of God hath not life." 1 John 5:12.

Eternal life is promised to those who have the Son. Victory over death and the grave is promised through Jesus Christ our Lord: "Thanks be to God, which giveth us the victory through our Lord Jesus Christ." 1 Corinthians 15:57.

When Jesus comes, He brings the gift of immortality to His faithful ones: "This corruptible must put on incorruption, and this mortal must put on immortality. . . . Then shall be brought to pass the saying that is written, Death is swallowed up in victory. O death, where is thy sting? O grave, where is thy victory?" 1 Corinthians 15:53-55.

The greatest gift that God can give to man is eternal life, victory over death forever! All other gifts are meaningless without it. And it is yours for the taking! Your decision is the greatest decision you will ever make; your eternal future depends upon it! This priceless gift of eternal life is promised to everyone who accepts Christ as his Saviour and Lord.

And the cost? Only a surrendered heart. A heart cleansed and changed. A proud, selfish heart made new at the foot of the cross. Christ made it all possible at Calvary. What more could He do? And eternal life can be yours if you want it enough. Because He lives, we have a glorious hope—a hope beyond the grave!

Is There Really a Hell?

Dr. Samuel Hopkins, an eloquent preacher of the nineteenth century, held audiences spellbound with his horrendous descriptions of the agonies of hell. It is said that the word pictures he painted were so vivid one could almost hear the crackling of the flames as he spoke of the fate of the unsaved. The following quotation was taken from his writings:

"The smoke of their torment shall ascend up forever in the sight of the blessed ... before their eyes. ... This display of Divine character and glory will be in favor of the redeemed, and most entertaining, and give the highest pleasure to those who love God. ... Should the eternal torment and fires be extinguished, it would in a great measure ... put an end to the happiness and glory of the blessed."—*Works of Samuel Hopkins, D.D.*, pages 457, 458.

Incredible, isn't it? Yet, nineteenth-century ministers vied with each other to make the pain and agony of hell more graphic. One preacher said the fires of hell are so hot that if a sinner were suddenly taken out and plunged into the hottest fire on Earth he would freeze to death! Robert Ingersoll, one of the world's best known infidels, might have been a prince of preachers were it not for his father's statement that God had infants in hell who would burn forever. Young Ingersoll said, "If that is what God does, I hate Him!" His logical mind could not conceive of such injustice. He turned from a God whom he mistakenly believed to be a tyrant who delights in the agonies of the lost.

Some preachers thought hellfire would frighten people into being good. If salvation comes through fear, millions should have flocked to the churches after listening to the descriptions given by some of the early preachers. But would a God who gave His only begotten Son to die on the cross, a God who said He was "not willing that any should perish, but that all should come to repentance" (2 Peter 3:9), burn sinners forever in the fires of hell because they failed to accept His salvation? That's a good question! Many sincere people have turned from Christianity because they could not harmonize these two contrasting pictures of God's character and justice so commonly taught.

However, the real question to be answered is, "Where in the Bible is such a doctrine of eternal fiery torment to be found?" And the amazing answer is that it isn't there! As you turn the pages of the Bible, you will discover that it talks about hell—a literal, burning hell—but not the kind pictured to frighten people into becoming Christians.

Let's turn to the New Testament and discover what Jesus taught about the fate of the unsaved, or the wicked. One day while He was teaching by the Sea of Galilee, a crowd pressed in to listen to Him. Seeking a spot where everyone could see and hear Him, Jesus got into a boat and pushed out a little from the shore. Nearby, men were sowing in their fields. Jesus could watch them as they worked. Directing the attention of the people to the fields, He spoke several parables. One concerned the fate of the unsaved.

"The kingdom of heaven is likened unto a man which sowed good seed in his field: But while men slept, his enemy came and sowed tares among the wheat. . . . But when the blade was sprung up, and brought forth fruit, then appeared the tares also. So the servants of the house-holder came and said unto him, Sir, didst not thou sow good seed in thy field? from whence than hath it tares? He said unto them, An enemy hath done this." Matthew 13:24-28.

The servants wanted to pull out the tares, but the master said, "In the time of harvest I will say to the reapers, Gather ye together first the tares, and bind them in bundles to burn them: but gather the wheat into my barn." Matthew 13:30.

Later the disciples came and asked Jesus to explain the parable to them. So Jesus said: "He that soweth the good seed is the Son of man; the field is the world; the good seed are the children of the kingdom; but the tares are the children of the wicked one; the enemy that sowed them is the devil; the harvest is the end of the world; and the reapers are the angels." Matthew 13:37-39.

Now notice what Jesus said: "As therefore the tares are gathered and burned in the fire; so shall it be in the end of this world." Matthew 13:40. According to Jesus, punishment will come at the end of the world. That is when the tares, or the wicked, will be gathered and burned. This is a future date. The fires of hell are not burning now; the wicked who have died certainly are not being punished in the fires of hell now. Peter wrote, "The Lord knoweth how to deliver the godly out of temptations, and to reserve the unjust unto the day of judgment to be punished." 2 Peter 2:9.

According to the Bible, when a man dies he does not go immediately to his reward. He must first be judged and sentenced. Doesn't that make sense? Isn't that the only fair way? Think for a moment: Would a just God send a person to suffer in hell and then centuries later call him up to stand trial to see if he deserved that punishment? Would that be justice? Hardly! The teaching that a man goes immediately to heaven or hell at death undermines God's love and justice. Small wonder God is so misunderstood and feared.

Job tells us what happens when a man dies: "Yet shall

he be brought to the grave, and shall remain in the tomb." Job 21:32. And notice what Job said concerning the wicked who die: "Do ye not know . . . that the wicked is reserved to the day of destruction? they shall be brought forth to the day of wrath." Job 21:29, 30.

You see, when Jesus comes back to this Earth He will reward every man. "The Son of man shall come in the glory of his Father with his angels; and then he shall reward every man according to his works." Matthew 16:27.

The Bible teaches that unrepentant sinners will be punished. How could it be otherwise? In the courts, justice demands that lawbreakers be punished according to the laws of the land. Yet God does not enjoy the punishment of the wicked as some preachers have stated. Isaiah calls it His "strange act." See Isaiah 28:21. But a God of justice has no other choice. The inhabitants of Earth rebelled against God's government of love. They refused to obey His laws, and sin has its penalty. "The wages of sin is death." Romans 6:23.

However, God's heart of love goes out to mankind, for Peter wrote, "The Lord . . . is longsuffering to us-ward, not willing that any should perish, but that all should come to repentance." 2 Peter 3:9.

God gave His own Son to die in our place on Calvary's cross to satisfy the claims of a broken law. For this reason, no one needs to perish. But in God's government, everyone has perfect freedom to choose either to accept or to reject the forgiveness and salvation of God. A loving, compassionate God urges man to choose salvation: "I have set before you life and death, . . . therefore choose life, that both thou and thy seed may live." Deuteronomy 30:19.

But those who refuse salvation, those who reject the sacrifice of Christ, must one day lose the priceless gift of eternal life that God offers. They will die for their sins. God has no choice, for sin and sinners will be destroyed. But you may rest assured that no one is suffering in some fiery chasm out on the edge of the universe today!

Maybe you wonder where such an idea originated. It came from the master deceiver, Satan! And it has been passed along from paganism to Christianity.

In the Garden of Eden, Satan told Eve, in contradiction of God's words, "Ye shall not surely die." Genesis 3:4. That lie has been passed on through the centuries! You see, if man does not die, he is immortal. Therefore, those who believe this lie of Satan reason that if wicked man is immortal, if he never dies, then he must burn forever in hell for his sins.

But God did not say that the wages of sin is continuing life in torment! Never! The love and justice of God could never be vindicated if He allowed sinful man to burn forever. What unspeakable cruelty! How diabolical! Even in man's faulty justice, he would never sentence the vilest criminal to such a fate. And yet, many accuse a loving, merciful God of such tyranny and cruelty!

The real punishment that the sinner will suffer is the loss of eternal life. To think they chose a few short years on Earth, which were often filled with worry, heartache, and tears, instead of life everlasting in a glorious Earth made new, where there will be only peace and love and harmony—forever! The real punishment will be seeing what could have been theirs.

But Jesus said that the tares, or the wicked, would be gathered and burned at the end of the world. Isn't that speaking of a burning hell? Indeed, but the interesting thing is that God's Word says that hell was prepared for the devil and his angels. As Christ passes sentence upon those who have rejected salvation, He will say, "Depart from me, ye cursed, into everlasting fire, prepared for the devil and his angels." Matthew 25:41. Jesus said He was going to prepare a place for man when He returned to heaven. See John 14: 2, 3. But if man rejects God and His salvation and chooses to follow Satan, man will also share in the fate of the devil and his angels.

"Wait a minute," you say. "Everlasting fire sounds like it will be forever." Well, let's read verse 46 of the same chapter in Matthew: "These shall go away into everlasting punishment: but the righteous into life eternal." Matthew 25:46. It is the punishment that is everlasting, not the punishing. God said that the wages of sin is death. That is final—everlasting. The state of being dead will never end. The punishment is eternal in its consequences. An example is found in the book of Jude:

"Even as Sodom and Gomorrha, and the cities about them in like manner, giving themselves over to fornication, and going after strange flesh, are set forth for an example, suffering the vengeance of eternal fire." Jude 7. The inhabitants of Sodom and Gomorrah had become so vile that they had to be destroyed. But Abraham's nephew, Lot, and his family lived in Sodom. God sent angels to lead Lot and his family out of the city before the fire fell and cities were destroyed.

You remember the story: Lot and his wife and two daughters were led out of the city, and the angel said to them, "Escape for thy life; . . . lest thou be consumed." "Then the Lord rained upon Sodom and upon Gomorrah brimstone and fire from the Lord out of heaven." Genesis 19:17, 24.

The Bible tells us that everyone and everything was destroyed, even the grass surrounding those cities. Sounds like an atomic explosion, doesn't it? Jude said those cities would be destroyed by "eternal fire." Jude 7. Are Sodom and Gomorrah burning now? Of course not. But the effects have been eternal. Peter said the destruction of those cities was an example to us of what is in store for those who live ungodly lives. "Turning the cities of Sodom and Gomorrha into ashes condemned them with an overthrow, making them an ensample unto those that after should live ungodly." 2 Peter 2:6.

One day while instructing His disciples, Jesus remarked, "If thy hand offend thee, cut if off: it is better for thee to enter into life maimed, than having two hands to go into hell, into the fire that never shall be quenched." Mark 9:43. Here Jesus pictures the fires of hell, or the fire which shall burn the wicked up, as being unquenchable. The same terminology is used in connection with the destruction of Jerusalem: "If ye will not hearken unto me to hallow the sabbath day, . . . then will I kindle a fire in the gates thereof, and it shall devour the palaces of Jerusalem, and it shall not be quenched." Jeremiah 17:27.

The fires kindled by the Babylonians when they destroyed Jerusalem were unquenchable. No one could put them out. But after the flames destroyed the city, the fires went out.

We use the same terminology today. If a fire breaks out in a building and cannot be contained, or put out, we say that it is unquenchable. We do not mean that it will never go out. The fires of Jerusalem are not burning today. They burned until there was nothing more to burn, and then they went out.

The wicked will be burned up very quickly—like stubble, Malachi says: "Behold, the day cometh, that shall burn as an oven; and all the proud, yea, and all that do wickedly, shall be stubble: and the day that cometh shall burn them up, saith the Lord of hosts, that it shall leave them neither root nor branch." Malachi 4:1.

The fire will be unquenchable. The wicked will cease to be. The effects of the fire will be eternal—everlasting. There will be nothing left of the wicked. In fact, Malachi says, "And ye shall tread down the wicked; for they shall be ashes under the soles of your feet." Malachi 4:3.

David wrote, "The wicked shall perish . . . ; into smoke

shall they consume away." Psalm 37:20. Obadiah says, "They shall be as though they had not been." Obadiah 16.

But you say, "That is just man's body that will be destroyed. His soul will live forever." Is that what the Bible teaches? Jesus said, "Fear not them which kill the body, but are not able to kill the soul: but rather fear him which is able to destroy both soul and body in hell." Matthew 10:28. In fact, Ezekiel makes it clear that "the soul that sinneth, it shall die." Ezekiel 18:4.

And doesn't that make sense? Think for a moment. Christ came to be our substitute, to die for our sins, to take our punishment. Did Christ suffer on the cross forever and ever? No, He died! That was man's punishment—death. "The wages of sin is death." Romans 6:23.

No doubt you are thankful to know that the teaching of eternal hellfire is not biblical and that no one is burning in hell now. However, some people cannot understand how a God of love could permit anyone to be destroyed, regardless of how wicked he has been. It is not a pleasant experience for the Lord. "I take no pleasure in the death of anyone, declares the Sovereign Lord." Ezekiel 18:32, NIV. But God has no choice if He is to preserve life on Earth.

It is somewhat like the PBB crisis in Michigan. In 1973 dairymen in Michigan noticed that many of their cows were becoming ill. Milk production dropped drastically. Cows got thinner, and many calves came stillborn. No one could find the cause of the mysterious illness.

Rick Halbert, a dairyman in Battle Creek, set out on a relentlesss search for the cause. Eleven months later it was identified: polybrominated biphenyl—PBB. The cattle had been poisoned by a fire retardant which had accidently been mixed with cattle feed at the farm bureau. Once the mill became contaminated, it poisoned all feed from that plant. As soon as the seriousness of the problem became known, it was recognized that unless some drastic action were taken, the lives of all livestock, as well as humans, in Michigan would be endangered.

Rick's wife, Sandra, kept a daily journal of the PBB experience at their ranch. Later it was compiled into a book titled *Bitter Harvest*. It tells the bitter story of the dairymen as they helplessly watched their once beautiful herds sicken. They did everything they could to make them well, but the contamination only spread. Finally the decision was made that the contaminated cattle must be destroyed to protect the lives of other livestock as well as the lives of the people living in Michigan.

The dairymen did not want their cattle destroyed. They loved their animals. But there was no alternative! It was the only safe and merciful thing to do. Many dairymen wept as more than 30,000 head of cattle, 1.5 million poultry, and thousands of hogs and sheep were destroyed.

Just like the dairymen in Michigan, God loves the sinner. He wants to help him. He urges every man to choose to be saved: "Let the wicked forsake his way, and the unrighteous man his thoughts: and let him return unto the Lord, and he will have mercy upon him; and to our God, for he will abundantly pardon." Isaiah 55:7.

But man has a choice, and God must honor that choice. It is the only loving thing to do. For, you see, heaven would be a miserable place for those who have chosen a lifestyle contrary to God's Word. Think for a moment: In heaven there will be no casinos for the gambler, no saloons for the alcoholic, no heroin for the addict, no places of sinful pleasure, no money for the greedy to hoard. Don't you suppose that heaven would actually seem like hell to these people?

And if they refuse to accept God's salvation, if they refuse to be cleansed by the blood of Christ, the deadly virus of sin spreads. Just like the cattle contaminated by PBB, the wicked carry the contamination of sin which endangers the lives of everyone in the universe. So sin and sinners must be destroyed. It is the only safe and merciful thing to do.

"But when will this take place?" you ask. The Bible tells us that the righteous dwell with Christ during the millennial period, and at the end of that time the wicked dead will be raised. This is the "resurrection of damnation" spoken of by Jesus when He said, "Marvel not at this: for the hour is coming, in the which all that are in the graves shall hear his voice, and shall come forth; they that have done good, unto the resurrection of life; and they that have done evil, unto the resurrection of damnation." John 5:28, 29.

The wicked will be raised, just as they went into the grave. Then John says, "I John saw the holy city, new Jerusalem, coming down from God out of heaven, prepared as a bride adorned for her husband." Revelation 21:2. What a sight! What a contrast will be seen as the magnificent city descends from heaven with all the saved, glorified and youthful. And what a sense of loss must sweep over the multitudes of the unsaved as they see what might have been theirs! The devil has robbed them of their dearest possession—eternal life!

Now they stand arraigned before God on the charge of high treason against His government. Their destiny is fixed by their own choice. They hear the sentence of death passed upon them; they fall to their knees and acknowledge that God is just. God's wisdom, justice, and goodness stand fully vindicated. For "we shall all stand before the judgment seat of Christ. . . . Every knee shall bow to me, and every tongue confess to God." Romans 14:10, 11.

The wicked do not repent. They only regret the fearful results of sin—the sentence of death, the second death. No doubt Satan and his angels must also tremble at the thought of their sentence of doom. However, the Bible tells us that, in a last desperate effort to overthrow God and take the city, Satan marshals all the millions of the wicked into one vast army and sets out to surround it. John, the beloved disciple, gives an account of what will happen as they come to take the city: "And they went up on the breadth of the earth, and compassed the camp of the saints about, and the beloved city: and fire came down from God out of heaven, and devoured them." Revelation 20:9.

And what about the devil? "And the devil that deceived them was cast into the lake of fire and brimstone." *"This is the second death.* And whosoever was not found written in the book of life was cast into the lake of fire." Revelation 20:10, 14, 15, emphasis supplied.

Peter described that day: "The elements shall melt with fervent heat, the earth also and the works that are therein shall be burned up." 2 Peter 3:10.

As the flames envelop the earth, a God of love must weep—weep just as Jesus wept that sad day as He looked at Jerusalem and cried out from the depth of His heart, "O Jerusalem, Jerusalem, thou that killest the prophets, and stonest them which are sent unto thee, how often would I have gathered thy children together, even as a hen gathereth her chickens under her wings, and ye would not!" Matthew 23:37.

Friend, that will be Earth's saddest day. It will also be the saddest day for God, for His Son, for the holy angels, for the saved, and for the lost. Tears of sadness and farewell will flow. How could it be otherwise? But, as always, a God of love shows His unfailing kindness and concern, for we read that "God shall wipe away all tears from their eyes; and there shall be no more death, neither sorrow, nor crying, neither shall there be any more pain: for the former things are passed away." Revelation 21:4.

Isn't that good news? And best of all, God promises, "Affliction shall not rise up the second time." Nahum 1:9. Never again will Planet Earth be contaminated with the virus of sin. But there is more good news. Peter wrote, "Nevertheless we, according to his promise, look for new heavens and a new earth, wherein dwelleth righteousness." 2 Peter 3:13.

Friend, Jesus wants to share eternity with you. He wants to share the beauty and pleasure of the earth made new with you. He has paid the price for your redemption on Calvary, and He invites you to accept that sacrifice. But the choice is *yours*.

And, friend, when you make that decision, Christ will be there to help you. Whatever the problem, whatever the difficulty, He is always there. Won't you reach out to Jesus right now? He is reaching out to you!

How Can I Change for the Better?

On October 26, 1967, after ruling twenty-six years on the Peacock Throne, the Shah of Iran, in a dazzling ceremony, crowned himself and his wife king and queen of the 2,500-year-old Persian throne. He said he had waited that long because he did not want to be a king of poor people. So, with enormous oil riches at his disposal, he set out to turn his country into a first-rate industrial power.

However, oil riches and Westernization challenged the old ways in a deeply conservative Islamic nation. Muslims were offended by Western influences, and that, coupled with the corruption and injustices of the shah's regime, generated a "back to basics" drive in Iran.

In an interview with Dennis Mullin, the shah stated, "Nobody can overthrow me. I have the support of 700,000 troops, all the workers and most of the people."—*U.S. News and World Report,* June 1978, page 37. Yet six months later the shah was forced to flee Iran! His old foe, the Ayatollah Khomeini, who had been in exile fifteen years, returned amid shouts of victory!

How did it happen? Journalists reported that Khomeini and his followers were armed with something far more powerful than the shah's military might: devotion to Islam, a religion whose 600 million followers are scattered over the Middle East from Morocco to Pakistan. A religion founded in the desert thirteen centuries ago by Mohammed.

Islam, the youngest of the four great world religions, venerates Allah and Mohammed, its founder. The great rallying call of the Muslim is, "There is one God, Allah, and Mohammed is his prophet."

Born in A.D. 570 in the city of Mecca, Mohammed claimed that the angel Gabriel appeared to him in a vision and gave him the words of the Koran, the Muslim's ultimate authority.

Mohammed died at the age of sixty-one. His grave in Medina is tightly guarded around the clock. Parts of his body are enshrined in various mosques throughout the Middle East. No resurrection was ever claimed for Mohammed.

Another great religion in the Middle East is Judaism. Its father, Abraham, died at the age of 175, about 1900 B.C. He was buried in Canaan in the cave of Machpelah. The Jews claim no resurrection for Abraham. The grave was the end of his long life.

Buddhism's founder, Siddhartha Gautama, or the Buddha, died in 483 B.C. Relics of his body, including hair and teeth, have been enshrined in pagodas throughout the Buddhist world. No resurrection was ever claimed for the Buddha. Death ended his career.

Today, young people are asking, "What difference is there between Christianity and the other great religions of the East? All have had great teachers; all encourage their adherents to be good persons. Why do Christians claim that their founder, Jesus Christ, is superior to the founders of the other religions?" The answer is the empty tomb. The followers of these other religions often challenge Christians to show them where their leader is entombed, saying, "You Christians have nothing."

Yet the tombs of Mohammed, Abraham, and Buddha are evidence of death and decay. The empty tomb of Christ is evidence of His power over death! For the angel said to the women, "Why seek ye the living among the dead? He is not here, but is risen." Luke 24:5, 6. There is not a shrine in the world that can boast one part of the body of Christ. The Roman seal could not hold Him in the tomb. Mountains of rock could not have held Him. The difference between Christianity and every other religion is an empty tomb! Only Christians claim the resurrection of their founder. A religion that does not have an empty tomb and a coming King is not enough. It does not meet man's needs. For if there is no empty tomb or coming King, the inhabitants on Planet Earth are doomed to a meaningless oblivion.

That is the message the apostle Paul proclaimed when he said, "If Christ has not been raised, our preaching is useless and so is your faith." "And if Christ has not been raised, your faith is futile; you are still in your sins. Then those also who have fallen asleep in Christ are lost." 1 Corinthians 15:14, 17, 18, NIV.

When the Jewish religious leaders asked Jesus to give them a sign of His divinity—proof that He was the Son of God as He claimed—He stated that His resurrection would be the only sign. Jesus staked His authority on His resurrection.

Jesus announced His death and resurrection when He said, "Destroy this temple, and in three days I will raise it up." John 2:19. Thinking Jesus spoke of the temple, the Jews scoffed at Him, saying, "It has taken forty-six years to build this temple, and you are going to raise it in three days?" John 2:20, NIV.

They missed the point completely! Jesus was not speaking about bricks or stones, "But he spake of the temple of his body." John 2:21.

The miracle of His resurrection authenticated Jesus' claim to be the divine Messiah. "After he was raised from the dead, his disciples recalled what he had said. Then they believed the Scripture and the words that Jesus had spoken." John 2:22, NIV.

Many others witnessed Christ's resurrection. More than 500 people either saw Him, talked with Him, walked with Him, or ate with Him after His resurrection. Even angels testified that Christ had risen!

Let us roll back the curtain of time and relive the last few hours of the crucifixion weekend. As three bruised bodies hung from crosses on Calvary's hill, the skies darkened, lightning flashed, the ground shook, and the veil in the temple split from top to bottom as Jesus triumphantly cried out, "It is finished." John 19:30, NIV. Later Pilate consented to the request of Joseph of Arimathea and Nicodemus to bury Jesus' body before sunset that Friday.

Matthew gives several interesting details about events that occurred the next day, the Sabbath. The chief priests and scribes remembered Jesus' prediction to rise on the third day, so they went to Pilate with a request: "Sir, we remember that that deceiver said, while he was yet alive, After three days I will rise again. Command therefore that the sepulchre be made sure until the third day, lest his disciples come by night, and steal him away, and say unto the people, He is risen from the dead." Matthew 27:63, 64.

Pilate sent a century of Roman soldiers to guard the tomb, but all the soldiers in the world could not have kept Him there! On Sunday morning "there was a great earthquake: for the angel of the Lord descended from heaven, and came and rolled back the stone from the door, and sat upon it. His countenance was like lightning, and his raiment white as snow: and for fear of him the keepers did shake, and became as dead men. And the angel answered and said unto the women, Fear not ye: for I know that ye seek Jesus, which was crucified. He is not here: for he is risen, as he said." Matthew 28:2-6.

Later that day Christ appeared to the disciples and

showed them His nail-scarred hands and pierced side. The Bible says that "the disciples were overjoyed when they saw the Lord." John 20:20, NIV.

Christ appeared to various people at various times and places. Paul, a contemporary of Christ, mentions some of these eyewitnesses of Christ after His resurrection:

"He appeared to Peter." 1 Corinthians 15:5, NIV.

"Then to the Twelve." 1 Corinthians 15:5, NIV.

"After that, he appeared to more than five hundred of the brothers at the same time." 1 Corinthians 15:6, NIV.

"Then he appeared to James." 1 Corinthians 15:7, NIV.

"Then to all the apostles." 1 Corinthians 15:7, NIV.

"And last of all he appeared to me also." 1 Corinthians 15:8, NIV.

These eyewitnesses to His resurrection provide evidence that Christ lives. However, Thomas was not with the other disciples when Christ appeared to them, and he said he would not believe Christ had risen unless he could put his hands in His pierced side and see the nail prints in His hands.

Later, Jesus appeared to the disciples with Thomas present. Jesus asked Thomas to look at His hands and feet and feel His side. Then Thomas said, "My Lord and my God." John 20:28. Jesus replied, "Thomas, because thou hast seen me, thou hast believed: blessed are they that have have not seen, and yet have believed." John 20:29.

Numerous first- and second-century historians add their testimony about the resurrection. Josephus, a Jewish historian of the first century A.D., wrote this fascinating passage:

"Now there was about this time Jesus, a wise man, if it be lawful to call him a man, for he was a doer of wonderful works,—a teacher of such men as receive the truth with pleasure. He drew over to him both many of the Jews and many of the Gentiles. He was [the] Christ; and when Pilate, at the suggestion of the principal men among us, had condemned him to the cross, those that loved him at the first did not forsake him, for he appeared to them alive again the third day, as the divine prophets had foretold these and ten thousand other wonderful things concerning him; and the tribe of Christians, so named from him, are not extinct at this day."—*Antiquities*, 18:3.3.

Josephus was a Jew, writing to please Romans. This story would hardly be pleasing to them! He surely would not have included it unless it were true. Christ's resurrection would have been the only motive for writing as he did.

And what motivated the disciples, cowering in despondence and doubt, hiding as they did behind locked doors, to rally and go forth proclaiming a crucified, risen, and coming Lord with unmitigated zeal and boldness? Surely, it could not have been a wrapped corpse in a tomb! It had to be a risen Christ!

What caused hundreds of thousands of Christian martyrs to courageously face death rather than recant? The answer is inscribed on the tombs in the catacombs of Rome: "Goodbye until we meet again." "Until tomorrow." Words etched in hope, for they believed the promise made by a risen Lord: "Because I live, ye shall live also." John 14:19.

The resurrection of Christ and the promised resurrection of His followers became the heart of the message proclaimed by His followers. In fact, on the day of Pentecost, Peter and the disciples set the city of Jerusalem aflame by boldly preaching a risen Christ. Peter said:

"Men of Israel, listen to this: Jesus of Nazareth was a man accredited by God to you by miracles, wonders and signs, which God did among you through him, as you yourselves know. This man was handed over to you . . . ; and you, with the help of wicked men, put him to death by nailing him to the cross. But God raised him from the dead." "We are all witnessess of the fact." Acts 2:22-24, 32, NIV. Stunned and deeply moved by Peter's inspired words, the crowd responded, "Men and brethren, what shall we do?" Acts 2:37. Peter replied, "Repent and be baptized." Acts 2:38, NIV.

To show that they believed in Christ's resurrection, His victory over sin and death, the Bible says, "Then they that gladly received his word were baptized: and the same day there were added unto them about three thousand souls." Acts 2:41.

The apostle Paul showed the true significance of baptism by paralleling it with the death, burial, and resurrection of Christ. "Don't you know that all of us who were baptized into Christ Jesus were baptized into his death? We were therefore buried with him through baptism into death in order that, just as Christ was raised from the dead through the glory of the Father, we too may live a new life." Romans 6: 3, 4, NIV.

Baptism to the early Christian was a public demonstration of his belief in the death, burial, and resurrection of Christ. Christ had washed away his sins. "Knowing this, that our old man is crucified with him, that the body of sin might be destroyed, that henceforth we should not serve sin." Romans 6:6.

Have you ever wished you could bury the past? Wipe out the mistakes and guilt and start over again? When the baptismal candidate repents and confesses his sins, he is placed under the water as a symbol of the death and burial of his old life of self and sin. Then he is raised from the watery grave to a new life in Christ, symbolizing the resurrection of our Lord.

What could more beautifully symbolize death to sin and the beginning of a new life than baptism by immersion?

Christian baptism had its origin with John the Baptist, a rugged prophet who appeared in the wilderness of Judea boldly preaching repentance. All roads leading to the Jordan River were crowded with people going to listen to him. The

Bible says, "Then went out to him Jerusalem, and all Judaea, and all the region round about Jordan, and were baptized of him in Jordan, confessing their sins." Matthew 3:5, 6.

Closing the door to His carpenter shop and bidding His mother farewell, Jesus also made His way to the Jordan. When John caught sight of Jesus, he recognized Him and said, "Behold the Lamb of God, which taketh away the sin of the world." John 1:29.

When Jesus asked to be baptized, John at first refused, saying, "I need to be baptized by you." Matthew 3:14, NIV. But Jesus insisted, "Let it be so now; it is proper for us to do this to fulfill all righteousness." Matthew 3:15, NIV.

John recognized that Jesus had no sinful past to confess. And Jesus certainly did not need to demonstrate His belief in His own resurrection! Jesus asked to be baptized because He wanted to identify with man. He wanted to leave us a perfect example to follow. So John immersed Jesus in the Jordan, for that is what the word *baptism* means. The Bible says that as soon as He was baptized, "he went up out of the water. At that moment heaven was opened, and he saw the Spirit of God descending like a dove and lighting on him. And a voice from heaven said, 'This is my Son, whom I love; with him I am well pleased.' " Matthew 3:16, 17, NIV.

On the wings of a dove God sent His love and words of encouragement to Jesus, but He did something else. As Jesus walked up out of the water and stood with dripping clothes on the muddy banks of the Jordan, God publicly introduced Him as His Son—the anointed One.

Christ's baptism marked the beginning of His public ministry, for Peter told Cornelius, "God anointed Jesus of Nazareth with the Holy Ghost and with power: who went about doing good, and healing all that were oppressed of the devil; for God was with him." Acts 10:38.

Jesus Himself did not baptize, but the Bible records that His disciples did: "The Pharisees heard that Jesus was gaining and baptizing more disciples than John, although in fact it was not Jesus who baptized, but his disciples." John 4:1, 2, NIV.

And notice Christ's last recorded command just before His ascension: "Go ye therefore, and teach all nations, baptizing them in the name of the Father, and of the Son, and of the Holy Ghost: teaching them to observe all things whatsoever I have commanded you: and, lo, I am with you alway, even unto the end of the world." Matthew 28:19, 20.

Perhaps you wonder what mode of baptism Jesus' followers practiced after He returned to heaven. No doubt they followed Jesus' example since they were His disciples. Paul, one of His most ardent followers, says that there is only "one Lord, one faith, one baptism." Ephesians 4:5.

The only detailed account of baptism after the cross is recorded in the book of Acts—a baptism conducted by Philip, the evangelist. As Philip walked along the dusty road to Gaza he saw an Ethiopian treasurer riding in an official chariot of that country. When the chariot stopped, Philip noticed that the official was reading from the scroll of the prophet Isaiah. The Ethiopian invited Philip to ride along with him and explain the meaning of Isaiah 53, which gave the details of the crucifixion of the Messiah. The Bible says, "Then Philip began with that very passage of Scripture and told him the good news about Jesus." Acts 8:35, NIV.

What a Bible study that must have been, bouncing along in that chariot! Not only did Philip tell about Jesus, but he evidently explained the significance of baptism, for the Bible says that when they came to a pool of water, the Ethiopian asked, "See, here is water; what doth hinder me to be baptized?" Acts 8:36. "Nothing," Philip said. "If thou believest with all thine heart, thou mayest." Acts 8:38. The Ethiopian official "ordered the chariot to stop. Then both Philip and the eunuch went down into the water and Philip baptized him." Acts 8:38, NIV.

Philip immersed the Ethiopian treasurer in the water just as John immersed Christ when He was baptized. The eunuch was anxious to demonstrate his acceptance of a risen Christ, and the Bible says that he "went on his way rejoicing." Acts 8:39, NIV.

That is what happens when we bury the old life of sin and start a new life in Christ!

Clearly, immersion was the mode of baptism practiced by the early Christian church. In fact, there is no evidence in the New Testament for any other method of baptism. Early church historians and findings by archaeologists both show that immersion was the mode of baptism until the twelfth and thirteenth centuries.

James Cardinal Gibbons wrote: "For several centuries after the establishment of Christianity Baptism was *usually* conferred by immersion; but since the twelfth century the practice of baptising by infusion has prevailed in the Catholic Church, as this manner is attended with less inconvenience than Baptism by immersion." "The Church exercises her discretion in adopting the most convenient mode, according to the circumstances of time and place."—*The Faith of Our Fathers,* 94th edition, page 277.

Many tourists today visit St. John's Church, located in the ruins of the biblical city of Ephesus in Turkey. This church was built as a memorial to the disciple John. The third general council of the church took place in this building in A.D. 431. Of special interest is the baptistry, circular in shape, about twelve feet in diameter and four feet deep, with stairs leading down into the font on two sides.

Baptism by immersion was still practiced in Ephesus in the fifth century. The Roman Catholic Church was still baptizing by immersion as late as the fourteenth century.

Most people have heard of the old bell tower in front of the Cathedral of Pisa in Italy, more commonly known as the Leaning Tower of Pisa. Along with the cathedral and the leaning tower is a baptistry, a round building that encloses a pool about twenty feet across and four feet deep that was constructed in the fourteenth century. Thirteen hundred years after Christ's ascension, the mode of baptism was still by immersion!

There are dozens of such cathedrals with large baptismal fonts in Europe. Sixty-six are found in Italy alone, whose construction dates between the fourth and fourteenth centuries.

But how important is the rite of baptism? Is it really necessary to be baptized? Jesus told Nicodemus, "Unless a man is born of water and the Spirit, he cannot enter the kingdom of God." John 3:5, NIV.

No doubt Nicodemus, the proud Pharisee, anticipated entrance into God's kingdom as a natural-born, devout Jew. However, Jesus made it clear that anything less than a complete transformation of life by the power of the Holy Spirit—as signified by water baptism—was inadequate. He said, "Whoever believes and is baptized will be saved." Mark 16:16, NIV. How can a Christian prepare for baptism? Jesus told His disciples, "Go ye therefore, and teach all nations, baptizing them." Matthew 28:19. Teaching precedes baptism. Jesus said the baptismal candidate is to be taught "to obey everything I have commanded you." Matthew 28:20, NIV. In other words, an individual preparing for the sacred rite of baptism needs to understand Jesus' teachings and be willing to obey them.

But more than a mere knowledge of doctrines is needed. There must be a commitment of one's life to Christ. When a person unites with Jesus, he naturally begins to live Christ's way. He does not want to do anything Jesus would not agree to.

The second step in preparing for baptism is total belief in Christ. When the Ethiopian asked Philip if he could be baptized, Philip said, "If thou believest with all thine heart, thou mayest." Acts 8:37.

The third step is repentance. Peter said, "Repent ye therefore, and be converted, that your sins may be blotted out." Acts 3:19. Repentance means to be deeply sorry for one's sins and to turn from them. This can only come from a heart that has been to Calvary, a heart touched and softened by the sacrifice made on the cross to save us from our sins.

Perhaps you have wished at times that you could change your life for the better—but you haven't known just how. By following these steps in preparation for baptism, you may truly become a new person—from the inside out. Through God's power you can be changed—reborn.

If you have not understood the meaning and importance of baptism before, or if you have not had the privilege of following Christ in this sacred ordinance of baptism by immersion, the same question and invitation is given to you that was given to the apostle Paul: "Why tarriest thou? arise, and be baptized, and wash away thy sins." Acts 22:16.

How Can I Live Longer and Be Healthier?

A young college student listened thoughtfully as her minister described the beauties and benefits of the earth made new. The promises he read seemed almost too good to be true. "God shall wipe away all tears from their eyes; and there shall be no more death, neither sorrow, nor crying, neither shall there be any more pain." Revelation 21:4. "The inhabitant shall not say, I am sick." Isaiah 33:24.

Greatly impressed, the young woman exclaimed, "Wow! That's wonderful! But, pastor, I'm interested in the here and now. I want more than just 'pie in the sky by and by.' Isn't God interested in what happens to me now? Do I have to wait for heaven to have health and happiness?"

That's a good question, especially when we consider soaring medical costs. It has been estimated that Americans spend more than $600 billion a year for medical care. Disease is the world's costliest commodity.

But how much is it worth to be well? Ask the terminal cancer patient or the person suffering from emphysema. Ask the parents of a child dying from leukemia or the older person deformed by arthritis. They will tell you that good health is priceless. That it is a blessing never fully appreciated until it is lost.

God is concerned about our health and happiness here and now. In the book of John we read, "Beloved, I wish

above all things that thou mayest prosper and be in health."
3 John 2. Jesus said, "I am come that they might have life,
and that they might have it more abundantly." John 10:10.

Jesus wants us to have a happy, joyous, exuberant life.
He wants us to live life to it fullest!

For decades the lifestyle of the Orthodox Jew has been of
considerable interest to medical researchers. Their cancer
mortality rate is far less than that of other Americans, and they
seem less prone to other catastrophic illnesses. Do Jewish
people have a hereditary factor that gives them immunity to
the leading killers which strike down other Americans?

It is interesting to note that when Jews become Ameri-
canized, living and eating as Americans, their cancer rate
and that of other diseases are the same as the average
American. The secret lies in their health practices, their nutrition and lifestyle.

When God brought the Israelites out of Egypt, He reminded them of some very important rules and regulations
concerning healthful living. After outlining His plan for good
health, He gave a most remarkable promise to those who
followed His instructions: "If thou wilt diligently hearken to
the voice of the Lord thy God, and wilt do that which is right
in his sight, and wilt give ear to his commandments, and
keep all his statutes, I will put none of these diseases upon
thee, which I have brought upon the Egyptians." Exodus
15:26.

What an amazing promise! Commenting on the fulfillment of this promise, the psalmist tells us, "There was not
one feeble person among their tribes." Psalm 105:37.

"Well," you say, "probably the Egyptians didn't have the
same diseases we have today."

A team of specialists from around the world gathered at
the Manchester Medical School in England in 1975 for the
express purpose of performing autopsies on the Egyptian
mummies in that museum. These mummies dated back to

1900 B.C. The findings were remarkable. The ancient Egyptians suffered from many illnesses common to modern man: heart disease, cancer, vascular diseases, arthritis, hepatitis, tetanus, trichinosis, et cetera.

Although Egypt was the educational and cultural center of the world during Moses' lifetime, its medical knowledge and remedies were very similar to those of the African witch doctor today! In 1552 B.C., not long before the birth of Moses, a famous medical book was written in Egypt called the Papyrus Ebers. This book lists scores of remedies or "cures" for a host of diseases, infections, and accidents.

For slivers embedded deep in the tissue it recommends rubbing worm's blood and horse dung into the wound. Small wonder that lockjaw took a hefty toll! For snake bite, Papyrus Ebers recommended drinking water poured over an idol. The person who had lost his hair was told to rub into his scalp a tonic made from horses' hoofs, date blossoms, and dog heels boiled in oil!

The Bible tells us that "Moses was educated in all the wisdom of the Egyptians." Acts 7:22, NIV. His writings are filled with instruction concerning sanitation, quarantine, personal hygiene, and nutrition, but not once did he prescribe any of the cures listed in Papyrus Ebers.

The reason is simple. The Egyptians, like many physicians today, were concerned with *cures.* God is concerned with *prevention.*

Black death and leprosy were the two most terrible plagues of the Middle Ages. It was the principles of public health, given by God and taught by Moses after the Exodus, that finally brought these scourges under control. Millions of lives were saved as scientists turned to the church leaders for help during these plagues. George Rosen wrote:

"Leadership was taken by the Church, as the physicians had nothing to offer. The Church took as its guiding principle the concept of contagion as embodied in the Old Testament. . . . This idea and its practical consequences are defined with great clarity in the book of Leviticus."—George Rosen, M.D. *History of Public Health,* pages 63-65. What a shame that 60 million people died from these plagues when the Bible principles of public health were there all the time! God designed our bodies. He knows exactly how they function. He understands the principles necessary to keep us in good health. He knows how we can avoid disease.

When we purchase a new car we receive an owner's manual. It tells what fuel to use, which oil to put in the crankcase, and when it should be changed. It suggests how often to service the car and how to drive it to secure optimum performance.

Manufacturers give us an owner's manual to help us keep the car in the best operating condition. They made it, and they know how it works best. Given the high cost of repairs, most of us try hard to follow the manufacturer's recommendations so we can avoid a trip to a garage.

That's how it is with our bodies. God gave man a wonderful body with almost limitless possibilities. It has many delicate parts to care for. God made us, and He knows exactly what is necessary to keep our bodies healthly and operating at peak efficiency. We certainly want to follow His instructions! One trip to the hospital can wipe out a lifetime of savings, so let's go back to the Garden of Eden and notice some of the things God told Adam and Eve that can promote good health. The Bible says that after God created them, He gave them work to do—some useful activity and exercise. "And the Lord God took the man, and put him into the garden of Eden to dress it and to keep it." Genesis 2:15. After Adam sinned, God increased his work: "In the sweat of thy face shalt thou eat bread, till thou return unto the ground." Genesis 3:19.

Perhaps Adam did not understand that an inactive body deteriorates. Exercise improves the tone of the muscles and blood vessels. The lungs become more efficient, able to process more air with less effort. The heart is more efficient, pumping more blood with each beat. Energy-producing oxygen is carried to the tissues, which improves the overall condition of the body.

Exercise protects the body from many diseases and slows down the aging process.

Before sin came, God gave Adam and Eve a perfect diet to sustain and promote their health. "God said, Behold, I have given you every herb bearing seed, which is upon the face of all the earth, and every tree, in the which is the fruit of a tree yielding seed; to you it shall be for meat." Genesis 1:29. In modern language we would say they were given fruit, grains, and nuts. This was their food.

God also gave them the right to eat of the tree of life, which was in the Garden of Eden. This fruit supplied their diet with a special life-giving substance that insured eternal youth and health. After Adam and Eve sinned, God separated them from the tree of life and added vegetables to their diet: "Thou shalt eat the herb of the field." Genesis 3:18. This was man's total diet until the Flood. It must have been a very good diet, for the people before the Flood lived to be hundreds of years old. The oldest man that ever lived was Methuselah: "All the days of Methuselah were nine hundred sixty and nine years: and he died." Genesis 5:27.

After the Flood, man's life span decreased markedly. Noah's son, Shem, lived 600 years, his grandson 239 years, his great-grandson 175 years. By the time of King David, man's life span had decreased to 70 years.

The Flood destroyed plant life on the earth, and Noah's supply of food was exhausted after he and his family had lived in the ark for a year and ten days. So God allowed Noah and his family to eat animals as an emergency measure. See Genesis 9:3, 4.

Of course, not all plants and animals were good for

food. God gave certain guidelines for the food He considered to be good for man to eat. There was a distinction between "clean" and "unclean" animals. It is interesting to note that this distinction did not originate during the time of Moses. God instructed Noah which animals to take with him into the ark, and how many of the clean and unclean. "Of every clean beast thou shalt take to thee by sevens, the male and his female: and of beasts that are not clean by two, the male and his female." Genesis 7:2.

Evidently Noah knew which animals God considered clean or unclean. Otherwise, God would not have given him those instructions.

After God brought the Israelites out of Egypt He gave Moses dietary principles and regulations to protect their health and longevity. Leviticus 11 and Deuteronomy 14 give the first instruction regarding clean and unclean animals as food. Deuteronomy 14 gives a list of the animals, fowl, and fish God said were clean to use for food. "These are the beasts which ye shall eat: the ox, the sheep, and the goat, the hart, and the roebuck, and the fallow deer, and the wild goat, and the pygarg, and the wild ox, and the chamois." Deuteronomy 14:4, 5.

God explained how to identify which animals are clean and which are unclean for food: "And every beast that parteth the hoof . . . and cheweth the cud among the beasts, that ye shall eat." Deuteronomy 14:6.

If the animal chews the cud and parts the hoof it is safe for food. However, some chew the cud but do not part the hoof, "as the camel, and the hare, and the coney: for they chew the cud, but divide not the hoof; therefore they are unclean unto you. And the swine, because it divideth the hoof, yet cheweth not the cud, it is unclean unto you: ye shall not eat of their flesh, nor touch their dead carcase." Deuteronomy 14:7, 8.

Study this list of animals carefully, and you will see why

they were classified as unclean. Most of them are scavengers. God did not arbitrarily withhold something good when He gave these guidelines in the Bible. He knows which are healthful and which will cause disease and illness. "No good thing will he withhold from them that walk uprightly." Psalm 84:11.

Some people say, "But I love my ham and bacon. They taste so good! Why doesn't God want us to eat swine?"

The hog is a scavenger. The garbage eaten by pigs is digested and converted into food in a matter of hours. The cow, on the other hand, has a complex digestive system. It takes forty-eight hours for its food to be converted into flesh. It also has a more complex and refined elimination system, which removes many of the impurities from the system.

Pork is often infected with trichina larvae, or worms. When a person eats infected pork, the hard cyst surrounding the larva is dissolved. The trichina worm then burrows into the intestinal wall and multiplies. These worms enter the bloodstream and are carried to other parts of the body. Trichinosis can be a fatal disease, depending on the number of worms eaten. Often the disease is wrongly diagnosed as arthritis or food poisoning. Nor is trichinosis a disease of modern times only. Autopsies reveal that many mummies were infected with trichina worms!

God also gave instructions about which fish were good for food and which should be avoided: "These shall ye eat of all that are in the waters: whatsoever hath fins and scales in the waters, in the seas, and in the rivers, them shall ye eat. And all that have not fins and scales in the seas, . . . of all that move in the waters, and of any living thing which is in the waters, they shall be an abomination unto you." Leviticus 11:9, 10.

Dr. Bruce Hallsted spent years doing research for the army and navy health services to determine which fish were safe for human consumption and which were poisonous.

Servicemen who are shipwrecked or stranded in deserted areas need to know which fish are poisonous and which they can eat for survival. In 1965 his work was printed in three large volumes by the United States Government Printing Office. After all the research was done, Dr. Hallsted concluded that the rule of thumb for army and navy men to follow was the same one God gave to the Israelites 3,500 years ago: "Of all the creatures living in the water, you may eat any that has fins and scales." Deuteronomy 14:9, NIV.

God placed yet another restriction on man's diet: "It shall be a perpetual statute for your generations throughout all your dwellings, that ye eat neither fat nor blood." Leviticus 3:17. Orthodox Jews still follow these instructions today. When an animal is slaughtered, it is hung upside down so that the blood will drain out. Then the animal is butchered and soaked in a salt solution to draw out the rest of the blood. The fat is cut off the meat.

For years people thought this command forbidding the eating of fat and blood was merely a ceremonial restriction given by God. However, modern research confirms the wisdom of God's command. We now know that blood carries impurities: germs, viruses, and body wastes. Many diseases are passed on through the blood. We also know that highly saturated fats like those found in meat and dairy products cause a rise in the cholesterol level of the blood—an important factor in vascular and heart diseases.

How much sickness could be avoided if man would trust his Maker in deciding what is best to eat!

The importance of caring for our bodies can be understood only when we know what God has said in the Bible. The apostle Paul said, "What? know ye not that your body is the temple of the Holy Ghost which is in you, which ye have of God, and ye are not your own?" 1 Corinthians 6:19. Paul explains why we are not our own: "Ye are bought with a price: therefore glorify God in your body, and in your spirit, which are God's." 1 Corinthians 6:20.

Man is God's property by creation and by redemption. The price God paid for us was the sacrifice of His Son on Calvary. Because man has been redeemed at such an infinite price, he is obligated to glorify God in everything he does. "Whether you eat or drink or whatsoever you do, do it all for the glory of God." 1 Corinthians 10:31, NIV.

Every person who truly loves God will be careful to avoid anything that would destroy or defile his body. "If any man defile the temple of God, him shall God destroy; for the temple of God is holy, which temple ye are." 1 Corinthians 3:17.

Perhaps you wonder how we can defile our bodies. Paul lists several ways. "Be not deceived: neither fornicators, nor idolaters, nor adulterers, nor effeminate, nor abusers of themselves with mankind, . . . nor drunkards, . . . shall inherit the kingdom of God." 1 Corinthians 6:9, 10.

The Bible lists immorality and perversion as practices that defile the body. It also lists drunkenness. Solomon wrote: "Wine is a mocker, strong drink is raging: and whosoever is deceived thereby is not wise." Proverbs 20:1. And again: "Look not thou upon the wine when it is red, when it giveth his colour in the cup, when it moveth itself aright. At the last it biteth like a serpent, and stingeth like an adder. Thine eyes shall behold strange women, and thine heart shall utter perverse things." Proverbs 23:31-33.

Alcoholism is America's biggest health problem. More than half of all automobile accidents can be traced directly to a driver or pedestrian "under the influence." In more than half of all murders in the United States, either the killer or the victim, or both, have been drinking!

Alcohol impairs the body's ability to use vitamins, and the sugar in alcoholic drinks (as in most soft drinks) lessens the body's ability to fight infection. The alcoholic develops a fatty liver, and his chances of dying from cirrhosis of the liver are great. His life span is shortened by at least twelve years. And according to the latest statistics, one out of every ten who take the first drink becomes an alcoholic.

Recent research shows that a large number of brain cells die any time alcohol is introduced into the bloodstream and that drinking fathers and mothers have a significantly greater number of babies born with birth defects than do nondrinkers. But for the Christian, the use of alcoholic beverages has even greater consequences. Christians must have full use of their minds to avoid Satan's temptations. They cannot afford to impair their judgment or lose control of their ability to distinguish right from wrong.

Jesus refused the stupefying potion offered Him on the cross by the soldiers as a means of deadening the pain. Even though Jesus suffered excruciating pain, He would receive nothing that might becloud His mind.

A number of other common practices seriously impair good health. Those who smoke have a 1,000 percent greater chance of dying from lung cancer than do those who never smoked. And cancer is not tobacco's only killer. A smoker's chances of dying from heart disease are 103 percent greater than those who have never smoked on a regular basis. And emphysema claims more than 55,000 lives each year.

Research has shown that nicotine increases the buildup of cholesterol (the major cause of heart disease) along the inner walls of the arteries.

"Nicotine also causes the arteries to shrink. This combination of fat buildup and shrinkage of the arteries hinders the blood vessels from supplying enough blood to the heart, brain, extremities, and other organs. As the condition becomes worse, tissue damage often results.

"At this point it takes only a small blood clot caught in the constricted blood vessels to cause a heart attack or stroke."—How to Stop Smoking Without Gaining Weight, (a supplement of *These Times* magazine), page 10.

The person who smokes is also a prime target for senility because of diminished oxygen to the brain. And smoking also poses risks to unborn children: "Women who smoke during pregnancy are damaging their babies' blood vessels, a Danish cardiologist warned . . . at an international symposium in Chicago. . . . If you smoke yourself, you harm yourself. But the unborn child can't do anything about it—it has to smoke if you do."—*Chicago Tribune*, October 20, 1978.

The detrimental effects of smoking mothers on children include restricted fetal movement, growth retardation, and an increased chance of respiratory illness later in life—all due to nicotine and a diminished oxygen supply in the mother's blood. Newborn deaths are 27 percent higher in the infants of smoking mothers.

Cigarette smoking will contribute to the deaths of more than 300,000 Americans this year. That is six times as many deaths as occurred in Vietnam in ten years! Dr. Linus Pauling has said that every cigarette a person smokes takes fourteen and a half minutes off his life. God said, "Thou shalt not kill." Exodus 20:13.

Yet, how many people are killing themselves by the things they eat, drink, and smoke. Someone has said that the most common suicide weapons are knives, forks, and spoons; perhaps we need to include cups too.

"Caffeine, the drug contained in coffee, is classed in textbooks as both a stimulant and a poison. The fatal dose is listed as one-third ounce (10 grams). It would require the amount of caffeine contained in 80 to 100 ordinary cups of coffee, then, to prove fatal if taken in a single dose by mouth."—Harold Shryock, M.D., *You and Your Health*, vol. 1, page 413.

Tea and cola drinks also contain caffeine. All of these beverages are now being linked with heart disease, neurological disorders, and cancer of the bladder. If someone you knew had to dash off to another room to inject a couple of grains of caffeine into his veins every few hours, you would call him an addict. Yet how many are doing the same thing with coffee and cola drinks?

True temperance means to avoid using anything that is harmful, and to use moderately that which is good. Many people consume too much of that which is good, and this leads to another major health problem of the Western world: overweight.

"Someone has estimated that every pound of body fat calls for another two-thirds of a mile of new blood vessels. And the heart must pump blood through this extra system of vessels."—Harold Shryock, M.D., *You and Your Health,* vol 1, page 395.

The heart, kidneys, liver, and lungs of overweight persons are overworked. Overweight people suffer from sixteen diseases that are not common to their thinner friends.

One of the enemies of good health is the large amount of refined sugar consumed by Americans. In 1822, Americans consumed two teaspoons of sugar per day. By 1905 it was 20 teaspoons per day, and today's average American uses 34 teaspoons of sugar each day of the year. American consumption of sugar is higher than any other country in the world.

"Oh," you say, "I don't eat much sugar." Have you ever added up the amount you eat in one day? It may surprise you! Notice just a few items which the average American eats daily:

A piece of pie: 14 teaspoons of sugar.
Bottle of pop: 8 teaspoons of sugar.
Candy bar: 7 teaspoons of sugar.
Banana split: 24 teaspoons of sugar.
Doughnut: 6 teaspoons of sugar.

Pancake and syrup: 15 teaspoons of sugar.
Sugared cereal: 6 teaspoons of sugar.

If you eat sugar when you are ill it will be harder for your body to get rid of its infection. Sugar lowers the ability of white blood cells to destroy bacteria, thus reducing your resistance to infection. God wants us to take good care of our bodies so we can enjoy life at its best here and now. He wants us to be responsible, moral, joyous people. He wants us to have an abundant life—life in all its fullness. But how long and how healthfully we live depends on how we follow His instructions.

He wants us to be temperate not only in what we eat and drink, but in every other part of life. For example, He asks us to balance work with rest and relaxation. That is why He gave us the Sabbath. He knew that we need to forget our problems and our work and spend time with Him.

Jesus believed in vacations—getting away from the pressures and resting in a quiet place. After a hard day with the multitude, Jesus said to His disciples, "Come ye yourselves apart into a desert place, and rest a while." Mark 6:31. Your time away from a busy schedule may not be in the desert, although that can be a beautiful place at certain times of the year. But you may prefer a remote mountain area where the tall trees and deep lakes can calm your anxious heart. Wherever it is, you need to find a spot away from the crowded city and noisy freeways. If you can have fun at the same time, so much the better!

Yes, God wants you to have a little bit of heaven here and now and to be ready to live in the earth made new, where all the diseases and illnesses that plague our world will be forever banished.

"That really sounds good to me," you say. "I want to be there, but I have some habits that I just can't overcome."

There is good news today! God does not expect you to

do it on your own. In fact, Jesus said, "Without me, ye can do nothing." John 15:5. In our own strength we cannot overcome wrong habits. Our Saviour is right there, longing to help us.

Paul knew the secret. He said, "I can do all things through Christ which strengtheneth me." Philippians 4:13. With His help you can live an abundant, healthy, joyful life here and now, and enjoy eternal life on the earth made new, "by and by."

How Can I Know What Is Truth?

Mankind is born with an inexpressible craving for something he does not have. Subconsciously he seeks something he cannot describe, but which he knows he wants and needs.

Carl Jung once said that man was created with a "God-shaped vacuum," and Augustine echoed his analysis: "Thou has made us for Thyself, O God, and our hearts are restless till they find their rest in thee."

Like frightened mice in a maze, man seems to be running up one corridor and down another in his unending quest for inner peace, but the corridors are all dead-end! So man in his restless boredom seeks to fill the void in his life with fame, fortune, material possessions, and leisure-time activities, only to discover when the prize is won that there is no lasting satisfaction.

Sooner or later chances are that in a lonely night of sleeplessness, the haunting question of an ancient prophet will echo from the past: "Why do you spend . . . your labor for that which does not satisfy?" Isaiah 55:2, RSV. Jesus understood the transitory satisfaction of possessing "things." He said, "A man's life does not consist in the abundance of his possessions." Luke 12:15, RSV.

Men today are weary of chasing elusive rainbows. They sense the need of a power outside themselves. God allowed the children of Israel in the wilderness to become hungry so they would recognize their need of Him: "He humbled thee, and suffered thee to hunger, ... that he might make thee know that man doth not live by bread only, but by every word that proceedeth out of the mouth of the Lord." Deuteronomy 8:3.

God allows modern man to sense a restlessness, an inner hunger, so that he will reach out and let God satisfy his longings. Today we see a great interest in various forms of religion. New churches are rapidly springing up across America. In fact, *Melton's Encyclopedia* lists 1,187 "primary" denominations in the United States alone, plus hundreds more that have split off the mainline churches! *Time* magazine, reporting on these sects and schisms, stated:

"What in heaven's name are the Church of the Four Leaf Clover, the Church of the Fuller Concept, and the Psychedelic Venus Church? Or the Infinite Way, the Faithists, Pragmatic Mysticism, and Soulcraft, Inc.? Answer: just a handful of the U.S. denominations described in an unbelievable compendium called the *Encyclopedia of American Religions*."—*Time*, July 16, 1979.

Some of these religious groups draw large numbers of young people to their cause. You see them on sidewalks and in airports selling flowers, candles, or ginseng tea. Others congregate on street corners chanting to the rhythm of tinkling bells and monotonous drumbeats.

Preachers from storefront churches or TV and radio programs claim to be teaching the one true faith. Catholicism has found a new vitality since the days of the charismatic Pope John XXIII. As today's pope makes his way around the world, millions jam the streets to honor him. In Chicago the worshiping crowd sang, "He's got the whole world in his hands." In the Middle East, Ayatollah Khomeini has sparked an incredible Islamic revival. Mormons, Jehovah's Witnessess, Pentecostals, and Seventh-day Adventists are multiplying at record rates.

Each of these religions claims to present God's truth for today. Each claims to be God's special people with a message of guidance for everyone on Earth. Each says, "We are the one!" "This is the truth." Yet the briefest consideration of those claims makes it obvious that they cannot all be true. For while each claims the Bible as the foundation for its beliefs, their teachings are most divergent.

How can the man on the street ever sort out the claims and counterclaims of these religious organizations and know for certain what is the real thing? Does God really have a special group within Christendom that He recognizes as His church today? Evidently so, for Paul wrote, "There is but one body and one Spirit—just as you were called to one hope when you were called—one Lord, one faith, one baptism; one God and Father of all." Ephesians 4:4, 5, NIV.

The Reverend John Milner says, "There is but one inquiry to be made, namely, 'Which is the true church?' . . . By solving this one question . . . you will at once solve every question of religious controversy that ever has ever been, or that ever can be agitated."—*The End of Religious Controversy*, page 95.

That's quite a statement! Perhaps Reverend Milner has placed his finger on the heart of the question which occupies the quiet moments of millions. But where do we start? There are so many denominations, and there is so much confusion in the religious community. Why didn't God make it easier to sort it all out so that a person could quickly find His last-day church?

According to Scripture, Jesus never intended that there should be so much confusion, and certainly not all these denominations. Just before His crucifixion He prayed, "that they may all be one. Father! May they be in us, just as you are in me and I am in you. May they be one, so that the world will believe that you sent me." John 17:21, TEV.

Jesus wanted the world to recognize His followers by their unity and love. He did not want any divisions in His church. In fact, Paul wrote, "there should be no schism in the body." 1 Corinthians 12:25. However, he also pointed out that apostasy would come, and with it division! We read:

"Take heed therefore unto yourselves, and all the flock, . . . to feed the church of God. . . . For I know this, that after my departing shall grievous wolves enter in among you, not sparing the flock. Also of your own selves shall men arise, speaking perverse things, to draw away disciples after them." Acts 20:28-30.

As we turn the pages of church history, we discover that false teachers did arise. Some people accepted their heresies and left. Others became confused. Disciples were drawn away, and there was a gradual branching off from the original body. Yet through it all God has had a church that remained faithful to the teachings of Christ.

"But," you say, "Wouldn't it take a lifetime to study in depth the teachings of every religion to find which is God's true church?" Indeed it would. But there is a simpler way, a better way.

Secret Service agents tell us that it is quite easy to distinguish a genuine dollar bill from a counterfeit. They study the characteristics of the genuine bill in depth. They know the fiberous texture of the paper, the color and fastness of the ink, the symbols, and the proper order of serial numbers of genuine dollar bills. As they examine a particular bill, they can quickly compare it with the distinguishing features they have learned about the genuine. If it lacks any one of these characteristics, it is a counterfeit.

And it is the same with God's church. You don't have to spend exhaustive hours studying the teachings of every denomination and schism in order to discover the characteristics of God's true church. God does not leave man to guess which one it is, for He has given us the facts in His Word: "Surely the Lord God will do nothing, but he revealeth his secret unto his servants the prophets." Amos 3:7.

Revelation, which is perhaps the most compelling prophetic book in the Bible, predicts the apostasy and religious confusion that exists in these last days of Earth's history. It foretells the conflict between Christ's church and Satan. Chapter 12 gives a panoramic view of church history from Christ's time to the end of the world: "There appeared a great wonder in heaven; a woman clothed with the sun, and the moon under her feet, and upon her head a crown of twelve stars: And she being with child cried, travailing in birth, and pained to be delivered." Revelation 12:1, 2.

Here God pictures a woman in white, clothed with the sun, standing on the moon with a crown of twelve stars on her head. What does it all mean? In Bible prophecy a woman represents God's people—His church. The prophet Jeremiah wrote: "I have likened the daughter of Zion to a comely and delicate woman." Jeremiah 6:2. And who is "Zion"? Through Isaiah God said, "Say unto Zion, Thou art my people." Isaiah 51:16.

As we link these two texts, we see that God used a virtuous woman to represent His true church. The apostle Paul uses the same terminology to describe the Corinthian church: "I have espoused you to one husband, that I may present you as a chaste virgin to Christ." 2 Corinthians 11:2.

However, John was also shown another woman, which he describes in Revelation 17: "I saw a woman sit upon a scarlet coloured beast, full of names of blasphemy. . . . And the woman was arrayed in purple and scarlet colour, and decked with gold and precious stones and pearls, having a golden cup in her hand full of abominations and filthiness of her fornication: And upon her forehead was a name written, MYSTERY, BABYLON THE GREAT, THE MOTHER OF

HARLOTS AND ABOMINATIONS OF THE EARTH." Revelation 17:3-5.

This symbolic language describes an impure, adulterous woman—the false church, or that part of Christianity which has been unfaithful to Christ and has compromised in its relationship to the world. James used similar words to describe those who forsake God's teachings and join the world: "Ye adulterers and adulteresses, know ye not that the friendship of the world is enmity with God?" James 4:4.

A fallen woman, then, represents a false church, and a pure woman represents a pure church.

Let's look again at the prophecy of the pure woman. "She being with child cried, travailing in birth, and pained to be delivered." "And the dragon stood before the woman which was ready to be delivered, for to devour her child as soon as it was born." Revelation 12:2, 4.

Who is this dragon that stood before the woman to devour her child as soon as he was born? "There was war in heaven: Michael and his angels fought ... and the dragon fought and his angels." "And the great dragon was cast out, that old serpent, called the Devil, and Satan, which deceiveth the whole world: he was cast out into the earth, and his angels were cast out with him." Revelation 12:7, 9.

Revelation also describes the child: "She brought forth a man child, who was to rule all nations with a rod of iron: and her child was caught up unto God, and his throne." Revelation 12:5.

Only one child in the history of the world was to "rule all nations with a rod of iron," and be "caught up unto God, and to his throne," and that was Jesus. Speaking of the second coming of Christ, John said, "Out of his mouth goeth a sharp sword, and with it he should smite the nations: and he shall rule them with a rod of iron." Revelation 19:15.

Paul tells how Jesus was "caught up unto God's throne," when God "raised him from the dead, and set him at his own right hand in the heavenly places." Ephesians 1:20.

The war that began in heaven moved to our world. Working through pagan Rome, Satan tried to take Jesus' life as soon as He was born. Herod, the Roman governor, decreed that all male children two years and under should be killed, but an angel warned Mary and Joseph to escape with Jesus into Egypt.

The devil dogged Jesus' steps throughout His ministry, hoping to block God's plan to save the fallen world. As Christ's body hung on the cross, Satan thought he had won the battle. But an empty tomb was Satan's Waterloo. Christ arose and ascended to His Father's throne. The prophecy was on schedule, just as predicted.

Failing in his attempt to destroy God's Son, Satan turned his wrath on the woman, or the Christian church. All but one of Christ's disciples died a martyr's death. Paul was beheaded outside the walls of Rome. Christians were tortured and thrown in dungeons, many sealing their testimony with their blood. As long as the apostles were alive the church stood firmly for the truth. But with second- and third-generation Christians came compromise and apostasy. "Toward the latter end of the second century, most of the churches assumed a new form; the first simplicity disappeared as the old disciples retired to their graves."—*Ecclesiastical Research*, page 51.

In the fourth century, Emperor Constantine tried to hold the Roman Empire together by uniting pagans and Christians in one great system of religion. As a result, Christianity lost much of its old stigma, becoming, in fact, very popular. Heathen people were baptized into the church who brought many of their pagan beliefs and practices with them. One historian wrote, "The new Christians were, as far as thinking and habits went, the same old pagans. . . . Their surge into the churches did not wipe out paganism. On the contrary, hordes of baptized pagans meant that paganism had diluted the moral energies of organized Christianity to the point of impotence."—*Centuries of Christianity: A Concise History*, page 58.

However, during this time many Christians remained faithful to God's truths and protested the changes that had crept into the church. They refused to compromise their position, and many were persecuted for their stand. Soon the Roman emperors issued edicts making it a crime punishable by death to reject the false practices of the state church. Historian Archibald Bower writes, "Great numbers were driven from their habitations with their wives and children, stripped and naked ... [and] many of them [were] inhumanly massacred."—*The History of the Popes*, volume 2, page 334.

Foreseeing it all, John wrote, "The dragon ... persecuted the woman which brought forth the man child." Revelation 12:13. And what happened to the woman? She "fled into the desert to a place prepared for her by God, where she might be taken care of for 1,260 days." Revelation 12:6, NIV.

Notice that God tells the time that His people were to be persecuted: 1,260 days. We have already discovered that each day in Bible prophecy stand for a year of literal time. Ezekiel wrote, "I have appointed thee each day for a year." Ezekiel 4:6. So the oppression of God's faithful people, as predicted in Revelation, was to continue for 1,260 years.

History accurately confirms this Bible prophecy. Justinian ordered the Roman general, Belisarius, to wipe out three Arian powers that opposed the church in Rome. The last of these powers was eliminated in 538 A.D., and Justinian declared the bishop of Rome to be "the head of the church, the true and effectual corrector of heretics." The reign of intolerance for so-called "heretics" began. Faithful Christians who continued to cherish the truths revealed in God's Word found that the only way to preserve their faith was to flee, just as Revelation predicted. The woman fled into the wilderness.

The Waldenses, Albigenses, Huguenots, and other faithful Christians fled to the Alps in northern Italy and southern France, settling in secluded valleys, remote caves, and high mountains. They were hunted down as common criminals, and many were slain. Their crime? They would not give up the teachings of Jesus. Millions of Christians died rather than compromise their faith. Some historians estimate the death toll to be as high as 50 million. And many of those who died were martyred by other professed Christians who believed they were doing the will of God!

God's truth finally triumphed. The Bible, long chained to monastery walls and cathedral pulpits, was translated into the language of the common people and scattered throughout the world. No longer was God's truth to be hidden. It must be revealed!

Courageous Reformers boldly proclaimed God's Word. Some, like Huss and Jerome, were burned at the stake. Others, like Luther, Wycliffe, and Tyndale, were hunted and persecuted. However, with the discovery of America, new freedom and a new refuge were provided for the persecuted Christians of Europe. On the shores of a newborn nation was laid the foundation of civil and religious liberty. France commemorated America's freedom by presenting the Statue of Liberty to the people of the United States. Inscribed on the pedestal of the statue are these words:

Give me your tired, your poor,
Your huddled masses yearning to breathe free,
The wretched refuse of your teeming shore,
Send these, the homeless, tempest-tossed, to me:
I lift my lamp beside the golden door.

The era of compromise and persecution predicted in Revelation 12 finally came to an end in 1798, when the atheistic government of Napoleon sent General Berthier to take the Pope captive—exactly 1,260 years after the period of persecution began in 538.

At the end of the eighteenth century, when this prophetic time period came to a close, God still had a group of faithful believers who clung to the Bible and its teachings. The prophecy foretold that Satan turned his fury upon the church of God that remained after this prophetic period: "The dragon was wroth with the woman, and went to make war with the remnant of her seed." Revelation 12:17.

"What does John mean by "the remnant" of the woman's seed? Most women are familiar with a remnant. All the yardage on a bolt of cloth is the same pattern, the same color, and the same texture, but when all the cloth has been sold except a yard or so it is called a remnant, meaning the last part of the bolt.

This illustration makes it easy to understand what the prophecy meant by the remnant of the church. It is the last part of the original church—God's last-day church. Translating Revelation 12:17 literally, we would say, "The devil was angry . . . and went to make war with the last-day church." Satan is furious that God's people still follow God's truths in these last days.

John describes two characteristics by which we can recognize this remnant, last-day church: "The dragon was wroth with the woman, and went to make war with the remnant of her seed, which keep the commandments of God, and have the testimony of Jesus Christ." Revelation 12:17. "The remnant" are those who *keep the commandments of God*—not only the Ten Commandments, but all the commands given in God's Word.

But doesn't every church teach that Christians should obey God's commands? Yes, but many religious bodies today teach their members, in one way or another, to disobey some of God's instructions. For example, some congregations are taught to bow before images. Others ignore the sacredness of God's name. And most of the religious world has lost sight of the memorial of creation described in the fourth commandment: "Remember the sabbath day, to keep it holy. Six days shalt thou labour, and do all thy work: But the seventh day is the sabbath of the Lord thy God." Exodus 20:8-10.

Try something. Drive down the street on a Saturday morning, the seventh day of the week, and look for a church that keeps the fourth commandment. You'll do a lot of looking. For, you see, that is one of the distinguishing characteristics of God's true church.

Not only was God's remnant, or last-day, church to keep the commandments of God, but the prophecy also says that it will "have the testimony of Jesus." Revelation 12:17. John tells us that "the testimony of Jesus is *the spirit of prophecy.*" Revelation 19:10, emphasis supplied. God's last-day church will have the gifts of the Spirit, including the spirit of prophecy.

God gives several other characteristics to help us in our search for His last-day church. His people will be engaged in the mission of reaching the world with the gospel, for Jesus commissioned His church: "Go ye therefore, and teach all nations, baptizing them in the name of the Father, and of the Son, and of the Holy Ghost: teaching them to observe all things whatsoever I have commanded you: and, lo, I am with you alway, even unto the end of the world. Amen." Matthew 28:19, 20.

The command to preach the everlasting gospel in all the world is symbolized in Revelation 14 by three angels flying in the heavens. The first part of this three-fold message emphasizes two great truths to be shared with every person:

"I saw another angel fly in the midst of heaven, having the everlasting gospel to preach unto them that dwell on the earth, to every nation, and kindred, and tongue, and people,

Saying with a loud voice, Fear God, and give glory to him; for the hour of his judgment is come: and worship him that made heaven, and earth, and the sea, and fountains of waters." Revelation 14:6, 7.

This is a warning to those living in Earth's last hours to remember that the day of judgment has come. It is also a reminder of the great memorial of God's creative power, the seventh-day Sabbath.

The second part of this three-fold message is found in verse 8: "There followed another angel, saying, Babylon is fallen, is fallen, that great city, because she made all nations drink of the wine of the wrath of her fornication." Revelation 14:8. This message calls God's true people to separate from the confused religious world. Their attention is to be called to the apostasy in religion today.

The last, and most solemn, appeal is given in the third portion of this prophecy: "The third angel followed them, saying with a loud voice, If any man worship the beast and his image, and receive his mark in his forehead, or in his hand, The same shall drink of the wine of the wrath of God." Revelation 14:9, 10. The world is to be warned against worshiping the beast and his image or receiving his mark. The reception of any of the three brings the seven last plagues.

Jesus said, "Other sheep I have, which are not of this fold: them also I must bring, and they shall hear my voice; and there shall be one fold, and one shepherd." John 10:16. God has faithful followers in all churches, but there will come a time when there will be one fold, or one church.

Jesus said His sheep will have to be called out of these other folds that have not carefully followed the teachings of God's Word. John the revelator predicted that time: "I heard another voice from heaven, saying, Come out of her, my people, that ye be not partakers of her sins, and that ye receive not of her plagues." Revelation 18:4.

God's faithful followers will be called out of the religious error and confusion that exists at the end of time. His people are identified in Revelation 14: "Here is the patience of the saints: here are they that keep the commandments of God, and the faith of Jesus." "And I looked, and behold a white cloud, and upon the cloud one sat like unto the Son of man, having on his head a golden crown, and in his hand a sharp sickle." Revelation 14:12, 14.

Let's briefly review some of the distinguishing characteristics of God's last-day church as given in the Bible:

1. God's remnant church was to appear after the period of terrible persecution which ended in 1798.
2. They will have the faith of Jesus which leads them to keep all the commandments of God.
3. They will proclaim the special warning messages of Revelation to all the world to prepare a people for Jesus' return.
4. They will have the gifts of the Spirit, including the gift of prophecy.

All churches may look alike at first glance, but as you study God's description of the genuine in His Holy Word, it is quite easy to eliminate the ones that do not measure up.

Perhaps you have been searching, trying to cull through the confusion in the religious world today, looking for God's last-day church. As we have studied this remarkable prophecy, you can clearly see that God does have a special message, and a special people to carry that message to the whole world. But it is not enough to know these biblical facts. To have the peace and happiness that come from a complete walk with Jesus Christ it is also necessary for you to step out and follow the truth as revealed in God's Word, for Jesus said, "If ye know these things, happy are ye if ye do them." John 13:17.

error and confusion that exists in the world about him. Has not God, the Designer, made plain the blueprint to the operator of the machine, man? Indeed they have! The human mind that is of the value of God, and the mind of Jesus. Paul looked, and beyond a while found it, ". . . upon the cloud one sat like unto the Son of man, having on his head a golden crown, and in his hand a sharp sickle" (Revelation 14:14).

Let's briefly review some of the distinguishing features of God's faithful church as given in the Bible:

1. God's true church will be present everywhere at the end of earth's probation, which closed in 1798.

2. It will have the holy commandments within hearts because it accepts the commandments of God.

3. It will proclaim the everlasting saving message of Revelation to all the world to prepare a people for Christ's return.

4. It will have the gift of prophecy, including the gift of prophecy.

All of these may look strange at first glance, but as you study the book more of the blueprint of the Holy Word, it is not easy to eliminate the truths that do not measure up. Perhaps you have been wondering, "Why is this truth in our day, not in the rich and troubled older, locked-in? God's law-day church. As we understand this hereafter able (mainly), you can clearly see that God does have a special message and especially people to carry that message to the whole world. But it is not enough to know these things on earth. "Follow the peace and happiness that come from serving with truly Jesus. "that the Lord does care for you to help out and follow the Path" as revealed in God's word. As Jesus said, "If ye know these things, happy are ye if ye do them" (John 13:17).

We believe in God in Jesus . . . Christ . . .
We believe in the Holy Ghost . . . bodies . . . etc.

What Can I Do When I'm Taken to Court?

I dreamed that the great judgment morning
　　Had dawned, and the trumpet had blown;
I dreamed that the nations had gathered
　　To judgment before the white throne;
From the throne came a bright shining angel
　　And stood on the land and the sea,
And swore with his hand raised to heaven,
　　That time was no longer to be.

And oh, what a weeping and wailing,
　　As the lost were told of their fate;
They cried for the rocks and the mountains,
　　They prayed, but their prayer was too late.

What a solemn day, when the lives of men pass in review before the Judge of all the earth! Every human being
who ever lived has a case pending before the judgment bar
of God, the supreme court of the universe! Every person has
an appointment. The apostle Paul says that God has "appointed a day, in the which he will judge the world." Acts
17:31. No one will be excused. No one can escape the summons. The Bible clearly states that "we must all appear before the judgment seat of Christ." 2 Corinthians 5:10.
Whether we believe it or not, whether we like it or not,

whether we profess to be Christians or not, we must all appear. God has no favorites. When a person is summoned by the court in heaven, he must appear. "So then every one of us shall give account of himself to God." Romans 14:12.

The decision of heaven's court will be irrevocable, for there is no higher court of appeal. It will forever seal the destiny of every person.

But before a verdict can be given, or sentence passed, there must be a trial or investigation. Let us turn to the Bible and study its description of this court session in heaven. The prophet Daniel wrote, "As I looked, thrones were set in place, and the Ancient of Days took his seat. His clothing was as white as snow; the hair of his head was white like wool. His throne was flaming with fire. . . . Thousands upon thousands attended him; ten thousand times ten thousand stood before him." Daniel 7:9, 10, NIV.

Here Daniel pictures God, the Father (the Ancient of Days) seated upon His eternal throne, with countless angels in awesome silence standing before Him. Now notice what Daniel saw next: "I saw in the night visions, and, behold, one like the Son of man came with the clouds of heaven, and came to the Ancient of days, and they brought him near before him." Daniel 7:13.

Here the Son of God is pictured standing before the Ancient of Days. How very much like a courtroom on Earth! There is the presiding Judge, the Ancient of Days. There are witnesses, the holy angels who have seen and recorded everything. And standing before the throne is Jesus, man's lawyer, or advocate, for John said, "We have an advocate with the Father, Jesus Christ the righteous." 1 John 2:1.

Everyone seems to be there except the one who is to be tried! However, the Bible says that "the court was seated, and the books were opened." Daniel 7:10, NIV. Evidently these books contain a record of the deeds of those who stand trial, for Solomon wrote, "God shall bring every work into judgment, with every secret thing, whether it be good, or whether it be evil." Ecclesiastes 12:14. Malachi adds, "Then they that feared the Lord spake often one to another: and the Lord hearkened, and heard it, and a book of remembrance was written before him for them that feared the Lord, and that thought upon his name." Malachi 3:16.

King David also knew about these heavenly records, for he said, "Record my lament; list my tears on your scroll— are they not in your record?" Psalm 56:8, NIV.

Of course God knows all about us, for David also wrote, "O Lord, you have searched me and you know me." "You are familiar with all my ways." "All the days ordained for me were written in your book before one of them came to be." Psalm 139:1, 3, 16, NIV.

God does not need records or books. He knows all about us. These records of our lives are kept for the benefit of the universe, so there will be clear evidence of our deeds and motives and of God's love and justice in dealing with every case.

Our accountability to God is a solemn thought. Everyone must account for the most precious gift of all: life! This is what Solomon meant when he wrote, "Rejoice, O young man, in thy youth; and let thy heart cheer thee in the days of thy youth, and walk in the ways of thine heart, and in the sight of thine eyes: but know thou, that for all these things God will bring thee into judgment." Ecclesiastes 11:9. In other words, Solomon was saying, Go ahead and have a good time while you are young. Live life to its fullest, but remember God will hold you accountable in the judgment!

Jesus said, "Every idle word that men shall speak, they shall give account thereof in the day of judgment. For by thy words thou shalt be justified, and by thy words thou shall be condemned." Matthew 12:36, 37.

Someone has estimated that the average person speaks enough words in one week to fill a book of 320 pages! In sixty years, that could mean more than 3,000 such books! What will your library of books have to say in the judgment? Remember that God will judge not only your words and actions but also the motives that prompted them. "He will bring to light what is hidden in darkness and will expose the motives of men's hearts." 1 Corinthians 4:5, NIV. There will be no erasures, no cover-ups in that day. Men may fool their friends and even their families, but no one can fool God. He reads the secrets of the heart!

On the day of judgment we will find ourselves in one of two positions. Our entire record of past failures will have been covered by the blood of Jesus, or it will stand to condemn us. And, of course, it is not what we profess, but what we are that makes the difference. We are told that when Jesus comes, "He shall reward every man according to his works." Matthew 16:27.

Maybe you wonder why we are judged by our works if we are saved by grace. That is a good question. Certainly works cannot atone for one's sin. However, they do indicate how complete one's surrender is to Christ and how much we love Him. Many people profess to be Christians, but a mere profession of faith in Christ is of no value unless it is demonstrated by loving works.

Dr. Sakae Kubo wrote, "Let us consider what it would mean if the judgment were not based on works. By what would God judge us—our skin, our race, our social class, our education, our looks, our talents, our strength, our membership in the church, our mere profession of Christ? God can judge us only by our works—good or bad."—*Your Summons to Court,* page 20.

Good works obviously are not done by the true Christian to earn merit. It is a love relationship with Jesus that motivates His followers to do good works. Summing up in the book of Ecclesiastes, Solomon said, "Let us hear the conclusion of the whole matter: Fear God and keep his commandments: for this is the whole duty of man. For God shall bring every work into judgment." Ecclesiastes 12:13, 14.

Since man's relationship to Christ is to be judged by his conduct, there must be some clear standard by which to measure that conduct. In our judicial procedures on Earth the usual purpose of a court trial is to determine whether a crime has been committed, if a law has been broken. Only when a law has been violated can a man be found guilty. In God's judgment there is a law or standard, and James makes it clear which law that is: "So speak ye, and so do, as they that shall be judged by the law of liberty." James 2:12.

In the previous verse, James mentioned two of the Ten Commandments: "Do not commit adultery," and, "Do not kill." Obviously, God's Ten Commandment law is the standard by which the lives of men will be judged. The judgment will simply show on which side we stand in the great conflict. Are we with Christ? Have we let Him live out His life in us? Have we had a supreme love for His will as expressed in His law? Is it our joy to follow that will in the Lord's strength? Has He written His law in our hearts?

When immigrants decide to become citizens of the United States, they are required to pledge their allegiance to this country, promising to be loyal citizens and to uphold the laws of the land. So it is with Christians. When they accept Christ and desire to become citizens of His kingdom, God asks them to pledge their love and allegiance to Him and to uphold the laws of His government.

However, not all immigrants remain faithful to their solemn vows. Some appear to be loyal citizens of the land, but later are found to be subversive. When this is proved, their citizenship is revoked and they are deported.

Likewise, not all Christians remain faithful to their vows. It is not enough to be declared righteous now. We must maintain our relationship with Jesus until He comes. It is not enough to *profess* that we are His followers. We must allow

Him to live His perfect life in us. Jesus said, "Not everyone who says to me, 'Lord, Lord,' will enter the kingdom of heaven, but only he who does the will of my Father who is in heaven." Matthew 7:21, NIV.

The whole controversy between good and evil, between Christ and Satan, is about God's character of love, and the law is a written standard of that character. No wonder it figures so prominently in the final judgment!

But a most astounding fact that is scarcely known by modern Christians is that the heavenly court is in session now! In fact, the Scriptures reveal that God's judgment began in the year 1844. That is why, in the closing chapters of the Revelation, John outlines the world's last warning and invitation in these words:

"I saw another angel fly in the midst of heaven, having the everlasting gospel to preach unto them that dwell on the earth, and to every nation, and kindred, and tongue, and people. Saying with a loud voice, Fear God, and give glory to him; for the hour of his judgment is come: and worship him that made heaven, and earth, and the sea, and fountains of waters." Revelation 14:6, 7.

This message does not say that God's judgment *will* come. It says that "the hour of his judgment *is* come."

The second part of this threefold message calls God's people out of the false religious systems that exist in the last days. And finally, God warns His people to beware of worshiping the beast power of Revelation 13: "If any man worship the beast and his image, and receive his mark in his forehead, or in his hand, the same shall drink of the wine of the wrath of God." Revelation 14:9, 10.

Now notice verses 14 and 15, which follow the proclamation of the three angels' messages: "I looked, and behold a white cloud, and upon the cloud one sat like unto the Son of man, having on his head a golden crown, and in his hand a sharp sickle. And another angel came out of the temple, crying with a loud voice.... Thrust in thy sickle, and reap: for the time is come for thee to reap; for the harvest of the earth is ripe." Revelation 14:14, 15.

Let us now pause to investigate this subject in greater depth. God's final judgment began in 1844. How do we know that? The key is found in a most remarkable prophecy in the book of Daniel: "Unto two thousand and three hundred days; then shall the sanctuary be cleansed." Daniel 8:14.

This is the longest time prophecy in the Bible. In prophecy we note that a prophetic day represents a year: "I have appointed thee each day for a year." Ezekiel 4:6. This 2,300-day period began at the command of King Artaxerxes to rebuild Jerusalem and restore its government. The Israelites had been captives in Babylon for seventy years, and they longed to go home and rebuild their beloved city, Jerusalem. Finally, in the year 457 B.C., the king issued the long-awaited decree.

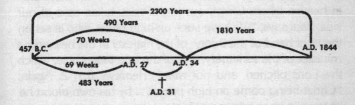

Twenty-three hundred years from that date terminates in A.D. 1844. That year God's court convened in heaven, and God began to judge the world. For more than a century now, God's court has been in session. This is also heaven's Day of Atonement, which we will discuss next.

When we sin, we ask God to forgive our sins because Jesus died in our place to pay the debt for our sins. However, before Calvary, men had no sacrifice to look back to, so by faith they looked forward to the time when the Lamb of God would die for them. In ancient Israel, men and women daily brought their sacrifices to the sanctuary. By sacrificing an innocent animal, they acknowledged their belief in a Saviour who would come and die to make it possible for them to be forgiven. Then the priest symbolically transferred their sins to the sanctuary by sprinkling some of the animal's blood before the veil.

One day each year, the children of Israel held a solemn service called the Day of Atonement. The people of Israel viewed this day as a day of judgment. Ten days before the Day of Atonement the trumpets were blown to remind the Israelites that it was time to take inventory of their lives, to repent and confess their sins. All who failed to do this were banished from the camp. "On that day shall the priest make an atonement for you, to cleanse you, that ye may be clean from all your sins before the Lord." Leviticus 16:30.

The book of Hebrews makes it plain that the earthly sanctuary and its service was an illustration of the sanctuary in heaven where Christ, our High Priest, takes care of our sins. Paul says, "We have such an high priest, who is set on the right hand of the throne of the Majesty in the heavens; a minister of the sanctuary, and of the true tabernacle, which the Lord pitched, and not man." Hebrews 8:1, 2. Again: "Christ being come an high priest . . . by his own blood he entered in once into the holy place, having obtained eternal redemption for us." "Christ is not entered into the holy places made with hands, which are the figures of the true; but into heaven itself, now to appear in the presence of God for us." Hebrews 9:11, 12, 24.

Christ's death on Calvary provided a complete sacrificial atonement for our sins. "Wherefore he is able also to save them to the uttermost that come unto God by him, seeing he ever liveth to make intercession for them." Hebrews 7:25.

In the judgment our relationship and attitude toward Christ will determine His attitude toward us, for He said, "Whosoever therefore shall confess me before men, him will I confess also before my Father which is in heaven. But whosoever shall deny me before men, him will I also deny before my Father which is in heaven." Matthew 10:32, 33.

You do not have to stand alone in the judgment! If you have confessed Christ, He will confess you before His Father. If you are Christ's, He is your Advocate, and you will appear as though you had never sinned, for you will receive credit for the perfect life of obedience that Christ lived on Earth.

Those who love and follow Christ with all their hearts and souls have nothing to fear about the judgment. Jesus will present the merits of His own shed blood to cover every confessed sin, for John wrote, "The blood of Jesus Christ his Son cleanseth us from all sin." 1 John 1:7.

We are living in Earth's last hours. Heaven's pre-advent judgment has been in session since 1844. This judgment probably began with Abel, the first righteous person who died on Earth. Paul wrote, "The time is come that judgment must begin at the house of God." 1 Peter 4:17. The judgment begins with those who profess to be God's people. Can't you picture in your mind Abel's day in court? As his case comes up, God sees from the record that he accepted the death of the Lamb of God. One of his last acts was the sacrifice that he offered, showing his faith in a coming Redeemer. See Genesis 4:1-4. The life of Christ was credited to his account. His sins were all covered by the blood of Christ. You can be assured that years ago in the judgment, Jesus, Abel's Advocate, stretched out His nail-scarred hands and said, "Father, My blood paid Abel's debt."

And can't you just hear those countless angels shout, "Keep Abel's name in the book of life!"

And his name is still there, just as Christ promised: "He

that overcometh, the same shall be clothed in white raiment; and I will not blot out his name out of the book of life, but I will confess his name before my Father, and before his angels." Revelation 3:5.

No doubt, Judas' name also has been raised in court. Judas was a follower of Christ, one of His disciples. He was not all bad, but his life did not measure up to his profession. He did not love Christ supremely. At times he was drawn to Christ, but one weakness led to another until he sold his Lord for thirty pieces of silver! Then in anguish he hanged himself.

Jesus loved Judas. He even stooped to wash his dusty feet that night of the last supper. He hoped to touch that proud heart. He wanted to be able to stand by him in the judgment as his Advocate. But Judas turned away. How sad it must have been for Jesus to review Judas' name in the judgment. Judas had only his own righteousness in the judgment, and the Scripture says that "we are all as an unclean thing, and all our righteousnesses are as filthy rags." Isaiah 64:6. Only those who have continued to make Christ first in their life can wear Christ's robe of righteousness. Without that robe no one can be vindicated in the judgment. So Judas' name was wiped out of the book of life.

It is a solemn time in which we live. Like the Israelites, we need to be taking inventory of our lives. We need to maintain our commitment to Jesus, because that is the only preparation we can make for our summons to court. Soon our probation will close, and the decree will go forth, "He that is unjust, let him be unjust still: . . . and he that is holy, let him be holy still." Revelation 22:11.

At that time, the mercy and pardon God has so long offered will be withdrawn. The saddest words in the human language will be the words of those who have postponed salvation, who have refused to accept Christ as their Lord and Advocate. They will say, "The harvest is past, the summer is ended, and we are not saved." Jeremiah 8:20.

Then Jesus returns to Earth, for we read, "Behold, I come quickly; and my reward is with me, to give every man according as his work shall be." Revelation 22:12.

Friend, Jesus longs to be your Attorney in the judgment. He longs for you to accept His sacrifice on Calvary. He longs to have you confess your sins so He can blot them out. He longs to have your name written in His book of life. John tells us that no one will enter the holy city, "but they which are written in the Lamb's book of life." Revelation 21:27.

Don't you want your name written there? Don't you want Jesus to stand by you in the judgment? All it takes is a surrendered heart. A heart that has been to Calvary. A heart that has invited Jesus to come in and reign supreme. And, oh, what a difference a heart fully committed to Jesus makes, not only in the judgment, but every day of your life!

Can I Know for Sure What the Future Holds?

Dreams! What could be more intriguing? Almost everyone has had a strange dream at one time or another. Some dreams are frightening, some happy. Some are sad and others are funny. Some dreams seem ever so real, some sheer nonsense. Some dreams we can remember vividly, while others elude us, never to be recalled. And, believe it or not, some dreams actually come true!

But perhaps the most remarkable dream ever recorded in the history of humankind occurred one night in the year 553 B.C. in the kingdom of Babylon. The dream is well documented, for it was written and told by the man who experienced it. The book of Daniel carries the account:

"In the first year of Belshazzar king of Babylon Daniel had a dream and visions of his head upon his bed: then he wrote the dream, and told the sum of the matters." Daniel 7:1.

Daniel, a prophet of God as well as a statesman at the court of Babylon, said that in his dream he saw the ocean being whipped around by the four winds of heaven. He was fascinated by the foaming, restless waves, and as he gazed at the scene, he was startled to see animals coming up out of the water. "Four great beasts came up from the sea, diverse one from another." Daniel 7:3.

"Well," you say, "that dream doesn't seem so strange or remarkable." But wait, there's more! These four great

273

beasts were not ordinary creatures of the sea. In fact, they weren't ordinary animals at all. Daniel went on to describe what he had seen: "The first was like a lion, and had eagle's wings: I beheld till the wings thereof were plucked, and it was lifted up from the earth, and made to stand upon the feet as a man, and a man's heart was given to it." Daniel 7:4.

But hardly did Daniel have time to take in the scene before his eyes were riveted to another beast coming up out of the water. "Behold another beast, a second, like to a bear, and it raised up itself on one side, and it had three ribs in the mouth of it between the teeth of it: and they said thus unto it, Arise, devour much flesh." Daniel 7:5.

This lopsided bear was soon followed by yet another strange-looking beast: "Lo another, like a leopard, which had upon the back of it four wings of a fowl; the beast had also four heads; and dominion was given to it." Daniel 7:6.

I suppose if I had dreamed such a dream I would have been convinced that I was having a bad nightmare! Those thoughts may have crossed Daniel's mind. At any rate, he must have been puzzled and perplexed by the appearance of the first three beasts. But the most terrifying monster of all was yet to make its way out of the water.

"After this I was in the night visions, and behold a fourth beast, dreadful and terrible, and strong exceedingly; and it had great iron teeth: it devoured and brake in pieces, and stamped the residue with the feet of it: and it was diverse from all the beasts that were before it; and it had ten horns." Daniel 7:7.

This beast was so ghastly in appearance that Daniel couldn't think of any animal he had ever seen with which to compare it. It defied classification. Daniel seemed to be especially intrigued by the ten horns of this savage animal, and while he was thinking about the ten horns, he was amazed to notice another little horn pushing its way up among the ten. "I considered the horns, and, behold, there came up among them another little horn, before whom there were three of the first horns plucked up by the roots: and, behold, in this horn were eyes like the eyes of man, and a mouth speaking great things." Daniel 7:8.

Daniel now felt deeply concerned. He was convinced that this was no ordinary dream. But what was the meaning of it all? He wrote, "The visions of my head troubled me." Daniel 7:15. He was anxious to know the meaning of the dream he had dreamed and asked an angel to tell him the truth about all the beasts he had seen. "So he told me and gave me the interpretation of these things: 'The four great beasts are four kingdoms that will rise from the earth.'" Daniel 7:16, 17, NIV.

Here we have the key which unlocks the truth about these four beasts. The Bible says they represented four kingdoms that would come to power on the earth. We use the same symbolism today. When we see an eagle and a bear in an editorial cartoon, we immediately recognize that they represent the United States and Russia. When we see a lion we are reminded of England. God used this same method to depict nations long before man did.

What significance did the churning, restless ocean and the four winds have in Daniel's dream? Most prophetic symbols are used consistently throughout the Scriptures. In Revelation we read that "the waters which thou sawest ... are peoples, and multitudes, and nations, and tongues." Revelation 17:15. In other words, these four kingdoms, symbolized by four beasts, were to rise to power out of the populated areas of the world. The winds upon the sea fitly represent the strife and commotion coming from all directions that usually accompany the rise and fall of earthly kingdoms.

Although clothed as the prophecy may have been in symbolism, what Daniel saw in his dream was really a prophecy of things to come. God allowed Daniel to pull back the curtain of time and look far ahead into the future of the world. Of course, this was not the first time God allowed Daniel such a wonderful privilege. Fifty years had slipped by since God had revealed to Daniel King Nebuchadnezzar's dream of the monumental statue, but no doubt Daniel's memory was vividly refreshed now as he sensed the similarity between these two dreams.

The statue in Nebuchadnezzar's dream was unique in that it was composed of four sections: the head of gold, breast and arms of silver, belly and thighs of brass, and the legs of iron, with feet and toes a mixture of iron and clay. As Nebuchadnezzar looked at this great metal man, he saw a rock cut out without human hands strike the statue on its feet and grind the image to powder. The rock then grew larger and larger until it covered the whole earth, and it stood forever.

Just like Daniel, King Nebuchadnezzar wanted to know what his dream meant. At that time Daniel was a very young man at the court of Babylon, and God gave him the interpretation of Nebuchadnezzar's dream. Looking the king squarely in the eye, Daniel said to him, "You are that head of gold." Daniel 2:38, NIV. Daniel actually meant that the head of gold represented Babylon, Nebuchadnezzar's kingdom, for he continued, "After you, another kingdom will rise, inferior to yours." Daniel 2:39, NIV.

The second kingdom, Medo-Persia, conquered Babylon in A.D. 538. This power, represented by the arms and chest of silver, was indeed inferior to the golden empire of Babylon, just as silver is inferior to gold. But this kingdom was not to last forever, for the Bible stated:

"Next, a third kingdom, one of bronze, will rule over the whole earth." Daniel 2:39, NIV. Two hundred years after the Medo-Persians had conquered the then known world, Alexander the Great (with his infantry, described by historians as Greek pirates "of bronze coming from the sea") crushed the Medo-Persian Empire in 331 B.C.

But this empire, symbolized by the belly and thighs of brass would also pass from the scene of history, for God predicted that "finally, there will be a fourth kingdom, strong as iron . . . [that] will crush and break all others." Daniel 2:40, NIV. And just as God predicted, the Roman armies defeated the armies of the Greek Empire in 168 B.C.

The giant Roman empire ruled for 600 years before it disintegrated. During the fourth century A.D. barbaric tribes from the north swept down over the empire, and by A.D. 476 Rome had been divided into ten segments, just as the Bible predicted: "Whereas thou sawest the feet and toes, part of potters' clay, and part of iron, the kingdom shall be divided." Daniel 2:41. The kingdoms that emerged from the break-up of the Roman Empire are the modern nations of Europe today:

Alemanni (Germans)	Bergundians (Swiss)
Franks (French)	Lombards (Italians)
Saxons (English)	Suevi (Portuguese)
Visigoths (Spanish)	Heruli (extinct)
Vandals (extinct)	Ostrogoths (extinct)

Finally Daniel came to the astounding climax of the interpretation of Nebuchadnezzar's dream: "In the days of these kings shall the God of heaven set up a kingdom, which shall never be destroyed: and the kingdom shall not be left to other people, but it shall break in pieces and consume all these kingdoms, and it shall stand for ever." Daniel 2:44.

According to the Bible, there will be no more world empires as we know them. God said that in the days of the kings represented by the ten toes, or the nations of Europe today, He will set up a kingdom to end all earthly kingdoms—one that will last forever.

As Daniel reflected on his vision of the four beasts, he couldn't help recognizing that Nebuchadnezzar's dream of the great image must be a parallel prophecy. What could better symbolize Babylon, the first world empire (represented by the head of gold in the towering statue), than a lion—the king of beasts and one of the symbols used by the ancient Babylonians themselves to represent their empire? Visitors to the excavated ruins of Babylon today can see lion-shaped bas-reliefs on baked-brick walls and monuments, often with eagle wings!

As the lion is noted for its strength and conquest, King Nebuchadnezzar's military conquests were unsurpassed. The rapidity with which Babylon gained power and spread its empire is appropriately symbolized by the eagle's wings. Jeremiah predicted that the Babylonian armies would invade ancient Israel and destroy her cities. Notice that God uses the same symbol of a lion to represent Babylon: "A lion has come out of his lair; a destroyer of nations has set out. He has left his place to lay waste your land." Jeremiah 4:7, NIV.

The proud, pompous king of Babylon envisioned his kingdom lasting forever. He apparently gave no thought to the idea that any other nation would ever rule the world. He inscribed on the bricks of his buildings "May It Last Forever."

However, God said the wings of the lion would be "plucked and a man's heart would be given it." In other words, Babylon would become so weak that it would no longer have the courage and boldness of one possessing a "lion's heart." And that's exactly what happened! After King Nebuchadnezzar's death, Babylon decayed both morally and politically.

During the reign of Belshazzar, Nebuchadnezzar's arrogant grandson, Cyrus the Mede laid siege to Babylon while Belshazzar foolishly feasted with his lords in the great banquet hall. As the bloodless hand etched those fiery letters of doom across the plastered wall, fear gripped every heart. The Bible says, "The king watched the hand as it wrote. His face turned pale and he was so frightened that his knees knocked together and his legs gave way." Daniel 5:5, 6, NIV.

Truly, the "heart of a lion" was replaced by that of a man. The prophet Jeremiah wrote concerning the soldiers of Babylon, "Babylon's warriors have stopped fighting; they remain in their strongholds. Their strength is exhausted; they have become like women." Jeremiah 51:30, NIV. The triumphant shouts of Cyrus's army could be heard above the terrified cries of Belshazzar's revelers, and that night, October 13, 539 B.C., the Babylonian kingdom (represented by the head of gold in the metal image and by the lion with eagle's wings in Daniel's dream) came to an inglorious end.

The kingdom or empire represented by the second beast—the bear—can be none other than the conquering nation of Medo-Persia, the same kingdom represented by the arms and chest of silver in the giant statue.

As Daniel watched the bear in his dream, he said, "It raised up itself on one side, and it had three ribs in the mouth of it between the teeth of it." Daniel 7:5.

What did this part of the prophecy mean? As we study history, we discover that the second empire was a dual dynasty, or a coalition government. The Medes and the Persians were united into one empire. However, before long the Persians became the dominant power in the dynasty. One side of this coalition was more powerful than the other. God predicted this shift in power years before it took place.

Daniel said that the bear had three ribs in its mouth between its teeth, but the Bible does not identify their meaning. However, most Bible commentators believe the three ribs represent Lydia, Babylon, and Egypt, the three principal territories that were devoured by the Medo-Persian armies.

The Persian Empire ruled for two centuries, but ferocious and strong as it may have been, God revealed to Daniel in the dream that another beast, or kingdom, would arise: "Lo another, like a leopard, which had upon the back of it four wings of a fowl; the beast had also four heads; and dominion was given to it." Daniel 7:6.

Just as a slow-moving bear proves no match for the agile leopard, so the Persian armies were unable to defend themselves against the swift advances of Alexander the Great.

In Nebuchadnezzar's prophetic dream the bronze belly and thighs of the image represented the third world empire of Greece, and so does the leopard in Daniel's dream. The four wings describe the great speed of Alexander's conquests. He defeated Darius III of Persia in the battle of Arbela in 331 B.C., thus becoming in less than ten years the ruler of the most extensive empire the world had ever known.

The leopard's four heads represent the four divisions of Greece. "Four kingdoms shall stand up out of the nation." Daniel 8:22. The New International Version states it this way: "Four kingdoms that will emerge from his nation but will not have the same power." Daniel 8:22.

History tells us that the Grecian Empire did indeed divide into four parts. Alexander died of a raging fever at the age of thirty-two, just seven years after his great victory at Arbela. Even before he was buried, a bloody, twenty-two-year power struggle began, first among his relatives and later among his military leaders. Finally, four of Alexander's generals gained control of the empire. Now the leopard beast, or Greece, had four heads! Cassander, Lysimachus, Ptolemy, and Seleucus.

Most people have trouble keeping one head going in the right direction. What do you suppose would happen if you had four? Chaos! Each head trying to be number one! That's exactly what happened to the Greek Empire. Alexander's four generals were greedy, ambitious men who wanted to attain the throne. "Each one whetted the sword against the other and the empire went down in a tangle of strife."—*Alexander the Great*, page 494.

The unrest and strife continued among the four parts of the empire till finally, "on June 22, 168 B.C., at the battle of Pydna, perished the empire of Alexander the Great, 144 years after his death."—Theodor Mounsen, *History of Rome*, book 3, chapter 10.

But what about the fourth nondescript beast that Daniel said would rise to power after the Greek Empire? The angel told Daniel that this fourth kingdom would be different from the other kingdoms. The beast representing it was extremely powerful, and it had enormous iron teeth that destroyed its prey. Here is pictured a cruel, vicious power. A more fitting description of the rise of the Roman Empire could hardly be found. It was more ruthless and brutal than all the previous empires, sometimes annihilating whole cities. When it didn't destroy or subjugate a people, it used them as slaves or sold them into slavery.

Daniel's monstrous beast had iron teeth, while the fourth kingdom in the metal image was represented by iron legs. Daniel was intrigued by this nondescript beast, and especially by its ten horns. He said, "I considered the horns, and, behold, there came up among them another little horn, before whom there were three of the first horns plucked up by the roots." Daniel 7:8.

The angel told Daniel that "the ten horns out of this kingdom are ten kings that shall arise." Daniel 7:24. No doubt Daniel's mind flashed back to the great metal image with the ten toes, representing the ten divisions of the Roman Empire, accomplished in A.D. 476 by the barbaric tribes of northern Europe. Seven of these kingdoms (nations) are still in Europe today.

But what interested Daniel most was the little horn that pushed itself up among the ten horns, uprooting three horns in its struggle for supremacy. Daniel noticed that "in this [little] horn were eyes like the eyes of man, and a mouth speaking great things." Daniel 7:8. This little horn troubled Daniel. He wrote, "I Daniel was grieved in my spirit . . . , and the visions of my head troubled me." Daniel 7:15.

Why did this description of the little horn cause Daniel such concern? Because "the same horn made war with the saints, and prevailed against them." "And he shall speak great words against the most High, and shall wear out the saints of the most High, and think to change times and laws: and they shall be given into his hand until a time and times and the dividing of time." Daniel 7:21, 25.

Daniel recognized that this prediction was no longer just about secular history, but that it had to do with God's people, for this little horn made war against the saints of God and actually prevailed against them for a period of time. Obviously, it was to be a hostile, persecuting power —a power or agency used by Satan to make war against God, His people, and His truth. Daniel said, "I . . . was deeply troubled by my thoughts, and my face turned pale, but I kept the matter to myself." Daniel 7:28, NIV.

All of this is but a background, or introduction, to the career of the little horn and the heavenly judgment. The identification of the little horn power and the part it was to play in the war against God and His people will be covered in the next chapter. Here we will simply say that the fourth beast and its horns will exist until the end of time, when God will give the kingdom to His saints.

In vision as Daniel watched the powers on Earth struggle to grasp political and religious dominance, his attention was suddenly shifted from Earth to heaven. "As I looked, thrones were set in place, and the Ancient of Days took his seat. His clothing was as white as snow; the hair of his head was white like wool. His throne was flaming with fire, and its wheels were all ablaze." "Thousands upon thousands attended him; ten thousand times ten thousand stood before him. The court was seated, and the books were opened." Daniel 7:9, 10, NIV.

Daniel saw God the Father, here called the Ancient of Days, come and sit upon a glorious throne. Evidently God came from some other part of heaven in order to commence this special work, for the Bible says, "Until the Ancient of days came." Daniel 7:22. He must have had to change locations in order to commence this particular work. Daniel saw God surrounded by myriads of angels, and "the judgment was set, and the books were opened." Daniel 7:10.

Daniel was shown the judgment in heaven, with God judging the world and the little horn power that made war against the saints. Daniel also saw the outcome of this judgment: "But the judgment shall sit, and they shall take away his dominion, to consume and to destroy it unto the end." Daniel 7:26.

Then Daniel saw something very special, very beautiful, happen after the Father was seated and the judgment was ready to begin: "I saw in the night visions, and, behold, one like the Son of man came with the clouds of heaven, and came to the Ancient of days, and they brought him near before him." Daniel 7:13.

Who is this distinguished Person called "the Son of man" that was presented before the Eternal Judge? Jesus applied this term to Himself more than forty times in the New Testament. To His astonished disciples He said, "The Son of man shall be betrayed into the hands of men: and they shall kill him, and the third day he shall be raised again." Matthew 17:22, 23.

To Judas, the traitor disciple, Jesus said, "Are you betraying the Son of Man with a kiss?" Luke 22:48, NIV. But the most significant statement was directed to the high priest who sat in judgment at Christ's trial: "Hereafter shall ye see the Son of man sitting on the right hand of power, and coming in the clouds of heaven." Matthew 26:64. Here Jesus unmistakenly identifies Himself as the Son of man that Daniel saw in his vision who "came with the clouds of heaven."

This almost sounds like Christ made His appearance at the court in heaven after God completed the judgment. But that couldn't be true, for the Bible states, "The Father judgeth no man, but hath committed all judgment unto the Son." John 5:22. But how can God the Father be Judge and yet not judge anybody? The answer is found in the book of Acts: "God ... has fixed the day on which he will have the world judged, and justly judged, by a man of his choosing; of this he has given assurance to all by raising him from the dead." Acts 17:30, 31, NEB.

That sounds a little unusual, but it is not a unique role that Christ will assume. We have seen such a thing happen in our time. President Jimmy Carter was requested to commute the sentence of Patty Hearst in 1979. He announced publicly that he would follow whatever recommendation came to him from the lawyers in the United States Department of Justice. You see, President Carter was the ultimate judge, but he chose to exercise his judicial responsibility by relying on the judgment of someone else.

And who could the Father better rely on to represent mankind than His Son, Jesus Christ, the One who lived on Earth as a man, with men, who understands perfectly the frailty of humanity? Jesus experienced the same temptations, disappointments, loneliness, poverty, and pain that men endure. He suffered persecution, ridicule, and betrayal, just as many of God's children have on Earth. God said, in effect, "I am the Judge, but My verdict will be whatever My Son recommends. He is your Advocate."

So we see that Christ has a dual responsibility at the court during the judgment. He is our Advocate, and He will also give the verdict or recommendation to His Father.

Perhaps Daniel became so interested in the little horn and what would finally become of it that he just leaped ahead and gave the complete story of its career, which actually takes place after the pre-advent judgment, when the affairs on Earth are scrutinized and the decision is made as to those who will make up God's everlasting kingdom. The kingdom was given to Christ as His dominion:

"There was given him dominion, and glory, and a kingdom, that all people, nations, and languages, should serve him: his dominion is an everlasting dominion, which shall not pass away, and his kingdom that which shall not be destroyed." Daniel 7:14.

Daniel goes on with more good news about this kingdom: "The kingdom and dominion . . . shall be given to the people of the saints of the most High." Daniel 7:27. God's people, His saints, will be joint heirs with Christ in taking possession of that everlasting kingdom: "The saints of the most High shall take the kingdom, and possess the kingdom for ever, even for ever and ever." Daniel 7:18.

This part of the prophecy parallels the rock in Nebuchadnezzar's dream that was cut out without hands and smote the image on the feet and became "a great mountain, and filled the whole earth." Daniel 2:35.

In these two parallel prophecies—Nebuchadnezzar's dream of the great image and Daniel's dream of the beasts — God summarized Earth's history from the time of ancient Babylon to the great day when Jesus comes in the clouds of glory to set up His everlasting kingdom of love and righteousness. Below is a completed outline of the two great prophecies and their climax as given in the two prophetic dreams:

First World Empire:

Babylon	605-539 B.C.	Gold head	Lion

Second World Empire:

Medo-Persia	539-331 B.C.	Silver arms/chest	Bear

Third World Empire:

Greece	331-168 B.C.	Brass belly/thighs	Leopard

Fourth World Empire:

Rome	168 B.C.— A.D. 476	Iron legs	Nondescript Beast

Ten kingdoms:

Nations of Europe	A.D. 476— second coming	10 Iron-clay toes	10 Horns

We today are living down in the feet of iron and clay. Time is running out for the earth and its inhabitants. This is the message that God is trying to share with each of us by His great prophecies. What a remarkable way to predict centuries of world history in but two short chapters of the Bible!

And come to think of it, wasn't the dream given to Daniel that night so long ago in Babylon a tremendous expression of God's love and concern for His people on Earth! You see, Jerusalem was in ruins. God's people, Israel, were in captivity in Babylon. Things looked pretty grim. But God, in this most unusual way, was telling Daniel, "I'm still in control. Kings may come and kings may go. Empires will rise and fall, but I have not forgotten My children on Earth, or My plan for them. Someday everything will come out right."

And, friend, kings and kingdoms have come and gone. The dual prophecies of the image and the beasts have almost reached their complete fulfillment. Jesus is soon coming to execute judgment and to restore the dominion lost by Adam and Eve so long ago. He wants all of His children on Planet Earth to be a part of that kingdom, to be ready for that glorious moment when our Saviour returns! For soon, very soon, our God is coming.

How Can I Spot a Counterfeit?

Have you ever been conned? Ripped off? Swindled? Most people have at one time or another. In fact, ever since 1626 when the early settlers traded $24 worth of colorful beads and cloth to the unsuspecting Indians for Manhattan Island, a record of swindling and fraud seems to have run throughout American history.

Only a few decades ago "con men" made thousands of dollars selling Grant's Tomb or the Woolworth Building to greenhorns on their first trip to New York. And unbelievable as it may seem, not too long ago an Italian immigrant paid a large sum of money to purchase the information booth in Grand Central Station. The swindler assured him that he could use it for a fruit stand!

Amusing? Perhaps. But it isn't only poor, ignorant greenhorns who are victimized by con artists. Listen: "No matter how intelligent or careful you are, at least once in your life you will be swindled, according to the National Better Business Bureau."—Curtis D. MacDougall, *Hoaxes*, page 61.

Unfortunately, it happens every day! In fact, one of the greatest swindles of the century took place in the late 1960s. David Stein, a brilliant young Frenchman, painted more than 400 imitations of the Old Masters: counterfeit Picassos, Chagalls, Renoirs, and Van Goghs, among others. He signed the names of the renowned artists to his paintings and passed them off as originals. They were masterpieces of deception—so much so that the experts declared them authentic!

To date only 110 of these 400 forgeries have been detected and recovered. Stein was apprehended in 1972 and served prison terms in Sing Sing and Paris for his crime. However, during his stay in prison, Stein had a change of heart and decided to paint under his own name. Today he is a noted artist and lecturer around the world. And what does he lecture about? What he knows best: "How to Spot a Fake."

Stein demonstrated that it isn't easy to spot a fake, even for experts. But clever as he may have been as a con man, Stein was just a "babe in the woods," so to speak, compared with Satan, the granddaddy of all con men. When it comes to swindling, cheating, deceiving, and counterfeiting, the devil stands without a peer.

Of course, Satan doesn't work openly. He works through other people, other powers and agencies. If he were an open enemy of God and truth there would be little danger that any Christian would be deceived. So he works under cover, sometimes masquerading in the very garb of religion—ingeniously mixing truth and error to draw men away from the true worship of God. This has been his all-consuming passion for thousands of years!

The first con job recorded in Scripture took place in the early hours of Earth's history when Satan, in the guise of a talking snake, appeared to Eve. He promised that she would be a liberated person, that her mind would expand, and that she would become like God. Satan told her that she would be a winner by disobeying God. And Eve was deceived. She believed the words of the master deceiver, and just as God said, she died. Not because she conscientiously believed a lie, but because she didn't believe God's warning and obey what God had said.

God's Word is our only protection against the shrewd deceptions of the devil. Whatever contradicts God's Word we may be sure is not true. You may think that because you are an intelligent person the devil can't con you. "I think I can hold my own," you say. Don't be too hasty in shrugging off the devil's ability to deceive. He's been in the business for over 6,000 years, and every moment of that time he has studied man's weaknesses. He has learned by experience the best strategy to use in deceiving his victims.

In fact, Satan was in the business of deceiving even before Earth's inhabitants were created. Under the pretense of bringing freedom to all the angels and giving them something much superior, Satan undermined God and His government by his subtle innuendos and lying propaganda. One third of the heavenly angels, with their great wisdom and intelligence, were conned by the devil's deceptions. The Bible gives this sad account:

"There was war in heaven. . . . And the great dragon was cast out, that old serpent, called the Devil, and Satan, which deceiveth the whole world: he was cast out into the earth, and his angels were cast out with him." Revelation 12:7-9.

Incredible as it may seem, Satan tried to con Jesus into uniting with him in his rebellion against God. Did you know that? It happened at the time of Jesus' greatest physical need, when He was most vulnerable. He had been fasting in the wilderness for forty days, preparing Himself for the bloodstained path He must travel to Calvary. He was faint from hunger, worn and haggard from mental agony, and who should happen to drop by to tempt Him in this critical moment but Satan. Satan, masquerading in the guise of an angel—not in the guise of the rebellious fallen angel that he was, but as a loyal heavenly angel. He tried to deceive Christ with the same con game that he had used so successfully with the other fallen angels and Eve, but, thank God, it didn't work!

Christ recognized and overcame each of Satan's temptations by citing God's Word. And Jesus warned His followers that they must be on guard against this great imposter. He said that in the last hours of Earth's history Satan's deceptions will be so overwhelming that "if it were possible, they shall deceive the very elect." Matthew 24:24.

Fortunately, God has provided His children with sufficient warning and information in the Bible to recognize and resist the deceptions of Satan. Through the prophet Daniel, God foretold the devil's master plan to delude and trap the whole world during Earth's last hours. In fact, God gives a detailed description of the means Satan would use to accomplish this final deception.

Daniel predicted that a powerful movement would arise, claiming to follow and speak for God, but which would directly subvert the Scriptures in its practice and doctrine. Daniel called this power the "little horn." You will remember that in the last chapter we studied the prophecy of the four strange animals that Daniel saw in his dream. The angel told Daniel, "These great beasts, which are four, are four kings, which shall arise out of the earth." Daniel 7:17.

First he saw a lion with eagle's wings which represented Babylon. The lopsided bear represented Medo-Persia, and the lepoard with four heads and four wings represented Greece. The most frightening of all the beasts represented the Roman Empire, and this beast and its little horn became the focal point of the prophecy. Daniel said: "After this I saw in the night visions, and behold a fourth beast, dreadful and terrible, and strong exceedingly; and it had great iron teeth: it devoured and brake in pieces, and stamped the residue with the feet of it: and it was diverse from all the beasts that were before it; and it had ten horns." Daniel 7:7.

Daniel had never seen an animal that even remotely resembled this fourth beast. But sensational and dramatic as its appearance may have been, one part intrigued Daniel more than anything else: "I considered the horns, and behold, there came up among them another little horn, before whom there were three of the first horns plucked up by the roots: and, behold, in this horn were eyes like the eyes of man, and a mouth speaking great things." Daniel 7:8. The "little horn" so troubled Daniel that he said, "I Daniel was grieved in my spirit . . . , and the visions of my head troubled me." Daniel 7:15.

Daniel explained why this part of the prophecy caused him such concern: "I beheld, and the same horn made war with the saints, and prevailed against them." "And he shall speak great words against the most High, and shall wear out the saints of the most High, and think to change times and laws: and they shall be given into his hand until a time and times and the dividing of time." Daniel 7:21, 25.

Daniel recognized that this prophecy was more than a prediction of secular history. It concerned God's people. The little horn power represented a persecuting power that would make war against God's people and actually prevail against them for a long period of time.

What an astonishing revelation! As Daniel envisioned the persecution and hardship that God's people would have to endure in the future, he became ill.

What is this little horn? Can we be sure to which power God is pointing so that we can avoid Satan's master deception? That's a very important question. In fact, the answer could mean the difference between eternal life or eternal death!

As we turn the pages of New Testament prophecy, we discover that the characteristics of the antichrist described there are identical to those of the little horn described by Daniel. The apostle Paul wrote to the Thessalonians concerning the work of this power in the last days: "He opposes and exalts himself over everything that is called God or is worshiped, and even sets himself up in God's temple, proclaiming himself to be God." 2 Thessalonians 2:4, NIV.

In Revelation John wrote, "There was given unto him a mouth speaking great things and blasphemies." "And it was given unto him to make war with the saints, and to overcome them." Revelation 13:5, 7. John also warned about this power during his lifetime: "This is that spirit of antichrist, whereof ye have heard that it should come; and even now already is it in the world." 1 John 4:3.

The Bible pictures a power operating in the world during New Testament times that would rise to great power and influence after the breakup of the fourth world empire and continue deceiving the world until the close of Earth's history. The great Protestant reformers studied these prophecies thoroughly. In fact, it was their interpretation of the prophecies of Daniel and Revelation that led them to break with the medieval church.

But was the interpretation of Daniel's prophecy by the reformers mere speculation, or does history confirm it? With the abundance of evidence given in Scripture and world history, there is no need for question. When we examine the unique characteristics of the little horn power, only one conclusion can be logically reached.

It's just like the "most wanted" posters in the post offices. A list of characteristics unique to each person is given: the color of his eyes, his height and approximate weight; any scars, tattoos, birthmarks, or defects; the aliases he uses, and a copy of his thumb print. Finally, there is the photograph. Many people resemble each other, even having some of the same general characteristics. But there is only one person in the world who can fit *all* of the distinguishing characteristics given on any one poster.

That's the way it is with the little horn. Only one power on Earth can perfectly match God's identifying characteristics so clearly cataloged in the book of Daniel. Let's examine the Bible's description of this little horn and see what history records concerning its fulfillment. Daniel described the fourth beast, or the fourth world empire of Rome, as "dreadful and terrible, and strong exceedingly; . . . and it had ten horns." Daniel 7:7.

The ten horns represented "ten kings that shall arise." Daniel 7:24. Instead of another world empire appearing on the scene of history at the fall of the fourth one, Bible prophecy predicted that there would be a division of the Roman Empire, resulting in ten lesser kingdoms. History confirms this portion of Daniel's prophecy. After ruling for six centuries, the great Roman Empire crumbled, weakened by internal strife, moral decay, prosperity, and ease. Its fall was, of course, hastened by the invasion of many Germanic tribes.

"As time passed, the barbarians could no longer be held back. In 376 several Germanic tribes broke through the Danube frontier, and others soon followed."—*Imperial Rome,* pages 146, 158. "When the last wave of the barbarian invasions had spent its force, the face of Europe had been transformed. Independent Germanic kingdoms had been established on the ruins of the Roman Empire."—*Church History,* page 175.

Historians tell us that the division of Rome was completed by A.D. 476. According to the English historian Edward Elliott, in his book *Horae Apocalypticae,* the following barbaric tribes came into being after the collapse of the Roman Empire in 476:

Alemanni (Germans)	*Burgundians (Swiss)*
Franks (French)	*Lombards (Italians)*
Saxons (English)	*Suevi (Portuguese)*
Visigoths (Spanish)	*Heruli (extinct)*
Vandals (extinct)	*Ostrogoths (extinct)*

These are the ten horns of the fourth beast that Daniel saw. And according to the prophecy, the little horn was to rise to great power *after* the ten horns, or divisions of the Roman Empire: "The ten horns out of this kingdom are ten kings that shall arise: and another shall rise *after* them; . . . and he shall subdue three kings." Daniel 7:24, emphasis supplied. In verse 8, Daniel said, "While I was thinking about the horns, there before me was another horn, a little one, which came up among them; and three of the first horns were uprooted before it." Daniel 7:8, NIV.

As we study history, we find that three of the ten horns, or kingdoms, were an obstruction to the supremacy of the church because of their religious differences.

However, the emperors of the eastern empire found ways to help the Bishop of the church at Rome by eliminating these three powers. In 493 the Heruli met their fate with the help of the Emperor Zeno. Another emperor, Justinian, exterminated the Vandals in 534 and then broke the power of the Ostrogoths in 538.

Thus, three horns of Daniel's prophecy were "plucked up by the roots," making the rise of the church at Rome a reality. It was at this time that Justinian made a decree establishing the Bishop of Rome as the political and religious leader of Western Rome. Notice this statement by the historian Thomas Hobbes: "If a man consider the original of this great, ecclesiastical dominion he will easily perceive that the papacy is no other than the ghost of the deceased Roman Empire sitting crowned upon the grave thereof."

The power which came up after the other ten kingdoms was none other than the Roman branch of the church in the Middle Ages. The Roman church had roots extending back to the early years of Christianity, to be sure. But it was not until A.D. 538, following Justinian's decree giving the Bishop of Rome political as well as ecclesiastical power, that the little horn became "more stout than his fellows." Daniel 7:20.

Daniel also predicted that the little horn would be *differ-*

ent from the other kingdoms: "He shall be diverse from the first." Daniel 7:24. Was this power different? Indeed it was! The other kingdoms were political powers, but the little horn was a church that wielded political power.

The prophetic finger would seem to point unerringly toward the Roman Church of the Middle Ages as the little horn of Daniel 7, just as the Protestant Reformers claimed.

Daniel gave another identifying characteristic of this little horn power: "I beheld, and the same horn made war with the saints, and prevailed against them." Daniel 7:21. He also said that power would "wear out the saints." Verse 25.

Did the church of the Middle Ages engage in persecution? Unfortunately, yes. The Inquistion, the crusades against the Huguenots, Waldenses, and Albigenses, the Thirty Years' War, the rack, the dungeon, the flames from the martyrs burned at the stake—all are historically linked to the church during the dark centuries of its supremacy. And why?

The answer is one of conscience. The martyrs were unwilling to compromise their belief in God and His Word. They refused to follow the man-made teachings of the Roman Church. For this they were branded as "heretics."

However shocking these revelations may be, God intended this prophecy to be a kind, loving warning against the errors and apostasy of the church, not against individuals of that church. We must never forget for a moment that there are loving and sincere Christians in every church, including those that have lost sight of truth or mixed it with error.

But we find that there is yet another very important distinguishing characteristic of this little horn power. The prophecy predicted that it would "think to change times and laws." Daniel 7:25.

Did the papal power in the Middle Ages attempt to change God's divine law? Yes, as noted in chapter 13, it changed the Sabbath—appealing primarily to tradition—

from Saturday to Sunday.

The last characteristic that we will study pinpoints when this power would be supreme and the length of time it would persecute the saints of God: "And they shall be given into his hand until a time and times and the dividing of time." Daniel 7:25.

Here we find more Bible symbols. The term *time* signifies one year—and the term *times* signifies two years, or 720 prophetic days. A "dividing of time" represents half a year, or 180 days. When we add a time (360 days), times (720 days), and the dividing of time (180 days), we arrive at a total of 1,260 prophetic days. According to the prophet Ezekiel, a prophetic day signifies one year. "I have appointed thee each day for a year." Ezekiel 4:6. The little horn power was to be supreme for 1,260 years.

History confirms the accuracy of this time period. The Ostrogoths, the last of the Arian kingdoms to oppose the Roman Church, were overthrown in the year A.D. 538, leaving the papacy free to develop her political and ecclesiastical power. Exactly 1260 years later, in 1798, the Roman Church's polictical power was broken by Napoleon's general, Berthier.

Now let's leap ahead to the climax of Daniel's great prophecy, for it has a very happy ending for the people of God.

Even though Daniel saw the various things that the little horn power would do—wearing out the saints of God and changing God's law—he said that this power would eventually come to an end. "The judgment shall sit, and they shall take away his dominion, to consume and to destroy it unto the end. And the kingdom and dominion, and the greatness of the kingdom under the whole heaven, shall be given to the people of the saints of the most High, whose kingdom is an everlasting kingdom, and all dominions shall serve and obey him." Daniel 7:26, 27.

What a glorious event, as God's eternal kingdom is

ushered in! The details of that kingdom are recorded earlier in the same chapter, as Daniel was given a vision of the second coming of Christ: "I saw in the night visions, and, behold, one like the Son of man came with the clouds of heaven, and came to the Ancient of days, and they brought him near before him. And there was given him dominion, and glory, and a kingdom, that all people, nations, and languages, should serve him: his dominion is an everlasting dominion, which shall not pass away, and his kingdom that which shall not be destroyed." Daniel 7:13, 14.

This kingdom will be established by the Lord Himself. What a contrast to the kingdoms this Earth has known! No armies, no prisons, no poverty, no sickness, no persecution. Just peace and love, beauty and gladness, forever and ever. And the good news is that Jesus wants to share that glorious kingdom with everyone everywhere. His invitation is given to all His children:

"Come, ye blessed of my Father, inherit the kingdom prepared for you from the foundation of the world." Matthew 25:34.

But even though God wants to save everyone, the choice is yours and mine to make. There will be only two classes of people in that day: those who choose to follow Christ and His Word, and those who choose to follow the arch-deceiver in his rebellion against God. To reject any portion of God's Word, or to follow the antichrist, is to choose the rebel angel as our leader and ultimately suffer his fate.

Will Religious Freedom Ever Disappear?

It was a high day in the Babylonian Empire, one that King Nebuchadnezzar had looked forward to with keen anticipation—and also one he would never forget as long as he lived. Sometime before, the king had dreamed a strange dream of a metallic image. After Daniel had revealed the dream and its interpretation, Nebuchadnezzar could think of nothing else.

The proud monarch was pleased when Daniel told him that the head of gold represented Babylon, but the thought that other kingdoms would follow seemed unbearable. In fact, the king wouldn't accept it. In defiance of God's prediction, the king ordered a gigantic statue made, similar to the one he had seen in his dream. However, instead of several metals, this image was all gold. Not just the head, but the entire body—everything! It was the king's way of signifying to the world that his kingdom would last forever.

The Bible gives this description of the great image: "King Nebuchadnezzar made an image of gold, ninety feet high and nine feet wide, and set it up on the plain of Dura in the province of Babylon." Daniel 3:1, NIV.

Accustomed as the Babylonians may have been to magnificent representations of their heathen gods, they had never seen one to equal the dazzling beauty of this one.

On the day appointed, thousands of VIP's assembled

on the plain of Dura to witness the dedication of Nebuchadnezzar's golden image. It was a thrilling day, for King Nebuchadnezzar himself would be there.

Suddenly a hush fell over the vast concourse. The trumpets sounded a fanfare, and the king's spokesman proclaimed loudly, "O people of all nations and languages, this is the king's command: When the band strikes up, you are to fall flat on the ground to worship King Nebuchadnezzar's golden statue; anyone who refuses to obey will immediately be thrown into a flaming furnace." Daniel 3:4-6, LB.

The music sounded, and all the people fell down and worshiped the statue. Well, not quite all the people. In that vast kneeling throng stood Shadrach, Meshach, and Abednego, three young Hebrews who refused to disobey God by bowing and worshiping an idol. Word soon reached the king.

Furious that anyone should dare defy his direct command, Nebuchadnezzar ordered the offenders to be brought before him. As the king looked at the three Hebrews, he recognized them at once. They were extraordinary men with great intelligence and many talents. He had assigned them many responsibilities in the past which they had faithfully and efficiently performed. Feeling somewhat kindly toward them, he decided to give them another chance. Calling them each by name, the king said, "Now when you hear the sound of . . . all kinds of music, if you are ready to fall down and worship the image I made, very good. But if you do not worship it, you will be thrown immediately into a blazing furnace." Daniel 3:15, NIV.

Not far away Shadrach, Meshach, and Abednego could see the smoke belching from the huge furnace. There could be no doubt about the king's intention. Would they disobey a direct command of God, rationalizing that perhaps it wouldn't hurt just once to bow to an idol—that they would be doing it to appease an angry king and save their lives?

Evidently such thoughts never crossed their minds, for they had been taught God's commandments from childhood, and one of those commands said, "Thou shalt not make unto thee any graven image. . . . Thou shalt not bow down thyself to them, nor serve them." Exodus 20:4, 5.

No consideration, not even that of life itself, could make them disobey God. For them, the commands of a sinful, finite man sank into insignificance when compared with the commands of the living God. They stood unmoved by the king's offer. Calmly and without hesitation came their reply: "O Nebuchadnezzar, we do not need to defend ourselves before you in this matter. If we are thrown into the blazing furnace, the God we serve is able to save us from it, and he will rescue us from your hand, O king. But even if he does not, we want you to know, O king, that we will not serve your gods or worship the image of gold you have set up." Daniel 3:16-18, NIV.

Of course, you remember the rest of the story. The king commanded that the furnace be heated seven times hotter than usual. Then he ordered the three Hebrews to be bound and thrown into the flames. The Bible says that the heat of the furnace was so intense that the soldiers who threw the Hebrews into the flames fell back dead.

Suddenly King Nebuchadnezzar shouted to his advisors, "Did not we cast three men bound into the midst of the fire? . . . Lo, I see four men loose, walking in the midst of the fire, and they have no hurt; and the form of the fourth is like the Son of God." Daniel 3:24, 25.

Forgetting his great dignity, the king ran to the opening of the furnace and called out, "Shadrach, Meshach, and Abednego, ye servants of the most high God, come forth, and come hither." Daniel 3:26.

The trio stepped out of the fiery furnace without a hair of their heads singed nor even the smell of smoke on their clothing! Imagine the impact this experience must have had on the heathen VIP's that day on the plain of Dura! Forgotten was the great golden statue set up with such pomp and ceremony. The lead story of the day, and many days to come, was the amazing experience of these three young Hebrews and how their God had saved them from the flames. It must have been told and retold thousands of times.

What a tremendous testimony to God's love and care for His faithful followers! Christ Himself came to deliver these three young men who refused to disobey God's commands, even when facing a white-hot furnace.

"Well," you say, "I'm certainly thankful that no one can dictate how I'm to worship. That would be terrible, having to choose between worshiping as someone else dictated or facing death like those three Hebrews!" Did you know that according to Bible prophecy, the greatest crisis in history is just before us? Like Shadrach, Meshach, and Abednego, every person living during Earth's last hours will be faced with a similar choice. A choice that will forever seal his destiny. A choice that will involve obedience to God and His commands or worshiping and obeying another power. And the penalty for obeying God will be death!

The most solemn warning ever given to Earth's inhabitants is recorded in the book of Revelation. Evidently God considers this message to be vitally important, for He said, "If any man have an ear, let him hear." Revelation 13:9. We must listen to this most urgent message!

"If any man worship the beast and his image, and receive his mark in his forehead, or in his hand, the same shall drink of the wine of the wrath of God, which is poured out without mixture into the cup of his indignation; and he shall be tormented with fire and brimstone in the presence of the holy angels, and in the presence of the Lamb." Revelation 14:9, 10.

Every person should carefully study this prophecy and make certain that he has nothing to do with the beast or his mark. Great blessings are promised to those who are loyal to God, who receive His seal, while the most terrifying warning in the Bible is given to those who receive the mark of the beast.

According to Bible prophecy, at the very end of time Earth's inhabitants will be divided into two groups: those who are loyal to God and obey His commandments, and those who worship the beast and receive his mark. Intense pressure will be brought to bear on those who refuse to worship the beast or receive his mark. They will be threatened with economic boycott: "He causeth all, both small and great, rich and poor, free and bond, to receive a mark in their right hand, or in their foreheads: And that no man might buy or sell, save he that had the mark, or the name of the beast, or the number of his name." Revelation 13:16, 17.

Eventually, a decree will be passed condemning to death those who refuse to worship the image of the beast. "He had power to give life unto the image of the beast, that the image of the beast should both speak, and cause that as many as would not worship the image of the beast should be killed." Revelation 13:15. Man says, "If you do not worship the beast, we will not buy anything from you or sell anything to you, and eventually we will kill you." God says, "If you worship the beast you will receive 'the wine of the wrath of God.' "

What is this wrath of God that is to be poured out upon the wicked? We find the answer in Revelation 15: "I saw another sign in heaven, great and marvellous, seven angels having the seven last plagues; for in them is filled up the wrath of God." Revelation 15:1. (Three of the seven last plagues are specifically targeted at the beast and those who worship him. In a later chapter we will study these plagues in detail.)

Of course, God would not pour out the seven last plagues upon mankind if He didn't first give them an opportunity to know what the mark of the beast is and how to avoid receiving it. No one need face this coming crisis unprepared. With His last warning message, God gives the key to unlock the prophecy so that we can understand what this power is, what its mark is, and how to avoid receiving it.

Let's turn to a prophecy found in Revelation and read about this beast power.

"I stood upon the sand of the sea, and saw a beast rise up out of the sea, having seven heads and ten horns, and upon his horns ten crowns, and upon his heads the name of blasphemy. And the beast which I saw was like unto a leopard, and his feet were as the feet of a bear, and his mouth as the mouth of a lion: and the dragon gave him his power, and his seat, and great authority. And I saw one of his heads as it were wounded to death; and his deadly wound was healed: and all the world wondered after the beast.

"And they worshipped the dragon which gave power unto the beast: and they worshipped the beast, saying, Who is like unto the beast? Who is able to make war with him? And there was given unto him a mouth speaking great things and blasphemies; and power was given unto him to continue forty and two months.

"And he opened his mouth in blasphemy against God, to blaspheme his name, and his tabernacle, and them that dwell in heaven. And it was given unto him to make war with the saints, and to overcome them: and power was given him over all kindreds, and tongues, and nations. And all that dwell upon the earth shall worship him, whose names are not written in the book of life of the Lamb slain from the foundation of the world." Revelation 13:1-8.

In this prophecy God again uses prophetic symbols to outline His warning to the world. As we studied the prophetic beast of Daniel 7, we discovered that God used beasts to represent kingdoms or ruling powers. Here in Revelation, we find pictured a composite beast made up of all four of

Daniel's great beasts. You will recall that the lion represented Babylon, the bear Medo-Persia, the leopard Greece, and the nondescript beast represented the Roman Empire. The beast of Revelation 13 is a power that succeeds these four great world empires. We are given seven characteristics which clearly identify this beast power. Only one power on Earth has all the characteristics used in this prophecy. Scripture and secular history make identification certain.

Speaking of the beast, John wrote, "The dragon gave him his power, and his seat, and great authority." Revelation 13:2. The dragon represents Satan: "There was war in heaven. . . . And the great dragon was cast out, that old serpent, called the Devil, and Satan, which deceiveth the whole world." Revelation 12:7-9.

Of course, Satan never steps into the battle in visible form. He works through other agencies, powers, and people. This chapter gives us a picture of the struggle between Satan and the church. "There appeared another wonder in heaven; and behold a great red dragon, having seven heads and ten horns, and seven crowns upon his heads. . . . And the dragon stood before the woman which was ready to be delivered, for to devour her child as soon as it was born. And she brought forth a man child, who was to rule all nations with a rod of iron: and her child was caught up unto God, and to his throne." Revelation 12:3-5. Here we see the dragon, or Satan, working through another power to destroy the man child, who is Jesus.

What nation was the devil working through at the time of Christ's birth? Did that ruling power attempt to take the life of Jesus when He was born? As we turn the pages of secular history, we discover that pagan Rome, under the Caesars, was ruling when Christ was born. Herod the Great decreed that all male infants in Bethlehem, up to the age of two, be slain in an attempt to kill Jesus when He was born.

A Roman governor, Pontius Pilate, condemned Christ

to death. Roman soldiers nailed Him to the cross, and a Roman seal secured the entrance to His tomb. Satan worked through pagan Rome to destroy Christ. And Jesus was resurrected and caught up to God and His throne as the prophecy predicted.

The prophecy predicted that this power, pagan Rome, would give its "seat" (or capital city), its "power," and "great authority," to the beast. Did pagan Rome fulfill this prophecy? And if so, who was the recipient?

History tells us that Constantine, the emperor of pagan Rome, donated his capital—the city of Rome—a treasury, and an army, to the Bishop of Rome! In A.D. 330 Constantine moved his capital to Byzantium and changed the name of the city to Constantinople in honor of himself.

When Constantine left Rome he gave his *seat* to the Pontiff. "The transfer of the emperor's residence to Constantinople was a sad blow to the prestige of Rome, and at the time one might have predicted her speedy decline. But the development of the Church, and the growing authority of the bishop of Rome, or the pope, gave her a new lease of life, and made her again the **capital**—this time the **religious capital**—of the civilized world."—Frank Frost Abbott, *A Short History of Rome,* pages 235, 236, emphasis supplied.

The Bishop of Rome became the head of the church and a king on a throne. A union of church and state followed. Most people are acquainted with the fact that Vatican City lies in the middle of Rome, the seat of the old Roman Empire. There, on approximately 109 acres, the papacy continues even today not only as a religious power but as a political power, to which most of the nations of the world send ambassadors or representatives.

Pagan Rome gave way to Papal Rome. We must keep in mind, of course, that the prophecy is talking about an organization, a system of theology, not individuals. A close study of the identifying marks of the beast power in Revelation 13 makes clear that it is the same power as was represented by the little horn of Daniel 7—which we considered in the previous chapter.

The prophet John said that this beast power would have a mark which he would try to force upon everyone. "He causeth all, both small and great, rich and poor, free and bond, to receive a mark in their right hand, or in their foreheads: and that no man might buy or sell, save he that had the mark, or the name of the beast, or the number of his name." Revelation 13:16, 17.

According to God's Word, this mark must be a symbol of rebellion or disloyalty to the government of God, for the Bible clearly describes those who will not receive the mark of the beast: "Here is the patience of the saints: here are they that keep the commandments of God, and the faith of Jesus." Revelation 14:12.

One group of people receive the mark of the beast, while the other is loyal and true to God by keeping all His commandments. The great issue to which this world is coming has something to do with the commandments of God.

God also has a mark, or a seal. It will be placed on the foreheads of His followers. "I saw another angel ascending from the east, having the seal of the living God: and he cried with a loud voice to the four angels, to whom it was given to hurt the earth and the sea, saying, Hurt not the earth, neither the sea, nor the trees, till we have sealed the servants of our God in their foreheads." Revelation 7:2, 3.

The final conflict of world history is over the the seal of God and the mark of the beast, between God's sign and a counterfeit sign. When we discover God's seal, or mark, it will be easy to discover the counterfeit mark that the beast power will enforce. God tells us what His sign or seal is:

"Moreover also I gave them my sabbaths, to be a sign

between me and them, that they might know that I am the Lord that sanctify them." Ezekiel 20:12.

"Speak thou also unto the children of Israel, saying, Verily my sabbaths ye shall keep: for it is a sign between me and you throughout your generations; that ye may know that I am the Lord that doth sanctify you." Exodus 31:13.

God said that the Sabbath is His sign or mark of authority. What does the beast power say is the mark of its authority? The following quotation is taken from a Catholic catechism:

"**Question:** How prove you that the church hath power to command feasts and holy days?

"**Answer:** By the very act of changing the Sabbath into Sunday, which Protestants allow of; and therefore they fondly contradict themselves by keeping Sunday strictly, and breaking most other feasts commanded by the same church.

"**Question:** Have you any other way of proving that the church has power to institute festivals of precept?

"**Answer:** Had she not had such power she could not have substituted the observance of Sunday, the first day of the week, for the observance of Saturday, the seventh day, a change for which there is no scriptural authority."—*An Abridgment of the Christian Doctrine,* page 58.

Sunday is the mark of the Catholic Church's religious authority, and it challenges Protestants to show why they have desecrated God's day and turned from the Bible Sabbath to follow a day that was instituted by custom, tradition, and a command of the Catholic Church.

Daniel predicted that this beast power would "think to change times and laws." Daniel 7:25. John predicted that Satan will try to force everyone to receive the mark of the beast: "He causeth all, both small and great, rich and poor, free and bond, to receive a mark in their right hand, or in their foreheads: and that no man might buy or sell, save he that had the mark, or the name of the beast, or the number of his name." Revelation 13:16, 17.

From a study of the prophecies in God's Word we can see that the time is not far distant when everyone, under threat of boycott and death, will be required to keep the first day of the week in direct violation of the command of God.

This idea is not new in America. For decades groups have advocated it. Pressure for Sunday legislation is being exerted upon many of our politicians at the present time. Some time ago the Supreme Court made a decision that will not be forgotten soon and will have repercussions in the coming months. It ruled that Sunday laws may be enforced, for they are no longer religious laws but laws designed to guard the health and welfare of the American people. However, in this decision, the late Justice William O. Douglas disagreed and made this dissenting statement to the majority decision of the Supreme Court:

"It seems to be plain that by these laws the States compel one, under sanction of law, to refrain from work or recreation on Sunday because of the majority's religious views about that day. The State by law makes Sunday a symbol of respect or adherence. Refraining from work or recreation in deference to the majority's feelings is within every person's choice. By what authority can government compel it?"—Warren L. Johns, *Dateline Sunday, U.S.A.,* page 154.

You will notice that he said that the state by "law" makes Sunday a symbol of respect or adherence. This is in accordance with the prophecy concerning this country that someday in the near future a national Sunday law will be passed forcing everyone to bow to the change that has been made in God's commandments by the beast power.

Many people ask, Does anyone have the mark of the beast now? No, not a single person has the mark of the beast yet. God has true followers in every church. When

Sunday keeping is enforced by civil law, every person must choose between allegiance to God by keeping His Sabbath or allegiance to the beast by keeping a man-made, counterfeit day—then and only then will anyone receive the mark of the beast.

To every soul will come the crucial test: Shall I obey God, or shall I obey man? It is not just a matter of days. It is a matter of masters.

Paul wrote, "Know ye not, that to whom ye yield yourselves servants to obey, his servants ye are to whom ye obey; whether of sin unto death, or of obedience unto righteousness?" Romans 6:16.

A most solemn moment will soon face every inhabitant on Earth. No one will be able to buy or sell who does not have the mark of the beast. First comes boycott, then the death decree. And for those who receive the mark of the beast, the seven last plagues.

But there is good news for those who choose to honor God and receive His seal. They may not be able to buy or sell, but God says, "Bread shall be given him; his waters shall be sure." Isaiah 33:16. And concerning the plagues to be poured out upon the earth, God promises: "Thou shalt not be afraid for the terror by night; nor for the arrow that flieth by day; nor for the pestilence that walketh in darkness; nor for the destruction that wasteth at noonday. A thousand shall fall at thy side, and ten thousand at thy right hand; but it shall not come nigh thee." Psalm 91:5-7.

Survival will not be easy. The Bible predicts that "there shall be a time of trouble, such as never was since there was a nation even to that same time." Daniel 12:1. But God gives a wonderful promise to those who choose to follow Him: "At that time thy people shall be delivered, every one that shall be found written in the book." Daniel 12:1.

John was shown a vision of those who gained the victory over the beast: "And I saw as it were a sea of glass mingled with fire: and them that had gotten the victory over the beast, and over his image, and over his mark, and over the number of his name, stand on the sea of glass, having the harps of God." Revelation 15:2.

Even now, God is pleading with His true followers to step out of the counterfeit religious systems to follow Him completely. "Come out of her, my people, that ye be not partakers of her sins, and that ye receive not of her plagues." Revelation 18:4.

Won't you this moment, without hesitation, step forward and place yourself on God's side, regardless of the cost?

How Can I Manage Stress?

Pastor George Vandeman tells the intriguing story of an old monastery perched atop a cliff in the beautiful country of Portugal. Visitors to this picturesque monastery were strapped into a huge wicker basket and pulled to the top of the cliff with an old, ragged rope. One day as a visitor settled himself into the basket for his precarious trip down the cliff, he asked the monk who would be lowering him, "Sir, how often do you get a new rope?" Calmly the aged monk replied, "Whenever the old one breaks."

Not a very comforting answer, to be sure! Yet, how many of us are rushing pell-mell through life on a threadbare rope? Pushing to the limit, continuously traveling in the fast lane with the throttle wide open—never giving a second thought that the rope might break, and that when it does, it can't be replaced.

Dr. Harold Shryock compares man's body to a finely tuned race car which is capable of maximum, all-out, open-throttle operation for only short periods of time. To push too hard too long could blow an engine. You see, a race driver deliberately removes his foot from the throttle occasionally so that the change in pressure within the motor will allow the lubricating oil to circulate more freely. Then he can again push the throttle to the limit—for a time.

Our intricately designed bodies are capable for short

periods of, producing all-out power, but we must have periods of reduced demands upon them, or something will break. However, slowing down isn't easy. We seem to be living in a world of jangled nerves: racing the clock, feeling the heat, conflicts on the job, traffic jams, family problems, racial tensions, fear, guilt, unemployment, hate, greed, worry, and on and on goes the list of deadly stressors. It has been estimated that as many as 75 percent of all complaints by patients are stress related.

Who can estimate the number of people who suffer silently from undue stress without seeking help? The number could be staggering. Perhaps there is scarcely anyone alive who has not found it hard at times to cope with someone or something. Stress management seminars, workshops, and retreats are cropping up everywhere. Physicians, psychiatrists, psychologists, and counselors are making millions trying to help people cope with stress. It seems that everyone has it and nobody wants it!

But strange as it may seem, a little stress isn't all bad. Dr. Hans Selye, considered the world's foremost authority on stress, wrote, "Stress is the spice of life. Since stress is associated with all types of activity we could avoid most of it only by never doing anything."—*Stress Without Distress,* page 85. However, he goes on to ask, "Who could enjoy a life of no runs, no hits, and no errors?"

Good question! Like so many others, we at times wish we could just sit in a rocking chair and rock, letting the rest of the world go by. But don't try it! Dr. Selye says that before long you would feel stressful about wasting time and being useless, and the sheer frustration of boredom would soon overcome you.

All worthwhile goals in life involve some stress to reach them, while the achievement of these goals brings meaning to life, fulfilling the basic human needs for accomplishment, self-esteem, and praise, which, in turn, alleviate many other serious forms of anxiety and stress. It is possible to set too many goals for ourselves to achieve or strive to reach unrealistic goals, which results in an overload of stress. Stress overload, either in a huge dose or in a series of small ones, cannot long be tolerated by our bodies without something giving way. As Selye says, "Our bodies are only as strong as the weakest vital part."

Yet in our society it seems that continuous, undue stress is a way of life. What executive doesn't feel the pressure to get ahead of the pack? Men race to build empires. They accumulate things, beat the competition, make a name for themselves. And in the process they sacrifice time with family, friends, and God. Today's high-pressure executive looks forward to some future time, retirement perhaps, when he can take "time to smell the roses," only to discover when it comes that the threadbare rope has raveled out and broken. As Dr. Selye so succinctly put it, they have been "so busy investing—there's no time to cash in."

But that isn't the way God intended that man should spend his time. He never planned for us to always travel in the fast lane. Many people are concerned. They want relief from tension and pressure. They're tired of the rat race. But, sad to say, too often people take the wrong road to relief. Robert Russell, health educator at the Kettering and Sycamore Medical Centers, says, "Often people under stress take the wrong road in dealing with it. Chemicals—drugs, alcohol, and tobacco—are among the stress relievers most frequently chosen by Americans."—"The Wrong Road for Managing Stress," Your Life and Health, stress issue, page 17. stress issue, page 17 At best, he says, these methods give only temporary relief, and often they have serious side effects contributing to much greater stress. Even vacations give only short-term relief; there's no permanent quieting of inner tension and restlessness.

Then how can a person cope with stress? We can't just

"chuck" it all and head for the hills. That's probably true, at least for most of us. We live in a world bombarded on every side with tension-producing sights, sounds, and smells, many of which we have no way of controlling.

But there's good news! There is an answer to human restlessness. The great theologian Augustine wrote about it centuries ago. Speaking about God, he said, "Thou hast made us for thyself, and our hearts are restless until they find rest in Thee."

Dr. Samuele Bacchiocchi echoes Augustine's statement in his book *Divine Rest for Human Restlessness:* "True rest is to be found not in *places* or through *pills* but rather in a right relationship with a Person, the Person of the Savior who says, 'Come to me, all you who are weary and burdened, and I will give you rest' (Matt. 11:28 NIV). Perfect rest and peace are not a human achievement but a divine gift."

This perfect rest and peace have their focal point in another of God's gifts, a special gift of time given to mankind at the end of creation week. For six days God had joyously worked in creating a new world. And what a world it was! Beautiful from pole to pole, beyond human comprehension or description. As the crowning act of creation, He made a beautiful thing. He said, "Let us make man in our image." Genesis 1:26.

Just think. Created in the very likeness of God! The very thought is awesome. What an interesting day that must have been for Adam and Eve, trying to understand it all. Drinking in all the wonders and beauties of a new world. All too soon they must have gazed in wide-eyed wonder as the blazing sun, in all its glory, began to edge over the western horizon, ending the sixth day of creation week.

But God's work of creation had not ended. The Bible says, "And on the seventh day God ended his work which he had made; and he rested on the seventh day from all his work which he had made." Genesis 2:2.

God rested, not because He was weary, for Isaiah 40:28 tells us that God never gets tired. God rested because He was finished, as one pleased with His accomplishments, viewing with satisfaction the work of His hands. Then God "blessed the seventh day, and sanctified it: because that in it he had rested from all his work which God created and made." Genesis 2:3.

God made this day an object of divine favor. He set the seventh day apart as holy time, a special day to continually remind man of his Creator and man's relationship to Him. As long as man remembered this day, he would never forget who he was or where he came from, for he would be eternally linked with God.

God designed this day especially to free man from all his secular interests and concerns. It was to be a twenty-four-hour oasis in this tension-filled world that would allow him to rest and worship God, letting his soul catch up to his body.

The Sabbath was the first full day of life for Adam and Eve. What a stupendous day it must have been! Their every glance was met with delightful creations fresh from the finger tips of an omnipotent God. But best of all, they were able to spend the day with God, resting, relaxing, and learning firsthand about the events of the first six days of creation. No day could have been more meaningful, joyful, or restful.

No doubt Adam and Eve had thousands of questions they wanted God to answer. After God had answered many of their questions, I can imagine Him saying, "There will be time for all your questions later." He may even have said, "That's why I made the Sabbath. Every week we'll have this special time to fellowship. I'm so pleased that you enjoy the things I've created. Every week, on this day, we'll walk and talk and rest together."

God made the Sabbath for man. Christ said so Himself:

"The sabbath was made for man."Mark 2:27. The Sabbath was made for man, not to make Adam and Eve holy and just, for they were holy and just. They were created perfect. It was a loving gift given to man that he might abide in the refreshing joy and sustaining rest of God.

After Adam and Eve sinned, their face-to-face fellowship with God was broken. God intended that through faith they should continually enter into His rest each Sabbath. But sad to say, as centuries passed many of Adam's descendents forgot the Sabbath, and soon they also forgot their Creator. That's why God had to send a reminder to man: "Remember the sabbath day, to keep it holy. Six days shalt thou labour, and do all thy work: but the seventh day is the sabbath of the Lord thy God: in it thou shalt not do any work, thou, nor thy son, nor thy daughter, thy manservant, nor thy maidservant, nor thy cattle, nor thy stranger that is within thy gates: for in six days the Lord made heaven and earth, the sea, and all that in them is, and rested the seventh day: wherefore the Lord blessed the sabbath day, and hallowed it." Exodus 20:8-11.

God planned that all nature should rest on the seventh day. He said that His children were not to do any work on that day. God said that people who work for us should also rest. He even said that our animals should rest on that day, for they too needed rest. No doubt God foresaw the restlessness, the stress and turmoil of today when He asked us to "remember" and rest on His day.

How does celebrating the Sabbath enable Christ to bring rest and peace to our stress-filled lives? Dr. Selye points out that much of man's stress is caused by a feeling that life has no meaning, that there is no hope. He has no sense of identity or self-esteem. That may have been why Alex Haley searched for his ancestral roots. But he didn't go back far enough. He only traced his roots back a few centuries.

"Through the Sabbath Christ offers us a much greater reassurance: the restful assurance that our roots can be traced back to God himself. ('So God created man in his own image.') . . . The assurance that our existence has value because it is not the product of *chance,* but of a personal choice on the part of a loving Creator."—*Divine Rest for Human Restlessness.*

Sometimes we feel that we are just a cog in a machine or a number in a computer. We have no sense of belonging to anyone or anything. But the Sabbath reminds us weekly that we belong to the Creator of the universe—that we are His children! Could anything be more reassuring? Could anything bring more of a sense of identity and self-esteem?

As we shut the world out and God in for this one day of the week, Christ's presence brings peace and tranquility to our stress-filled lives, just as His presence brought stillness and peace that stormy night to His disciples on Galilee. And what peace we can have trusting a God like that, not only on His special day, but every day as perplexities and pressures build. We can say with confidence, "Nothing will happen to me today that You and I can't handle together, Lord."

Doesn't that kind of faith bring rest from worry and fear? Doesn't it bring comfort to your troubled, stress-filled heart? As you lay aside your ordinary pursuits on the Sabbath, you will be able to experience the spiritual and restful presence of the Lord, for it is God's presence that brings rest to the Sabbath. "My Presence will go with you, and I will give you rest." Exodus 33:14, NIV.

Dr. Bacchiocchi says, "Because we enter into the spiritual presence and communion of the Lord on the Sabbath, the fourth commandment enjoins us to do all our work in six days in order that we can be free on the seventh day to 'have a vacation with God,' as Thomas Aquinas expressed it. Without the Sabbath vacation with God, our weekdays would be as tasteless as spaghetti without sauce or as food without salt." *Ibid.*, page 11.

The Sabbath was to be a day of rest—not a day of self-centered rest, but a day of divine-centered rest. Otherwise, it would truly be only a human holiday. God intended this day to be free from producing, achieving, competing, accumulating, and manipulating—a day free to rest and celebrate with God the works of His creation, His power, and His love. It is a day that teaches us that there is something far more important to do with our time and talents than serving self. It teaches us to be concerned with the welfare of all of God's creatures, man *and* beast.

All of life takes on more meaning as we contemplate God's creation. All men become brothers regardless of race, color, or status. All are created by God, and all are redeemed by Him. We all have one Father.

Perhaps the facet of true Sabbath keeping that brings the greatest release from tension and anxiety is the assurance of God's acceptance, forgiveness, and salvation: freedom from guilt. Guilt is the number one killer. There can be no long-term inner peace for the heart that is burdened with a load of sin and remorse. Nothing can sap one's vitality more than a sense of guilt.

God says that He is the One who can sanctify us, the One who can forgive and restore us into His fellowship and rest. He gave us the Sabbath as a sign of His willingness to do that: "Moreover also I gave them my sabbaths, to be a sign between me and them, that they might know that I am the Lord that sanctify them." Ezekiel 20:12.

Paul challenged the Hebrews to enter into the rest of God's salvation. He uses the Sabbath rest as a type of the rest that God wants to give each of us from our load of sin and guilt: "And God did rest the seventh day from all his works." "There remaineth therefore a rest to the people of God. For he that is entered into his rest, he also hath ceased from his own works, as God did from his. Let us labour therefore to enter into that rest." Hebrews 4:4, 9-11.

As we bring our guilt to the foot of the cross and slip our hand into God's hand and allow Him to bring peace and rest to our troubled hearts, our alienation is ended, and we can experience His acceptance, forgiveness, and salvation. We enter into His rest, just as we enter into God's rest on His holy day. This rest will continue throughout eternity, for the prophet Isaiah wrote, "And it shall come to pass, that from one new moon to another, and from one sabbath to another, shall all flesh come to worship before me, saith the Lord." Isaiah 66:23.

Our celebration of the Sabbath here is but a foretaste of the greater celebration and rest we will experience when Christ sets up His kingdom. The Sabbath is a precious legacy handed down from creation week for God's people to enjoy for all time to come.

Many people say, "I'd love to celebrate the Sabbath and honor God's special day. Tell me how I can experience it. How can I enjoy this special gift to the fullest?" Perhaps those questions can best be answered by asking another: How did Jesus celebrate the Sabbath when He was on Earth? Did He conform to the rituals and customs of the Jews in His day, or was there a difference?

Let's take a quick trip through the Gospels and spend a few Sabbaths with our Lord. There is no better example to follow. What did Jesus do on the Sabbath? Luke gives a brief glimpse of Jesus' activities on this day: "He went to Nazareth, where he had been brought up, and on the Sabbath day he went into the synagogue, as was his custom. And he stood up to read." Luke 4:16, NIV. Today we would say, "Jesus returned to His hometown, Nazareth, and on Saturday He went to church as usual, and read to the congregation."

On another Sabbath Jesus was teaching in one of the synagogues, and He spotted a crippled woman, bent over, not able to stand erect. She had been in that condition for eighteen years. "When Jesus saw her, he called her to him, and said unto her, Woman, thou art loosed from thine infirmity. And he laid his hands on her: and immediately she was made straight, and glorified God." Luke 13:12, 13.

Matthew tells of a time when he and the other disciples were with Jesus on the Sabbath. "At the time Jesus went through the grainfields on the sabbath." Matthew 12:1.

From the accounts given by Jesus' own followers and friends, we discover that Jesus always went to the synagogue on Sabbath. Sometimes He read. Sometimes He taught. Sometimes He healed, and sometimes He listened.

For Jesus, the Sabbath was a day to praise God and worship in His house. It was a day to teach and heal those "bound" by Satan, a day to fellowship with friends. It was a day to do good, to minister to people's spiritual needs and sometimes to their physical needs. Jesus Himself said, "It is lawful to do good on the Sabbath." Matthew 12:12, NIV.

Yet there appears to be a limit to what we might call "doing good." Jesus' followers, those who had been with Him, who had sat at His feet and learned from Him for over three years, refused to make the Sabbath a common work day. The Bible states that they took His body down from the cross and laid it in a new tomb on the preparation day, or Friday. The women who were with them watched how He was placed in the sepulcher. They made certain that the men placed the body of their Lord carefully and gently in the tomb. Then the Bible says that "they returned, and prepared spices and ointments; and rested the sabbath day according to the commandment." Luke 23:56.

In this hour of grief, Jesus' most devoted followers and friends laid aside the work of caring for the body of their Lord until after the hours of the Sabbath day. The Bible says they rested according to the commandment.

Jesus Himself rested on the Sabbath in the tomb. He

had rested on the seventh day of creation, and now He rested on the seventh day in the tomb after He finished His work of redemption.

Special promises are given to those who honor the sacred hours of the Sabbath:

"If thou turn away thy foot from the sabbath, from doing thy pleasure on my holy day; and call the sabbath a delight, the holy of the Lord, honourable; and shalt honour him, not doing thine own ways, nor finding thine own pleasure, nor speaking thine own words: Then shalt thou delight thyself in the Lord; and I will cause thee to ride upon the high places of the earth, . . . for the mouth of the Lord hath spoken it." Isaiah 58:13, 14.

The Sabbath is to be a delightful day. A day to remember and honor.

"That sounds wonderful," you say. "But how does it work? I'd like to know how real twentieth-century people do it."

Let's interview the Browns, a middle-class family living in a middle-sized city in the northwestern United States.

Bill is an architect. His wife, Marilyn, is a nurse who has worked only part time since the birth of their three children—Susan, Randy, and Mindy. Like most American families, the Brown's home is filled with endless activities and deadlines. "It gets pretty hectic at times," says Marilyn. "I don't know how we could make it without the Sabbath. It's the highlight of our whole week. After Sabbath we actually feel refreshed and ready for another week. Of course, not too long after the Sabbath ends, Bill and I begin thinking about how we can make the next Sabbath special for the children. We try to think of new ways to make it more meaningful to them."

"And that's a challenge," Bill says. "But it's worth the

effort. If the weather is good we love to be out in nature. Otherwise we do something for someone else. Sometimes we form a singing band with friends and visit nursing homes. Other times we visit someone who is sick, or we take food to someone in need."

Randy, age eleven, likes to head for the hills on a warm Sabbath afternoon. "After church we take a lunch and usually a few friends and go to a river up in the mountains," he says. "I love it! We try to see how many different birds we can see. My dad knows about every bird that flies, I think. And one of our friends knows most of the wildflowers, so it's a lot of fun. It's just neat being up there where it's quiet and peaceful. You forget that the rest of the world exists."

When it's cold and stormy, twelve-year-old Susan likes everyone to sit around the fire and play Bible games with Dad and Mom. "Of course we all love to hear Dad tell stories or listen to Mom read to us," she says.

What about seven-year-old Mindy? "What I like best is that the work is all done and we can just spend the whole time doing things together," she says.

Marilyn makes careful preparations for the Sabbath. "I start by making lists," she says. "I have a list for everything! I usually plan the menu for the next Sabbath. I try to do the shopping for groceries ahead of time so I can do my baking and cooking before Friday, which is our preparation day. I try to freeze some casseroles, salads, and desserts during the week. Perhaps that sounds strange to you, but it's biblical, you know. Exodus 16:23 says, 'The Lord has commanded that tomorrow is a holy day of rest, dedicated to him. Bake today what you want to bake and boil what you want to boil. Whatever is left should be put aside and kept for tomorrow.' [TEV]. That's wonderful advice, because I can rest on the Sabbath too."

"We all help Mother so she can enjoy Sabbath too," Susan says. "We all have our assigned duties on Friday mornings."

Randy explains that everyone gets up an hour earlier on Friday to help with the housework, and Mindy is proud that "every Friday morning we all change the sheets on our beds and clean our own rooms." Everyone has a job. Susan cleans the bathrooms, and Randy washes the car and brings in the wood.

"I'm the vacuuming expert around here," Bill says. "I've got it down to a science, too. I can do the whole job in twenty-five minutes!"

To keep the Sabbath special Marilyn makes the Sabbath meals tastier and more attractive. She puts out her best dishes, tablecloths, and napkins. If flowers are blooming in the yard, she cuts some for the table and the bathrooms. The children love that. She likes to make the Friday evening meal simple, but extra nice—usually a fruit salad, homemade cinnamon rolls, and open-face sandwiches.

It's Mindy's job to turn off the TV and put away all newspapers and magazines and books—except Sabbath ones, of course.

Everything is ready when sunset comes on Friday evening. "It's our way of welcoming in the Sabbath day," Bill says. "We like to gather around the piano and sing, and then we read something from the Bible and have a story or two. We also take time to share our experiences of the past week. It just keeps us tuned to each other and to God, and it builds a wonderful bond between all of us as a family. It helps to remind us of who we are and where we are going—it sort of keeps our priorities straight."

Mindy's favorite part of Sabbath is Sabbath School. "We sing and have Bible stories," she says. "I learn all about Jesus, and I have lots of friends there too!"

Every Sabbath morning finds the Brown family in church unless someone is seriously ill. They feel that they have a sacred appointment with God, and they don't want to miss it. It's a time when God can speak to them and they can praise Him. Yet it's more than an appointment with God. It's also a time to declare to the world that God is worthy to receive praise and honor and worship. It's a way of demonstrating loyalty and allegiance to Him as Creator and Redeemer. "We wear our very best clothes to church because God is there," Mindy explains. "I'd like to sing a song I learned at Sabbath School. Here goes." And she sang with gusto:

> Sabbath is a happy day,
> happy day, happy day.
> Sabbath is a happy day,
> I love every Sabbath.

What's Ahead for America?

O beautiful for spacious skies,
For amber waves of grain,
For purple mountain majesties
Above the fruited plain!

America! America!
God shed His grace on thee,
And crown thy good with brotherhood
From sea to shining sea.
                                —Katherine Lee Bates

God has extravagantly "shed His grace" upon America. The scenic wonders of her fifty states are limitless! Massive mountain ranges, like the protruding vertebrae of giant dinosaurs, divide the continent.These mountains, with their spectacular waterfalls and gushing streams, twist in and out of fertile valleys.

The towering Rockies of the West snuggle tightly in blankets of snow, only to burst into exquisite beauty at the climax of winter's chill. And what could equal the ever-changing hues of the shifting sands and flowering cacti of the Southwest deserts with their ghostly, silhouetted rock formations standing guard over the desert floor—or the splendor of Mount Hood's magnificent sunsets?

Unless, of course, it would be the grandeur of Arizona's Grand Canyon. Its vastness is breathtaking. In fact, it has been called the most spectacular sight on Earth.

Is it any wonder that this great land has captured the imagination of people around the world? Truly, they say, it is a land flowing with milk and honey.

But surprising as it may seem, it wasn't the beauty of the New World that beckoned the Pilgrim fathers to these shores, nor was it an obsession with wealth or fame. They were a profoundly committed people, with a consuming desire to know God's will. And they wanted the freedom to follow His will as they understood it. For centuries, this freedom had been ruthlessly denied many people of the Old World. The oppression that they experienced kindled the fires of the Reformation.

The Pilgrims were certainly aware of what had gone before—the Inquisition, the massacre of the Huguenots, the slaughter of the Waldenses, the burnings at the stake, the hangings, the whippings, and the imprisonments.

This history was still fresh in the minds of the Pilgrims. In virtually all the countries of Europe, whether under Catholic or Protestant rule, freedom of religious belief and practice was unknown except to those who belonged to the established church. England's James I, who authorized the 1611 English translation of the Bible—the Book that proclaims "liberty and justice for all"—declared that the Puritans would have to conform to the teachings of the Church of England, or he would harry them out of the land or hang them. So the sparks of persecution spread, fanned on by the Protestant Reformation. It was a difficult time for those who chose to worship God as their conscience directed.

"Hunted, persecuted, and imprisoned, they could discern in the future no promise of better days, and many yielded to the conviction that for such as would serve God according to the dictates of their conscience, England was ceasing forever to be a habitable place."—*History of New England,* chapter 3, paragraph 43.

"When God's hand seemed pointing them across the sea, to a land where they might found for themselves a state, and leave to their children the precious heritage of religious liberty, they went forward, without shrinking, in the path of providence."—*The Great Controversy,* page 291.

Those sixty-four days crossing the Atlantic were a rough and trying voyage. The ailing *Mayflower* Pilgrims, numbering 102, set foot on the shores of the New World November 9, 1620. Sinking to their knees, they thanked God for a safe journey and for a new home. Soon the good news spread throughout the Old World of a land where everyone might enjoy the fruit of his own labor and obey the convictions of his own conscience. Thousands flocked to the shores of the New World.

By 1775 the struggle of the colonies for independence raged. On the evening of July 4, 1776, the Declaration of Independence was ratified after a moving appeal by Patrick Henry. This revered document, penned by Thomas Jefferson, declared: "We hold these truths to be self-evident, that all men are created equal, that they are endowed by their Creator with certain inalienable Rights, that among these are Life, Liberty, and the pursuit of Happiness."

Thirteen years after the Declaration of Independence was signed, the Constitution was ratified. The first ten amendments to the Constitution are known as the Bill of Rights, the first of which begins: "Congress shall make no law respecting an establishment of religion, or prohibiting the free exercise thereof."

This nation was established without the power of kingly authority and without a state church. Our forefathers were determined that America should enjoy the benefits of two great principles: civil liberty and religious freedom. Church and state were to be forever separated. America was destined to be a great land! The struggling, isolated colonies grew into a confederation of states, and the world was amazed at the peace and prosperity of a "church without a pope, and a state without a king."

We have studied the prophecies concerning empires past. History testifies to the accuracy of their fulfillment. But what about the United States? It would be surprising to discover that a land destined to become such a vibrant and dynamic nation, one with such significant developments in religious affairs, had been left out of Bible prophecy. Doesn't God say anything in Bible prophecy about this great land?

Indeed, He does! Fourteen centuries before Columbus discovered the New World, the prophet John foretold America's unique rise to power, the time she would come on the scene, her form of government, and her influence in world affairs.

In Revelation 13, John describes a beast power (which we considered in the previous chapter) that is identical to the "little horn" power described by the prophet Daniel.

But notice the next part of John's vision. The aged prophet saw another beast, or nation, rising to power at the same time that the first beast received its deadly wound. "I beheld another beast coming up out of the earth; and he had two horns like a lamb, and he spake as a dragon." Revelation 13:11.

There was something different about this nation. The other beasts arose out of the sea, or populated areas of the world. This nation came up out of the earth, or wilderness area. What young, peace-loving nation was growing in power and prominence in a wilderness area of the world in 1798, just as the papal power was "wounded unto death"? Only one nation can claim that prophetic distinction—the United States of America. In just two centuries she has become one of the most powerful nations on Earth.

It is significant that this lamblike beast has no crowns

on its horns, as did the beasts preceding it. In other words, it would be a nation without a king, having a church without a pope.

The Statue of Liberty has long been a symbol of the freedoms to be enjoyed within the borders of this land. But this will not always be so! The rest of the story is not so pleasant. A time will come when this nation, while appearing to be gentle as a lamb, will speak like a dragon, for the Bible says, "He spake as a dragon." Revelation 13:11. Sometime, somehow, a change will take place in the government of the United States. In fact, it is already taking place. Usually nations speak through their legislative enactments, or laws. And throughout history, whenever and wherever the dragon's voice has been heard, there has been persecution.

The prophecy continues with a most startling announcement. Speaking of America, the Bible says: "He exerciseth all the power of the first beast before him, and causeth the earth and them which dwell therein to worship the first beast, whose deadly wound was healed." Revelation 13:12.

Unbelievable as it may seem, the persecuting character of the first beast is to be duplicated by the lamblike beast turned dragon—or the United States. The prophecy states that this lamblike beast will "cause" them that dwell on the earth to worship the first beast.

"That could *never* happen in America," you say. "We are 'the land of the free and the home of the brave.' We have the Declaration of Independence, the Constitution, and the Bill of Rights to protect us from any infringement upon our liberties. We have a guarantee of separation of church and state. Any infringement of our liberties would be directly contrary to the principles of our government."

So it would! This can happen only if the principles of civil and religious liberty written into our Constitution are abandoned, or simply ignored. But the Bible clearly declares that it will be so, and incredible as it may seem, it's happening!

Continuing the prophecy concerning the United States, we read: "He doeth great wonders, so that he maketh fire come down from heaven on the earth in the sight of men, and deceiveth them that dwell on the earth by the means of those miracles which he had power to do in the sight of the beast; saying to them that dwell on the earth, that they should make an image to the beast, which had the wound by the sword, and did live." Revelation 13:13, 14.

These verses speak of "an image to the beast." To make an image or likeness of something, we copy it. For our government to copy the aims and policies of apostate religion, it would have to tear down the wall of separation between church and state. Religious power would have to so control our government that she would make and enforce religious laws, for the Bible says that she "causeth the earth and them which dwell therein to worship the first beast, whose deadly wound was healed." Revelation 13:12. This prophecy clearly indicates that the authority of this nation will be used to enforce some religious observance which will be an act of homage to an apostate religious power.

After God's dire prediction concerning the fate of those who worship the beast and receive his mark, (see Revelation 14:9-11), the Bible pictures those who are faithful to God: "Here is the patience of the saints: here are they that keep the commandments of God, and the faith of Jesus." Revelation 14:12. Since those who keep God's commandments are contrasted with those who worship the beast, it follows that keeping God's law, on the one hand, and its violation, on the other, will distinguish between the worshipers of God and the worshipers of the beast.

"The church, . . . after changing the day of rest from the Jewish Sabbath, or seventh day of the week, to the first, made the third commandment refer to Sunday as the day to be kept holy as the Lord's Day."—*Catholic Encyclopedia*, volume 4, page 153.

Here the papacy claims that its mark of authority in religious matters is its ability to change the law of God, instituting Sunday as a day of worship.

"The observance of Sunday by the Protestants is an homage they pay, in spite of themselves, to the authority of the [Catholic] Church."—*Plain Talk About the Protestantism of Today,* page 213.

If, according to the symbols of Bible prophecy, the United States is to exercise all the power of papal Rome and cause the people of the world to "make an image to the beast," it need only exalt, or legislate, the observance of Sunday as a day of worship and cause the rest of the world to accept it.

It is interesting to notice that the worship of the beast, or keeping the day it claims as its mark, will not always be a matter of voluntary choice. Religious legislation will be enacted, compelling people by threats of boycott and finally by the threat of death to worship the beast. "He had power to give life unto the image of the beast, that the image of the beast should both speak, and cause that as many as would not worship the image of the beast should be killed. And he causeth all, both small and great, rich and poor, free and bond, to receive a mark in their right hand, or in their foreheads: and that no man might buy or sell, save he that had the mark, or the name of the beast, or the number of his name." Revelation 13:15-17.

The time is not far distant when everyone will be required to keep holy the first day of the week instead of the day commanded by God.

Religious pressure is even now being exerted upon our politicians. Since 1980, Christian Voice has put out a comprehensive Presidential Biblical Scoreboard which rates every U.S. senator or representative on "moral-family" votes. It designates which legislators vote correctly, according to the Bible. It then urges the nation to put so-called Christians into public office so the nation can become offically a "nation under God." In doing so, it blatantly contradicts the Constitution, which clearly states that "no religious test shall ever be required as a qualification to any office or public trust under the United States."

For some time now, religious minority voting blocs have been organizing across America. Jerry Falwell, president of Moral Majority and the new Liberty Federation (of which Moral Majority is a part), writes in one of his recruitment letters: "Did you know that the Moral Majority is now the largest minority voting bloc in America? Did you know that the Moral Majority now represents more voters than labor, any ethnic or racial minority, or feminist group? This is a fact."

Reading again from the same letter: "Louis Harris, the famous pollster, recently declared that Moral Majority now represents 20 percent of the electorate. . . . Any political expert will tell you that this 20 percent can virtually determine who is elected and who is not elected to office in the years ahead."

Robert Grant is the director of Christian Voice, a group that reportedly intends to mold Christian and other "morally right-thinking people" into a potent political factor in American politics. Says Grant: "If Christians unite we can do anything. We can pass any law or any amendment, and that's exactly what we intend to do."—*Ministry,* December 1979.

In a recent editorial, Norman Cousins said that he believes the Moral Majority is on a collision course with the American tradition that draws a line between religious influence and religious control: "The moment religious forces seek to control government rather than to influence it they threaten the very society they seek to protect."—*Liberty,* March/April 1983, page 26.

Think for a moment! Wasn't Jesus Christ a moral and ethical leader—the greatest that ever lived? Of course. Yet, we find no evidence that He ever coerced people to follow Him. He was the greatest communicator, the greatest persuader, but He never organized political groups to press for legislative reforms in the society of His day. Jesus wanted people to change, but His was a mission based on love, respect, and free choice. That is the spirit of Christ. The spirit of coercion, threats, and force is not the spirit of love, but of Satan.

It is frightening that when a person is convinced that he is doing God's will, it is so easy to believe that anything he does in furtherance of that conviction is justified.

The prophet John said that "all the world wondered after the beast." Revelation 13:3. Surely, the deadly wound has been healed! Even the scar is disappearing! But "still to be closed is the most important rift of all—between the world's 350 million Protestants and about 800 million Catholics. . . . Today, however, hatchets are being buried at such a pace that many theologians say that Lutherans, Anglicans and some other denominations may reconcile with Rome long before Protestantism's next centennial."—*U.S. News and World Report,* November 14, 1983.

One religious writer, commenting on these prophecies over a hundred years ago, confidently stated: "The Protestants of the United States will be foremost in stretching their hands across the gulf to grasp the hand of spiritualism; they will reach over the abyss to clasp hands with the Roman power; and under the influence of this threefold union, this country will follow in the steps of Rome in trampling on the rights of conscience."—*The Great Controversy,* page 588.

Even the United States government has been willing to court the interests and favors of the Vatican. On January 10, 1984, while seemingly circumventing the democratic process, the White House and the Catholic Church announced that they had established diplomatic relations and that William A. Wilson, the President's personal envoy to the Vatican, had been nominated by the White House as the United States Ambassador to the Vatican. This action is totally contrary to a U.S. Supreme Court decision stating that neither a state nor the federal government "can pass laws which aid one religion, aid all religions, or prefer one religion over another."—*Everson* v. *Board of Education*, 1947.

This radical change in a longstanding national policy was accomplished with hardly a whimper of dissent in either house. The First Amendment to the United States Constitution was ignored, and the violation of the American principle of equality of all religions aroused no debate in either house. Someone said it was a "nonissue"—that no one cared. But that isn't true! *Not one religious denomination supported the legislation.* Opposition was formidable from conservative and religious groups. But this massive opposition was ignored by the administration and the media.

This action came as no surprise to the student of Bible prophecy, for this candid prediction is made concerning the United States: "He exerciseth all the power of the first beast [papal Rome] before him, and causeth the earth and them which dwell therein to worship the first beast, whose deadly wound was healed." Revelation 13:12. Amazing! The United States will lead all other nations in paying homage to the beast by ultimately honoring her day of worship.

It is very difficult to believe that such a radical departure from our government's principles of religious freedom could come about. But the Bible states that it will—and it is!

"All that dwell upon the earth shall worship him, whose names are not written in the book of life." Revelation 13:8. And that decree will be made by the lamblike beast, speaking as a dragon. As one writer says,

"When the leading churches of the United States, uniting upon such points of doctrine as are held by them in common, shall influence the state to enforce their decrees and to sustain their institutions, then Protestant America will have formed an image to the Roman hierarchy, and the infliction of civil penalties upon dissenters will inevitably result."—*The Great Controversy,* page 445.

Here we see the issue to which the whole world is being brought. According to Bible prophecy, the United States will be the primary moving force, the agent, for enacting legislation that will cause everyone to worship the beast. Then the world will unite in a crusade against those who refuse to comply with their repressive religious regulations. Civil penalties will be enforced, and finally those refusing to worship the beast will be declared deserving of death.

But the law of God's government, which includes the seventh-day rest and worship, instituted by the Creator Himself, deserves our loyalty and obedience. God's warning is clear: "If any man worship the beast and his image, and receive his mark in his forehead, or in his hand, the same shall drink of the wine of the wrath of God, which is poured out without mixture into the cup of his indignation." Revelation 14: 9, 10.

Uniting with this message of God's final warning to the inhabitants of the earth is heard God's loving call: "Come out of her my people, that ye be not partakers of her sins, and that ye receive not of her plagues." Revelation 18:14.

Many conscientious people have been confused. They have followed the beast unknowingly. As they hear God's call to come out of Babylon—the false systems of worship—they step out and join the ranks of those who refuse to worship the beast or to receive the plagues.

John saw in vision the triumphal celebration given in heaven for those who had been victorious over the beast and his image:

"I saw as it were a sea of glass mingled with fire: and them that had gotten the victory over the beast, and over his image, and over his mark, and over the number of his name, stand on the sea of glass, having the harps of God. And they sing the song of Moses . . . and the song of the Lamb, saying, Great and marvellous are thy works, Lord God Almighty; just and true are thy ways, thou King of saints." Revelation 15: 2, 3.

Friend, don't you want to be a part of that great celebration? Jesus says, "Behold, I come quickly." Revelation 22:12. Are you ready for the glory of the coming of our Lord?

How Can I Survive the Coming World Crisis?

Survivalists—rugged individualists convinced that doomsday is just around the corner—seem to be rapidly edging their way into the American consciousness. People from all walks of life—rich and poor, young and old, male and female—are preparing themselves, "just in case."

Survival is big business—a whole new industry is mushrooming. A survival mentality has spread to thousands of concerned Americans.

Thinking men and women today are questioning whether mankind can actually survive escalating crime, economic depression or collapse, contaminated and diminishing natural resources, civil insurrection, natural disasters, or nuclear attack. Dare we sit idly by and wait for the inevitable? A growing number of survivalists think not! If you want to survive the coming crises, they say, you have to prepare *now*. Tomorrow may be too late! "But," someone says, "aren't these survivalists just a bunch of overactive paranoiacs, trigger-happy extremists, or prophets of doom?" Perhaps that fairly describes some of them, but the majority of survivalists are rational, educated, thinking people seeking to find a way to survive any personal, national, or international disaster.

Robert K. Brown, editor of *Survive* magazine, writes, "After all, that's what survival and self-sufficiency is. Learning to prepare for the worst, while working for the best." Fall 1981, page 6.

"Well," you ask, "just what *are* some of these earth-shattering crises for which we need to prepare in order to survive? Is the coming rough time fact—or is it all in the imagination of a group of wild-eyed fanatics?"

Ralph and Suzanne may have thought so until a few months ago. Living in what they considered to be a rather secure middle-class neighborhood in the suburbs of Los Angeles, life seemed quite pleasant. Weekends and evenings, they pursued the diversions of the "good life": skiing, hang-gliding, auto races.

Suddenly it all changed. Within two weeks their home was burglarized three times. Their friends' home down the street was also burglarized, and the wife was raped and beaten by a gang of toughs. Ralph and Suzanne decided that the time had come to learn how to protect themselves.

They bought books and magazines dealing with self-protection and survival. They attended classes. They purchased firearms and soon acquired proficiency in using them. They even learned the art of pressing their own bullets!

Sound drastic? Perhaps. However, most survival books and magazines *urge* people to buy firearms for self defense. In fact, not long ago the mayor of Miami appeared on television to urge the citizens of that city to arm themselves for protection—as the police force could not answer all the emergency calls for help against criminals!

M. C. Adley, writing in *Survival* magazine concerning the use of guns for protection, said: "If you can get a permit to carry a concealed firearm, do so. If not, we can't recommend you violate the law. . . . If you do not take measures to protect your physical and mental well being, no one else is going to do it for you. As one sage is reported to have uttered, 'I would rather be judged by 12 today, than carried by six tomorrow.' "

Right or wrong, the possibility of people walking the streets with shotguns or concealed weapons is terrifying, to say the least! In the heat of passion anything can happen.

As Ralph and Suzanne continued studying and attending survival classes, they learned of another major crisis many are convinced is imminent—a total economic collapse. The national and world economy, many warn, is racing without brakes toward a precipice. The collapse of currency, astronomical interest rates, massive national indebtedness, and hyperinflation—these are but a few of the predictions of today's financial seers. Their books sell briskly, proving the lure of doomsday predictions to a jittery populace.

Many such prophets of disaster preach a radical change in lifestyle. Our problems are not just economic, they tell us. Something is spiritually wrong with America as well. The nerves of society are deadened with the morphine of tradition and are incapable of sensing the certainty of the crisis ahead. They advise citizens to buy gold, silver, and diamonds. Invest in goods. Ignore the banks. Accumulate food.

In his book *How to Prosper During the Coming Bad Years,* Howard J. Ruff writes: "The purpose of this book is to persuade you that the United States is about to enter its greatest test period since the Civil War—an inflationary spiral leading to a depression that will be remembered with a shudder for generations. . . . No one knows exactly where the breaking point is, but it's coming, and soon. . . . America is truly on the brink, and so is the rest of the world, because when we sneeze, the rest of the world gets pneumonia." Page 14.

Ruff then predicts a whole series of unpleasant events looming just ahead: massive unemployment, erosion of personal savings to nothing, the collapse of private and government pension programs, including unemployment, Social Security, and welfare funds, an international monetary holocaust that will sweep all currency and other paper fortunes down the drain, and finally—utter chaos!

Those preparing for the coming bad times as predicted by the prophets of doom are indeed stockpiling food, medical supplies, and water. And they are stockpiling guns, ammunition, and electronic surveillance equipment to protect themselves. Sound grim? Indeed! However, many feel the worst is yet to be told. Perhaps the most complex and frightening of all the survival scenarios is focused on the threat of radiation.

Dr. Helen Coldicotte, a pediatrician at Boston's Children's Hospital Medical Center, writes: "As a physician, I contend that nuclear technology threatens life on our planet with extinction. If present trends continue, the air we breathe, the food we eat, and the water we drink will soon be contaminated with enough radioactive pollutants to pose a potential health hazard far greater than any plague humanity has ever experienced."—*Nuclear Madness,* page 1.

She states that already dangerous concentrations of radioactive poisons have appeared in the milk our children drink. But think for a moment. What would be the level of radiation fallout and pollution in the event of World War III? Most of us cringe at the very thought! With all the exotic weaponry, with all the nuclear, chemical, and biological arsenals scattered over Planet Earth, such a conflict would be sheer madness! And for those who might survive, unimaginable privation, disease, and suffering would follow.

Is nuclear war a possibility? Most statesmen, military leaders, scientists, and historians think so!

Sir Charles Snow commented: "We know with the certainty of statistical truth that if enough of these weapons are made—by enough states—some of them are going to blow up through accident, folly, or madness."

No one knows when some madman will turn the key,

push the button, and drop the bomb. If indeed such an irrational act should trigger World War III, what would be our chances? According to information released by civil defense agencies, scientists, and medical researchers, the answer is not encouraging. Colin Bruce Sibley, physicist, author, and member of the Institute for Defense Studies, paints a grim scenario which he sees following the detonation of nuclear bombs. He pictures Europe and Britain as a graveyard. The major cities of America, Russia, and China annihilated. Millions dead or dying. Half the population of some large nations wiped out. Still more death and dying as radiation sickness sets in. No signs of life in the main target areas—where the ground is still extremely radioactive.

And for those who survive? Grim conditions beyond description. Water and food worth more than gold! Nonexistent medical care. Rodents spreading disease. Wild animals and dog packs roaming the country insane with hunger. No law—no order.

"Groups of self-appointed rulers and criminal elements attack peaceful survivors, looting, killing, raping, and attempting to subject survivors to their demands."—*Surviving Doomsday,* page 51.

Some may in fact survive such a holocaust, but the changes wrought by this huge exchange of nuclear weaponry would be long-term and unknown. No one can accurately predict the results of such radiation.

And what about the frightening use of chemical warfare? "Remember: One tiny drop of nerve agent deposited on any part of your skin will result in death."—*Surviving Doomsday,* page 37.

And, of course, what of the horrors of germ warfare? This unique form of madness clearly pinpoints man's inhumanity to man!

With all this in mind, survivalists believe that if we can't have a guarantee of peace, we should at least have a plan for survival and get ourselves prepared.

Sweden and Switzerland—both countries of long-standing neutrality—take the prospects of World War III seriously. They maintain highly developed civil defense programs, second only to the Soviet Union. Sibley writes: "Meanwhile, the Soviet Union possesses the largest and most comprehensive war survival program in the world today. The Soviet leadership never tires of reiterating that victory is impossible unless every Soviet citizen has undergone intensive practical and moral—psychological—civil defense training. . . . Russian citizens are being taught not be be deterred by the awful spectre of nuclear, chemical and biological warfare—but instead to prepare for its inevitability!"— *Surviving Doomsday*, page 5.

The Russians have also developed and tested plans for evacuating almost the entire population from their cities and towns. In fact, it has been reported that Russia has stockpiled enough food underground to feed its entire population for a year. And ironically, much of this food we sold or gave to them!

It seems that the Soviets are prepared to face a nuclear attack and to survive and inherit the scorched lands of a once-beautiful planet—that is, if all goes according to their plans! They *are* preparing!

Many survivalists believe that if our government isn't doing anything about civil defense in a tangible way, that private industry must. That's how L. Lande Blackmore, president of Survive Tomorrow, Inc., feels. He hopes to begin a trend of getting private developers to become actively involved in civil defense. Blackmore's corporation started construction of Terrene Ark I—earth shelter survival condominiums—in a little southwestern Utah town called La Verkin. "Should a national disaster, nuclear war, economic collapse, or civil disaster strike the United States, those on board Terrene Ark I will survive—if anyone will."—*Survive,* page 38. Blackmore's ark community is being built underground with roofs constructed of eight-inch reinforced concrete—topped by three-and-a-half feet of earth. Fully furnished, the units contain water and air purifiers, survival foods, and medical facilities. The price tag? Either $47,900 or $95,800, depending on the size—360 or 720 square feet. Many are already sold. People are getting ready for what seems to be the inevitable.

Blackmore's attempt to build an earth ark to provide an escape from coming destruction is reminiscent of another ark built for man's survival. We find the story in the first book of the Bible. "And God saw that the wickedness of man was great in the earth, and that every imagination of the thoughts of his heart was only evil continually." "The earth also was corrupt before God, and the earth was filled with violence." Genesis 6:5, 11.

God realized that if humanity were to survive, something had to be done with the problem of a human society bent upon self-destruction. So God said to Noah, "The end of all flesh is come before me; for the earth is filled with violence through them; and, behold, I will destroy them with the earth." Genesis 6:13.

God told Noah that the earth would be destroyed by water, and He instructed Noah to build an ark. Unlike Blackmore's Terrene, or earth ark, this was to be a water ark. Noah was to invite his family, friends, and neighbors to come aboard and escape the coming flood.

For 120 years, Noah the survivalist gave the warning, trying to persuade others to prepare for the catastrophe. But when the rains came and the flood covered the earth, only eight people survived the destruction of that civilization. God had sent the warning and provided a way out. But man was too busy and too unconcerned to recognize the ominous signs of the times. All but the eight who entered the ark paid their carelessness with their own lives.

"But as the days of Noe were, so shall also the coming of the Son of man be. For as in the days that were before the flood they were eating and drinking, marrying and giving in marriage, until the day that Noe entered into the ark, and knew not until the flood came, and took them all away; so shall also the coming of the Son of man be." Matthew 24:37-39.

You see, friend, whether or not the survivalists are right—whether or not buying gold and gems and stockpiling weapons and food will enable us to survive, whatever bad times lie ahead—survival must be more for us than just a few added years. More than merely continuing to exist. More than simply reproducing another generation that will have to face even greater crises. Survival must be *forever* if it is to be worth the fight at all!

The good news of the Bible—the news TV won't tell you—is that some who live on this dying planet *will* survive—and *forever!* Repeatedly, the Bible assures us that those who choose Jesus Christ as their Saviour and Lord will survive this world's worst to enjoy a new world's best.

Friend, are you filled with a nameless anxiety as your world seems to be hurtling toward some chilling economic, environmental, or nuclear disaster? Does fear cast its cold shadow over all that you do? Do you sometimes honestly wonder if you will personally live out your full lifespan, given the numberless sinister possibilities threatening your very existence?

For all you ever hear about it in the media, you could easily get the idea that the good news—the hopeful news—contained in God's Word is secret information. But your Bible is not bound or banned. It is not locked shut. If its messages of hope are secrets—then, as we have pointed out already in this book—they are *open secrets.*

One of those open secrets is that God is about to s⁺ in and reclaim His hijacked world and set its captive

And another open secret is that this mighty Creator-God loves you so much that He cannot seem to do without you. So He's coming soon to take you home

Oh, yes—this poor, wretched world is about to come to an end, all right. But it won't perish in a nuclear holocaust. It won't die of natural causes, either. It will end when its Maker—*our* Maker—creates it new again.

Are you tired of living in fear and hopelessness? Don't focus on the bad news. Let the TV newcasts keep on dredging up all the dark sludge of sin here on this expiring planet. Focus instead on the good news—the hope, the love, the joy, the peace—of soon meeting in person the best Friend you will ever have.